7 Strategies OF Highly Effective READERS

7 Strategies OF Highly Effective READERS

Using Cognitive Research to Boost K-8 Achievement

Elaine K. McEwan

CORWIN PRESS
A Sage Publications Company
Thousand Oaks, California

For information:

Corwin Press
A Sage Publications Company
2455 Teller Road
Thousand Oaks, California 91320
www.corwinpress.com

Sage Publications Ltd.
1 Oliver's Yard
55 City Road
London, EC1Y 1SP
United Kingdom

Sage Publications India Pvt. Ltd.
B-42, Panchsheel Enclave
Post Box 4109
New Delhi 110 017 India

Printed in the United States of America

Library of Congress Cataloging-in-Publication Data

McEwan, Elaine K., 1941-
Seven strategies of highly effective readers : using cognitive research to boost K-8 achievement / by Elaine K. McEwan.
     p. cm.
Includes bibliographical references and index.
ISBN 0-7619-4620-9 (cloth) — ISBN 0-7619-4621-7 (paper)
   1. Reading (Kindergarten) 2. Reading (Elementary) 3. Reading (Middle school)
I. Title: 7 strategies of highly effective readers. II. Title.
LB1181.2.M32 2004 372.41—dc22

                                    2003025005

This book is printed on acid-free paper.

04 05 06 07 08 10 9 8 7 6 5 4 3 2 1

Acquisitions Editor:	Robert D. Clouse
Editorial Assistant:	Candice Ling
Production Editor:	Julia Parnell
Copy Editor:	Marilyn Power Scott
Proofreader:	Cheryl Rivard
Typesetter:	C&M Digitals (P) Ltd.
Cover Designer:	Tracy E. Miller
Graphic Designer:	Lisa Miller

Contents

Instructional Aids

Preface

One of my biggest frustrations when I taught fifth grade was the inability to help those students who were unable to make sense of what they read. The basal reading series provided unit tests to measure comprehension, but the authors were strangely silent regarding what to do about those students who did poorly on the tests. When I encountered some of the same difficulties in my own reading of challenging textbooks and literature in high school and college, I developed some strategies to increase my comprehension and retention, but I had no theoretical background *or* practical framework for teaching them to students. My strategy instruction was haphazard and from my perspective largely ineffective.

After moving to a media center position, I taught my favorite strategies to upper-grade students in preparation for the traditional "research" and report-writing unit and came to believe that if all teachers embedded these lessons into their daily instruction, students would eventually use them independently. They would acquire the habits of the mind that are needed to understand and retain what is read. But my colleagues were not buying what I was selling. They were already overloaded with mandates and curriculum binders.

I became an elementary school principal in 1983, about the same time that a new body of research became available. It described some of the key cognitive strategies that highly skilled readers routinely use and explained how to teach them to students.[1] As my faculty and I explored ways to increase literacy levels in a low-performing school, we dipped our toes into the unfamiliar waters of schoolwide (K–6) strategy instruction. Our experimentation with strategy instruction (as well as a variety of other reading initiatives) was associated with rising achievement (McEwan, 1998).

Our instructional resources were limited to a few journal articles and simple handouts developed by our county reading specialist. Today there are multiple options for educators desiring to implement cognitive strategy instruction. Many of the books contain appealing instructional activities with catchy titles, samples of student work, and colorful photos of happy students and confident teachers. But most do not give their readers the "big picture" of cognitive strategy instruction—the relevant scientific research and the critical elements, particularly the need for explicit instruction. In my opinion, they fall short of preparing teachers for the challenges that confront anyone desiring to implement what I call *strategic reading instruction (SRI)*.

In addition to the popular strategy books, there is also a second option for those who want to implement strategy instruction—a group of edited academic volumes containing articles written by some of the most eminent cognitive psychologists and reading scholars.[2] These books explain the theory, summarize the current research, and offer research agendas for the future—all extremely important topics in these days of accountability, but they are challenging to read and provide few, if any, ready-to-use instructional activities.

Seven Strategies of Highly Effective Readers: Using Cognitive Research to Boost K–8 Achievement aims to combine the best of both of those worlds and offers a third option that is both research-based *and* practical. I know from my own administrative experience in raising student achievement in a low-performing school that strategy instruction is a necessary (albeit insufficient) piece of the reading puzzle (McEwan, 2002a). I also know the importance of selecting research-based strategies and instructional methods. All strategy instruction is not created equal. There is no point in wasting valuable instructional time on appealing activities that don't get results. The administrators and teachers who attend my workshops know that I frequently invoke the dean of American college basketball coaches, John Wooden, on that topic, who preached, "Do not mistake activity for achievement" (Wooden & Jamison, 1997, p. 20).

THE GOALS OF THIS BOOK

Cognitive strategy instruction has come a long way since my faculty and I first tinkered with it more than twenty years ago. My observations in retrospect are similar to those made by cognitive strategy guru Michael Pressley (2000):

> The scientific community has made great progress in learning how good readers decode and understand text; they have also made great progress in the last 25 years in demonstrating the potency of teaching students to use the processes that good readers use. I am thrilled by this progress. As it turns out, however, there are those who continue to argue against direct teaching of reading skills, believing that children's literacy development is best stimulated by immersion in literacy experiences alone. Moreover, in the same 25 years when so much scientific progress was made, the whole-language position was developed and came to predominate in the language arts marketplace. I am hopeful that during the second quarter century of my career, the scientific community studying reading will be as successful in the schoolplace as it has been in the marketplace of academic ideas during the first quarter century of my career. (p. 48)

I share Pressley's hopes for the next twenty-five years, and in some sense I have written this book in response to his wish for a more widespread dissemination of the research regarding the learning power to be found in the direct teaching of cognitive strategies. I have written *Seven Strategies of Highly Effective Readers* with the following goals in mind:

- To summarize and explain a substantial body of relevant scientific research as defined in the No Child Left Behind Act of 2000 as it converges around three areas of knowledge: cognitive science, reading comprehension, and strategic instruction[3]

- To define and explain the seven strategies that highly effective readers routinely use and that all educators need to employ in their own reading to become strategic teachers

- To give K–8 (kindergarten through Grade 8) educators a sampling of instructional activities to facilitate cognitive strategy instruction

- To present an instructional planning template that will assist educators in infusing cognitive strategy instruction into every subject and lesson they teach

- To convince educators that strategy instruction done well is not more work but, rather, the most effective and important work a teacher can do, not only for its power to boost student achievement but for the benefits that will accrue to students in their academic and future lives

SPECIAL FEATURES OF THIS BOOK

Seven Strategies of Highly Effective Readers contains the following features:

- Teacher Think-Alouds to help you model the use of cognitive strategies for your students
- Instructional templates to help you plan cognitive strategy instruction
- Instructional activities to assist you in modeling, explaining, scaffolding, and facilitating the seven strategies before, during, and after reading
- Reproducible forms, posters, props, and prompts that provide ready-to-use instructional assistance for both students and teachers

WHO THIS BOOK IS FOR

One of the biggest obstacles to implementing cognitive strategy instruction is lack of confidence. You are not alone if you feel a bit uneasy regarding how to become a strategic teacher. "Many of today's educators plan comprehension lessons with limited pedagogical knowledge" (Block, Gambrell, & Pressley, 2002, p. xvi). As I travel the country working with teachers and principals, many struggling to improve the literacy levels of at-risk students, we examine the curricular, instructional, and environmental variables that can be altered in their classrooms, schools, and district (Bloom, 1980; McEwan, 2001, 2002b). One variable that consistently emerges as needing change is comprehension instruction. Some attendees are eager to integrate cognitive strategy instruction into their already overloaded day, but they recognize that without a schoolwide or even districtwide commitment, what they do in their individual classrooms may be "too little and too late" to help their students. Others are hesitant and a bit embarrassed to think aloud. Still others are reluctant readers themselves and need help in learning how to become strategic readers before they can model the strategies they use in their own reading. Whether you are an eager beaver who can't wait to get started or someone who needs a little push to try something new, I have written this book for you, as well as for the following groups of educators:

- K–8 classroom teachers who need a practical, easy-to-read, research-based introduction to cognitive strategy instruction[4]
- Content-area teachers who want their students to understand and retain challenging subject-matter text
- Administrators at both the building and central office levels who wish to implement cognitive strategy instruction in multiple classrooms or buildings
- School, grade-level, or content-area teams of teachers who need assistance in planning for the implementation of cognitive strategy instruction
- University-level teachers of preservice and graduate reading courses who desire a more organized approach to cognitive strategy instruction
- Staff development specialists who need a user-friendly text to guide discussion and study groups around the topic of cognitive strategy instruction

OVERVIEW OF THE CONTENTS

Chapter 1 defines strategic reading instruction, describes what a cognitive strategy is, explains the important ways that strategies differ from instructional activities and reading skills, and briefly introduces the seven cognitive strategies that highly effective readers routinely use. Chapter 2 focuses on specific research-based teaching practices that will help your students mature into highly effective readers. You will discover how to become a strategic teacher who is able to motivate and facilitate the development of the seven strategies in your students.

Chapter 3 provides a crash course on the critical attributes of the seven strategies, knowledge that is essential for effective instruction, while Chapter 4 introduces a variety of instructional activities to successfully teach the strategies—activities that you can adapt and adopt to fit your own personal teaching style. Chapter 5 explains how to integrate strategic reading instruction into your grade-level or content-area classroom routines with the goal of developing lifelong strategic readers. Chapter 6 concludes *Seven Strategies of Highly Effective Readers* with a discussion of schoolwide strategic reading instruction implementation.

NOTES

1. Brown, Day, and Jones (1983); Palincsar and Brown (1984); Raphael (1982, 1984); Raphael and Gavelek (1984); Raphael and Wonnacott (1985); Roehler and Duffy (1984); Rosenshine and Meister (1984).
2. Block, Gambrell, and Pressley (2002); Block and Pressley (2002); RAND Reading Study Group (2002); Taylor, Graves, and van den Broek (2000).

3. I use the term *scientific research* as defined in the No Child Left Behind Act of 2000 (2002). "The term 'scientifically based research' (a) means research that involves the application of rigorous, systematic, and objective procedures to obtain reliable and valid knowledge relevant to education activities and programs; and (b) includes research that (1) employs systematic, empirical methods that draw on observation or experiment; (2) involves rigorous data analyses that are adequate to test the stated hypotheses and justify the general conclusions drawn; (3) relies on measurements or observational methods that provide reliable and valid data across evaluators and observers, across multiple measurements and observations, and across studies by the same or different investigators; (4) is evaluated using experimental or quasi-experimental designs in which individuals, entities, programs, or activities are assigned to different conditions and with appropriate controls to evaluate the effects of the condition of interest, with a preference for random-assignment experiments, or other designs to the extent that those designs contain within-condition or across-condition controls; (5) ensures that experimental studies are presented in sufficient detail and clarity to allow for replication or, at a minimum, offer the opportunity to build systematically on their findings; and (6) has been accepted by a peer-reviewed journal or approved by a panel of independent experts through a comparably rigorous, objective, and scientific review" (Olson & Viadero, 2002).

4. *Seven Strategies of Highly Effective Readers* could readily be used by high school teachers since the seven strategies of highly effective readers are especially applicable in Grades 9–12 and many of the instructional activities in Chapter 4 designed for middle school students could easily be adapted to the high school level. However, the challenge of creating think-alouds that would fully serve the needs of the K–12 grade span, as well as the inclusion of multiple activities for the primary grades, dictated the selection of a K–8 designation in the title. However, if you are a high school administrator or teacher, you will find much to inform strategic reading instruction in your high school.

Acknowledgments

There are hundreds of individuals who have contributed to this book in both large and small ways over the past five years. They include the administrators who invited me to share cognitive strategy workshops with their districts, schools, and county offices of education in Missouri, Texas, Nebraska, Georgia, Florida, Iowa, Washington, Oregon, and California. They include the teachers from whom I learned about what worked and what didn't work—both in my workshops and in their classrooms.

In addition, there are three individuals who have played major roles in the successful completion of this book:

• Robb Clouse, senior acquisitions editor at Corwin Press, never lost his vision for *Seven Strategies of Highly Effective Readers*, even as we continued to postpone the due date to accommodate my hectic workshop schedule. Robb's strong editorial and production support have made this book a reality.

• Jeanette Jackson, Nebraska reading teacher extraordinaire, read the manuscript in progress and managed to give me positive feedback just *when* I needed it and offer gentle, corrective feedback just *where* I needed it. Jeanette is an elegant lady who has encouraged and enriched my work.

• E. Raymond Adkins, my husband, intrepid travel companion and faithful copy editor, listened to me chatter endlessly about cognitive strategy instruction, not only in the dozens of workshops for which he provides patient and expert technological assistance but also during our myriad car trips from airports to workshop sites across the United States. On June 12, 2003, we rejoiced on the occasion of our tenth wedding anniversary and at the same time celebrated the fact that we had traveled together in all fifty of the United States during those ten years. I bless the day I married Ray. His gentle spirit and generous heart have contributed in vital though unseen ways to every one of my books, including this one.

Authors rarely credit airlines, hotels, and rental car agencies in their acknowledgements, but this book could not have been written without the hospitality and superior service of Southwest Airlines, Hilton Hotels, and Hertz Rental Car. A good share of this book was written in airports, airplanes, rental cars, and hotel rooms from Alaska to Hawaii and from Mississippi to North Dakota. I have written under palm trees and in blinding snowstorms, but "the book must go on." And it has.

I am especially grateful to my supportive readers. Thanks to Corwin Press and their wonderful marketing department, these readers number in the tens of thousands. A special thanks to those of you who have taken the time to write or call me. I think of you collectively whenever I am writing—imagining the challenges you face and knowing all too well the constraints within which you work. You are my heroes and heroines, and I commend you for the vision and commitment you bring to your classrooms, schools, and districts each and every day. This book is dedicated to you.

A special thanks is owed the following reviewers who carefully read and shared their candid observations with me. Their varied experiences and practical approaches helped me to make this a more teacher-centered book.

Lori Benton
Reading Specialist
Covina Valley USD
Covina, California

Aileen Carew
Reading Specialist
Bel Aire School
Tiburon, California

Cheri Howell
Reading Specialist
Covina Valley USD
Covina, California

Dr. Stevi Quate
Professor
School of Education
University of Colorado at Denver
Denver, Colorado

Dr. Timothy Rasinski
Professor
Kent State University
Kent, Ohio

About the Author

Elaine K. McEwan is a partner and educational consultant with The McEwan-Adkins Group, offering workshops in instructional leadership, team building, and raising reading achievement, K–12. A former teacher, librarian, principal, and assistant superintendent for instruction in a suburban Chicago school district, she is the author of more than thirty-five books for parents and educators. Her Corwin Press titles include *Leading Your Team to Excellence: Making Quality Decisions* (1997), *Seven Steps to Effective Instructional Leadership* (1998), *The Principal's Guide to Attention Deficit Hyperactivity Disorder* (1998), *How to Deal With Parents Who Are Angry, Troubled, Afraid, or Just Plain Crazy* (1998), *The Principal's Guide to Raising Reading Achievement* (1998), *Counseling Tips for Elementary School Principals* (1999) with Jeffrey A. Kottler, *Managing Unmanageable Students: Practical Solutions for Educators* (2000) with Mary Damer, *The Principal's Guide to Raising Math Achievement* (2000), *Raising Reading Achievement in Middle and High Schools: Five Simple-to-Follow Strategies for Principals* (2001), *Ten Traits of Highly Effective Teachers: How to Hire, Mentor, and Coach Successful Teachers* (2001), *Teach Them ALL to Read: Catching the Kids Who Fall Through the Cracks* (2002), *7 Steps to Effective Instructional Leadership, 2nd Edition* (2003), *Making Sense of Research: What's Good, What's Not, and How to Tell the Difference* (2003) with Patrick J. McEwan, and *Ten Traits of Highly Effective Principals: From Good to Great Performance* (2003).

McEwan was honored by the Illinois Principals Association as an outstanding instructional leader, by the Illinois State Board of Education with an Award of Excellence in the Those Who Excel Program, and by the National Association of Elementary School Principals as the National Distinguished Principal from Illinois for 1991. She received her undergraduate degree in education from Wheaton College and advanced degrees in library science (MA) and educational administration (EdD) from Northern Illinois University. She lives with her husband and business partner, E. Raymond Adkins, in Oro Valley, Arizona. Visit her Web site at www.elainemcewan.com where you can learn more about her writing and workshops and enroll in online seminars based on her books, or contact her directly at emcewan@elainemcewan.com.

The Power of Strategic Reading Instruction

There has long been a tradition in American schooling that comprehension is essentially unteachable and that the most teachers can do is set the stage for learning to occur. Comprehension instruction from this perspective was very limited since one learned to comprehend on one's own.

Mason, Roehler, & Duffy (1984, p. 301)

I have written a weekly education column for various small town newspapers for more than fifteen years and frequently receive questions from readers about comprehension difficulties. In response to one such question from the mother of a high school student lamenting her daughter's inability to understand, I wrote a brief article describing four strategies that might help her daughter's reading comprehension (McEwan, 2002a). Shortly after the column was published, I received the following note from another reader.

Dear Elaine,

I have been following your columns in the *Northwest Explorer* and enjoy your matter-of-fact teaching principles. In a recent column, you answered a parent regarding her daughter's lack of reading comprehension. At the end of the article, you said, "Very few teachers actually teach students how to read to learn," and suggested that there are several strategies that can improve reading comprehension for any age reader. I do hope you will address this in one of your future columns, hopefully soon, as I have always felt I lacked the ability to remember things of interest without memorizing what I wanted to remember. I am an avid reader but have trouble remembering names or even the title of a book I have just read. I am 57 years old and feel one can always improve their comprehension. (Personal communication, Phyllis Hiemenz, July 12, 2002)

I took Phyllis's suggestion and devoted several columns to describing a variety of procedures, prompts, and props that readers could use to acquire and perfect their cognitive strategy usage. I thought no more about Phyllis's reading problem until I began writing this book. It was then that I decided to get in touch with her to ask if she had been using any of the strategies. Here is her reply:

> Dear Elaine,
>
> Your description of four cognitive strategies [summarizing, monitoring-clarifying, questioning, and visualizing-organizing] was very helpful and I find myself reading more with a purpose rather than thinking that I will absorb it simply because I am reading it. I now question why I want to read a particular article and then what I want to get out of it.
>
> I have also realized that I shouldn't be so hard on myself when I can't remember everything, since we are individuals and what I remember about a book is what was important to me.
>
> The strategy I have used the most is the one where I write down key words as I read to help me comprehend and remember the important ideas. I have to admit I haven't done much book reading since I have been upgrading my skills on Microsoft Office and Excel. As I'm learning new skills, I still write down key words to help me remember since it's easy to overload on so much information at once. This way, when I am applying something new, I can quickly look at my outline and it helps me remember what to do (of course, not every time). I especially liked your example about the waitresses who served you recently and how easily you remembered the name of one because it was the same as your daughter's, but promptly forget the names of the others. This has helped me to realize that we do selectively remember what is relevant and important to us. *I hope this all makes sense.* (Personal communication, Phyllis Hiemenz, December 15, 2003).

Phyllis's note made perfect sense to me. Bransford (1979) calls the processing activities in which learners engage "acquisition activities" (p. 52) and observes, "Many people speak of their poor memories. What do they mean? Are they limited by inferior 'storage capacity' because of the makeup of their brain?" Bransford answers his question in the same way I answered Phyllis in my newspaper column: "It is the types of processing activities performed at acquisition that are important for learning and remembering. As these acquisition activities are changed, the ability to remember follows suit" (p. 52).

For a mature adult like Phyllis, who had long been frustrated by her inability to read text and automatically understand and remember it, the awareness that she can activate prior knowledge, connect what she is reading to what she already knows, summarize the key points or main idea while she reads, and monitor her comprehension comes as something of a cognitive epiphany. Hopefully your students will not have to wait as long as Phyllis did to discover the power of strategic reading. We know that students can acquire *strategic reading* habits through the delivery of *strategic reading instruction* by *strategic teachers*, and that the process can begin in preschool or kindergarten (Novak,

1998; Smolkin & Donovan, 2000; Williams, 2002). We can teach all students to become more *strategic readers.*

The four italicized terms in the previous sentences are described, defined, and discussed at depth throughout *Seven Strategies of Highly Effective Readers.* The following definitions are drawn from the literature and research in three areas: reading comprehension instruction, cognitive science, and teacher effectiveness.

- *Strategic reading* is the extraction and construction of meaning from text by teachers and students individually or by teachers and students jointly through the skillful and situational use of a repertoire of cognitive strategies: the seven strategies of highly effective readers. The following synonyms are used for *strategic reading* in this book: *real reading* and *reading to learn.*
- *Strategic reading instruction (SRI)* is the explicit, systematic, and supportive instruction of cognitive strategies by all teachers in all grade levels and content areas. Whenever students are expected to extract and construct meaning from text (i.e., read to learn), the seven strategies of highly effective readers will be modeled, explained, scaffolded, and facilitated. The following synonyms are used for SRI in this book: *cognitive strategy instruction* and *strategy instruction.*
- *Strategic readers* are students who employ grade-level-appropriate cognitive strategies to extract and construct meaning from text. The following synonyms are used for strategic readers in this book: *highly effective readers* and *skilled readers.*
- *Strategic teachers* are individuals who, in addition to having personal traits that signify character, teaching traits that get results, and intellectual traits that demonstrate knowledge, curiosity, and awareness (McEwan, 2002c),[1] are also able to model, coach, and facilitate their students' acquisition of cognitive strategies by drawing metacognitively on their personal strategic reading habits. The following synonym is used for strategic teachers in this book: *highly effective teachers.*

WHAT IS STRATEGIC READING?

According to Mortimer Adler (1940), reading is thinking (p. 43), while Edward Thorndike (1917) described reading as problem solving (p. 329). Adler and Thorndike were right, to a point, but more contemporary scholars focus their definitions of reading on meaning, most particularly the construction of meaning by the reader. The RAND Reading Study Group (2002) defined *reading comprehension* as "the process of simultaneously extracting and constructing meaning through interaction and involvement with written language" (p. 11). *Strategic reading,* as described and discussed in this book, assumes that the process of extracting and constructing meaning from challenging text can only occur through the automatic and expert use of cognitive strategies.

The cognitive processing that occurs during reading has fascinated a wide variety of scholars. My concept of what occurs during this process is akin to what Walt Whitman (as quoted in Gilbar, 1990) describes as "an exercise [or] a gymnast's struggle; [something] that the reader is to do for himself, must be on the alert [and] must . . . construct . . . the poem, argument, history, metaphysical essay—the text furnishing the hints, the clue, the start or [the] framework" (p. 39). Reading can often be hard work that leaves the reader exhausted.

Cognitive psychologists van den Broek, Young, Tzeng, and Linderholm (1999) theorized that the process of skilled reading consists of fluctuating activations of concepts in the brain that can come from one or more of four different sources: (1) the text that is currently being processed, (2) text that was processed immediately preceding, (3) concepts processed in even earlier reading cycles, or (4) background knowledge. Their hypothesized representation looks somewhat like a landform map, complete with peaks, valleys, plateaus, and plains (p. 75). Of course, the mental landscape of a skilled reader is neither a landform map nor an actual place. It is a theory or representation of what is happening in the mind of a skilled reader as memory is constantly changing to accommodate the dynamic results of cognitive processing. "The pattern of activations and deactivations is a result of the interaction of the text, the reader's attentional capabilities, his or her background knowledge, and the reader's criteria for comprehension, and hence for retrieval" (p. 78).

Pearson and Fielding (1991) summarize what happens during their version of strategic reading thus: "Students understand and remember ideas better when they have to transform those ideas from one form to another. Apparently it is in this transformation process that the *author's* ideas become [the] *reader's* ideas, rendering them more memorable. Examined from the teacher's perspective, what this means is that teachers have many options to choose from when they try to engage students more actively in their own comprehension: summarizing, monitoring . . . engaging visual representation, and requiring students to ask their own questions all seem to generate learning" (p. 847).

Perkins (1992) calls the processing that must go on in order for students to acquire more than a smattering of soon-to-be-forgotten facts *complex cognition*, and suggests that teachers will have to "sell" students on both the short- and long-term benefits of acquiring and using cognitive strategies.

> Complex cognition has more intrinsic interest and promises more payoff outside of school and later in life. But consider the cost to learners: complex cognition demands much more effort. It creates greater risk of failure. It introduces the discomforts of disorientation, as learners struggle to get their heads around difficult ideas. Peer status for complex cognition is certainly mixed; who wants to be known as a 'brain'? And very commonly, so far as grades and teacher approval go, complex cognition buys no more than the simpler path of getting facts straight and the algorithms right. No wonder, then, that students perfectly reasonably do not automatically gravitate toward complex cognition. (pp. 59–60)

The goal of this book is to convince you of the benefits of strategic reading so that you in turn can convince your students.

The most comprehensive and informative descriptions of what happens in the minds of skilled readers as they process text (or engage in the kind of complex cognition described by Perkins [1992]) can be found in a type of research called *verbal protocols*. Verbal protocols are verbatim self-reports that people make regarding what is happening in their minds as they think (James, 1890), solve problems (Duncker, 1926, 1945), and read (Pressley & Afflerbach, 1995). These transcripts are subsequently analyzed to answer specific research questions, such as: What is the influence of prior knowledge on expert readers' strategies as they determine the main idea of a text?" (Afflerbach, 1990b). As subjective as verbal protocols may seem to be, they are a valid and highly useful tool for providing "snapshots" and even "videos" of the ever-changing mental landscape that expert readers construct during reading. Pressley & Afflerbach (1995) conclude, based on their extensive collection of verbal protocols from expert readers, that reading is "constructively responsive—that is, good readers are always changing their processing in response to the text they are reading" (p. 2).

The question that most educators ask at this point is this: "Can *I* really teach *all* students how to become strategic, situational, constructively responsive readers?" This question is an important one that should always be asked by educators regarding any idea, program, or methodology that is being proposed for implementation in their schools and classrooms. The answer comes from cognitive science research.

WHAT IS STRATEGIC READING INSTRUCTION?

The solutions to the challenge of teaching students to read strategically are found in a vast body of research on cognitive strategy instruction derived from the discipline of cognitive science (National Reading Panel, 2000; Pressley, 2000; Pressley et al., 1995; RAND Reading Study Group, 2002; Rosenshine, 1997b; Rosenshine & Meister, 1984; Trabasso & Bouchard, 2000, 2002; Wood, Woloshyn, & Willoughby, 1995). Based on more than 200 scientific research studies and reviews, here is what we currently know about the power that cognitive strategies, taught well and consistently, have to increase students' abilities to understand and retain what they read:

- Skilled or expert readers routinely draw from a repertoire of cognitive strategies while they are reading challenging text.
- Students of all ability levels benefit from strategy instruction both as evidenced in increased understanding and retention and also in higher standardized test scores.
- The effectiveness of a variety of individual cognitive strategies in boosting student achievement is well supported by experimental research.
- The effectiveness of several multiple-strategy instructional approaches is well supported by experimental research.
- There are specific instructional methods to teach cognitive strategies to students that produce results.

Figure 1.1 presents a small portion of the scientific evidence for the power of cognitive strategy instruction to boost student achievement. Consult the previously cited research articles and literature reviews in this chapter for a comprehensive list of the applicable studies.

Research Evidence for Strategic Reading Instruction

Research Questions	*Research*
Which strategies do skilled readers use?	Afflerbach (1990a, 1990b); Afflerbach & Johnston (1984); Pressley & Afflerbach (1995)
Which students benefit from strategy usage?	Anderson & Roit (1993); Brown & Campione (1994, 1996); National Reading Panel (2000); Palincsar & Brown (1984); Pressley, Johnson, Symons, McGoldrick, & Kurita (1989); Rosenshine & Meister (1984); Rosenshine, Meister, & Chapman (1996); Trabasso & Bouchard (2000, 2002)
Which multiple-strategy approaches work best?	Brown, Pressley, Van Meter, & Schuder (1996); Lysynchuk, Pressley, & Vye (1990); Palincsar & Brown (1984); Pressley, El-Dinary, Gaskins, et al. (1992); Rosenshine (1997a); Rosenshine & Meister (1984)
Which instructional methods are most effective for teaching cognitive strategies?	Brown, Pressley, Van Meter, & Schuder (1996); Duffy (2002); Duffy et al. (1987); Gaskins & Elliot (1991); Gaskins, Laird, O'Hara, Scott, & Cress (2002); Marks et al. (1993); Morrow, Tracey, Wood, & Pressley (1999); Pressley, El-Dinary, Marks, & Stein (1992); Rosenshine (1997a, 1997b); Taylor, Pearson, Clark, & Walpole (1999)
What is the current status of cognitive strategy instruction?	Pearson (1996); Pressley, Wharton-McDonald, Mistretta-Hampton, & Echevarria (1998); Pressley et al. (2001); Wharton-McDonald, Pressley, & Hampton (1998); Wharton-McDonald et al. (1997)

Figure 1.1. Copyright © 2004 Corwin Press. All rights reserved. Reprinted from *Seven Strategies of Highly Effective Readers*, by E. K. McEwan. Thousand Oaks, CA: Corwin Press. www.corwinpress.com. Reproduction authorized only for the local school site that has purchased this book.

The scientific research evidence showing that we can directly and explicitly teach a repertoire of cognitive strategies to students in order to increase their capacities to understand and remember is (and has been for quite some time) an astounding educational breakthrough. A comparable breakthrough in the field of medicine, for example, was the discovery of a vaccine for polio. Unfortunately, the findings of the National Reading Panel (2000) regarding the power of cognitive strategy instruction did not make the front page of the *New York Times* as did the discovery of a vaccine for polio. In fact, "despite a significant body of research in the 1980's suggesting the effectiveness of strategy instruction, especially for lower-achieving readers, strategy instruction has not been implemented in many American classrooms" (Dole, 2000, p. 62). With the passage of the No Child Left Behind Act of 2000 (2002), educators can no longer afford to ignore this powerful body of research. It is precisely what we need to assist us in leaving no child behind.

Knowing that we do not need to wait for students to "catch on" to comprehension or "develop" a strategic reading approach or "bloom" as strategic readers when they become "ready" should encourage and hearten every teacher. Cognitive strategies *can* be taught to all of our students—now.

WHAT ARE THE SEVEN STRATEGIES OF HIGHLY EFFECTIVE READERS?

If you have read any of the recent comprehension and reading strategy books, you may well have been overwhelmed, as have I, by the sheer number and variety of "strategies" to be found. Where did they all come from? What's good, what's not, and how does one tell the difference? You may even be wondering if you are getting your money's worth in a book that gives you only seven. The strategies that I have chosen to feature in this book are the actual cognitive *processes* in which all skillful readers engage (Pressley & Afflerbach, 1995). These differ greatly from the hundreds of instructional activities developed by teachers, curriculum developers, and consultants (myself included), and we will explore those differences shortly. The seven strategies of highly effective readers are listed in alphabetical order and defined, in Figure 1.2.

I selected them for the following reasons: (1) They are used by skilled readers and known to be essential to proficient adult reading, (2) instruction in these strategies results in higher achievement on both teacher-made tests and standardized achievement tests, and (3) the majority of state standards and assessments expect students to demonstrate proficiency in the use of all of these strategies. Without a skillful marriage of content *and* SRI that begins on the first day of kindergarten and continues during every school day thereafter, the accomplishment of the stringent learning outcomes set forth in most state standards, especially with diverse learners, may well be impossible. SRI offers the promise, however, of making stiff standards, whether those of your school, district, or state, actually "stick" with students. The research evidence is shown in Figure 1.3.

Cognitive strategies are defined in various ways. They are sometimes called mental tools. Skilled readers routinely use these "mindtools" (Jonassen, 2000) to process what they read or what they hear (in the case of listening comprehension),

Seven Strategies of Highly Effective Readers

Strategy	Description
Activating	"Priming the cognitive pump" to recall relevant prior knowledge and experiences from long-term memory in order to extract and construct meaning from text
Inferring	Bringing together what is spoken (written) in the text, what is unspoken (unwritten) in the text, and what is already known by the reader in order to extract and construct meaning from the text
Monitoring-Clarifying	Thinking about how and what one is reading, both during and after the act of reading, for purposes of determining if one is comprehending the text, combined with the ability to clarify and fix up any mix-ups if necessary
Questioning	Engaging in learning dialogues with text (authors), peers, and teachers through self-questioning, question generation, and question answering
Searching-Selecting	Searching a variety of sources to select appropriate information to answer questions, define words and terms, clarify misunderstandings, solve problems, or gather information
Summarizing	Restating the meaning of text in one's own words—different words from those used in the original text
Visualizing-Organizing	Constructing a mental image or graphic organizer for the purpose of extracting and constructing meaning from text

Research Evidence for the Seven Strategies

Strategy	References
Activating	Afflerbach (1990a, 1990b); Bransford (1983); Brown, Smiley, Day, Townsend, & Lawton (1977); Dole, Valencia, Greer, & Wardrop (1991); Neuman (1988); Palincsar & Brown (1984); Pearson, Roehler, Dole, & Duffy (1992); Roberts (1988); Tharp (1982); Wood, Winne, & Pressley (1988)
Inferring	Cain & Oakhill (1998); Dewitz, Carr, & Pathberg (1986); Hansen (1981); Hansen & Pearson (1983); Oakhill, Cain, & Yuill (1998); Reutzel, & Hollingsworth (1988); van den Broek (1994)
Monitoring-Clarifying	Babbs (1984); Baker & Zimlin (1989); Baumann, Seifert-Kessel, & Jones (1992); Cross & Paris (1988); Elliott-Faust & Pressley (1986); Markman (1977); Miller (1985, 1987); Paris, Cross, & Lipson (1984); Paris, Saarnio, & Cross (1986); Schmitt (1988); Schunk & Rice (1985)
Questioning	Davey & McBride (1986); King (1989, 1990, 1992); King, Biggs, & Lipsky (1984); Nolte & Singer (1985); Rosenshine, Meister, & Chapman (1996); Singer & Dolan (1982); Smolkin & Donovan (2000); Wong, Wong, Perry, & Sawatsky (1986)
Searching-Selecting	Dreher (1993, 2002); Dreher & Guthrie (1990); Guthrie & Kirsch (1987); Guthrie & Mosenthal (1987); Kobasigawa (1983); Kuhlthau (1988); Spires & Estes (2002); Symons, MacLatchy-Gaudet, Stone, & Reynolds (2001)
Summarizing	Afflerbach & Johnston (1984); Afflerbach & Walker (1992); Armbruster, Anderson, & Ostertag (1987); Baumann (1983, 1984); Bean & Steenwyk (1984); Brown & Day (1983); Brown et al. (1983); Hare & Borchardt (1984); Rinehart, Stahl, & Erickson (1986); Taylor (1986)
Visualizing-Organizing	Alvermann & Boothby (1983, 1986); Armbruster, Anderson, & Meyer (1991); Berkowitz (1986); Borduin, Borduin, & Manley (1994); Gambrell & Bales (1986); Jones, Pierce, & Hunter (1988/1989); Pressley (1976); Shriberg, Levin, McCormick, & Pressley (1982); Sinatra, Stahl-Gemake, & Berg (1984)

similar to the ways that master tradespersons or artisans use their specialized tools. This analogy is an apt one and can be further extended to consider strategic teachers as cognitive masters and to refer to students as cognitive apprentices (Collins, Brown, & Holum, 1991; Collins, Brown, & Newman; 1990). Just as novices observe and learn from the experts in a particular trade or art, novice academics (students) learn from "mind mentors" (teachers) When teachers articulate their thinking about academic tasks and explain, model, and scaffold the use of cognitive strategies for students, these novice learners gain confidence and expertise, gradually reaching a point where, when they are confronted with a piece of challenging text, they are able to readily select the appropriate tool (cognitive strategy) from their personal "cognitive tool belts or boxes" (long-term memory) and apply it to their reading.

Cognitive strategies are also described as "behaviors and thoughts" (Weinstein & Mayer, 1986). Behaviors could include actions such as note-taking, generating key words, constructing a graphic organizer (e.g., a concept map or story grammar), previewing the text, looking back to check on an answer, writing a summary, retelling a story, or thinking out loud (i.e., rehearsing the steps or the ideas that are unclear or need to be remembered), or searching the Internet for an explanation or definition. Thoughts might include cognitive processes such as activating prior knowledge, monitoring comprehension, or inferring meaning. Skilled readers apply these strategies situationally, depending on their purposes for reading, the difficulty of the text, and their own experiences and background knowledge. If you prefer a more academic definition, strategies can be defined as "processes (or sequences of processes) that when matched to the requirements of tasks, facilitate performance" (Pressley, Goodchild, Fleet, Azjchowski, & Evans, 1989, p. 303). The seven cognitive strategies of highly effective readers should be part of every teacher's daily lesson plans and classroom conversations, but there are several other pieces of the reading puzzle that must also be in place for students to extract and construct meaning from text.

WHAT ARE THE PREREQUISITES FOR STRATEGIC READING INSTRUCTION?

We *can* teach all students how to extract and construct meaning from written text more effectively, but only if they have several other important pieces of the reading puzzle already in place (McEwan, 2002b): (1) fluency, (2) vocabulary, and (3) background knowledge. The ability to read both accurately and automatically is an essential, albeit insufficient, prerequisite for comprehension (Perfetti, 1985). Dysfluent readers who lack decoding skills and employ guessing as their strategy of choice will be unable to comprehend what they read, regardless of their comprehension abilities.[2] These students need explicit instruction in the code (the forty-four sound-spelling correspondences) combined with opportunities to practice their newly learned decoding skills to fluency. But even readers who can decode accurately will have comprehension difficulties if they are unable to retrieve words in under a second (Wolf & Bowers, 1999, 2000). Speed deficits that impair fluency should ideally be identified and remediated as early as possible in a student's school career, as they are particularly difficult to overcome if ignored or overlooked. Fluency (the ability to read at grade level speed and accuracy)[3], while essential, is not the only prerequisite for comprehension. Students must also have grade-level-appropriate vocabulary and background knowledge in order to comprehend.

If you reflect on your most recent experience with a standardized test, the Graduate Record Exam, for example, you no doubt recall one or two text selections that gave you sweaty palms. You *were* able to decode the words in the text. But that wasn't enough to understand what you were reading. Because the topics were unfamiliar to you, perhaps quantum physics or transcendentalism, you may have thought you were reading a foreign language. Even though you used every available strategy, without adequate background and vocabulary knowledge, you could do little to make sense of the impenetrable concepts.

Students encounter similar difficulties in their reading of unfamiliar text. One of the biggest frustrations for teachers in Grades 3–8, where "reading-to-learn" is the goal, has to do with the students who "read it, but don't get it" (Tovani, 2000). This pervasive problem is compounded with each passing school year as the number and size of content-area textbooks increase while the ability of students to extract and construct meaning from what they read seems to diminish. Some students may need an extra measure of instruction in the sound-spelling correspondences to boost their word identification abilities. Some students may have mastered the one-to-one correspondences but need more instruction in the "advanced code" (McGuinness & McGuinness, 1998), where two or more letters stand for one sound. Others may need to engage in the repeated oral reading of text at their independent reading level to increase fluency (Ihnot, 2001; LaBerge & Samuels, 1974; Mercer & Campbell, 2001). Cognitive strategy instruction, while of great benefit to listening comprehension, will not improve students' *reading* comprehension *if* they do not know how to read (i.e., decode fluently).

All students need to be intentionally taught as much vocabulary and content background knowledge as teachers can skillfully pack into the school day (Beck, Perfetti, & McKeown, 1982; McKeown, Beck, Omanson, & Perfetti, 1983; McKeown, Beck, Omanson, & Pople, 1985). In reality, all teachers must be ESL (English as a Second Language) or ELL (English Language Learners) teachers, teaching new vocabulary, connecting concepts constantly, and introducing their students to as broad and deep a knowledge of the world as they can (Hirsch, 2001). One of the most effective ways to increase vocabulary knowledge is to use newly introduced vocabulary in meaningful interactions with students. One of the best ways for students to acquire fluency, vocabulary, *and* background knowledge is to read a lot recreationally at their independent reading levels as well as to read a lot at their instructional levels guided in the acquisition of cognitive strategy usage by a strategic teacher. Reading a lot is known to accomplish three learning goals for students:

1. Increase vocabulary (Dickinson & Smith, 1994; Robbins & Ehri, 1994)

2. Develop fluency (LaBerge & Samuels, 1974)

3. Add to readers' domain knowledge, especially if they are encouraged to read expository text (Stanovich, 1993; Stanovich & Cunningham, 1993)

WHEN IS A STRATEGY *NOT* A STRATEGY?

I encounter confusion from time to time regarding just what a cognitive strategy is, and I can empathize because I was confused myself for a time by the sheer number of different things that educators called reading or comprehension strategies. However, a strategy is *not* a strategy when it is in reality one of the following: (1) an instructional activity using a variety of procedures, prompts, posters, and props to assist teachers in modeling, explaining, and teaching one or more cognitive strategies; (2) a study skill; or (3) a reading skill.

Instructional Activities Are *Not* Cognitive Strategies

The "reading strategies" or "comprehension strategies" found in many of the popular books are not, in my opinion, strategies at all. They are *instructional activities* containing *procedures, prompts, posters,* and *props* to assist classroom teachers in cognitive strategy instruction.[4] Instructional activities are the plans and procedures that teachers make and follow for the purpose of cognitive strategy instruction, the things that teachers and students "do" during cognitive strategy instruction.

These activities are often given catchy titles to make them more enticing to both teachers and students. One, for example, is called "click or clunk." After reading a portion of text, students are prompted to ask themselves if what they have read *clicks* (i.e., they understand it) or whether it *clunks* (i.e., they need to use a fix-up strategy (Klingner, Vaughn, & Schumm, 1998; Weaver, 1994, p. 157). Click or clunk is not a cognitive strategy, but a *prompt* to help students practice and internalize the monitoring-clarifying strategy. Another cleverly named prompt is "trash or treasure." It asks students to determine what portions of the text they are reading could be considered irrelevant and redundant (trash) and conversely, which parts of the text contain the important main ideas and details—treasure. This instructional activity and accompanying prompt are designed to assist students with one of the critical tasks of summarizing—determining what's important and what's not.

In another clever prompt, questions are described as "thick [important and global questions] or thin [incidental clarifying questions]" (Harvey & Goudvis, 2000, p. 90). Harvey and Goudvis also suggest a favorite *prop* of many students and teachers—sticky notes. They recommend that students code their responses to what they have read and write reactions and questions regarding their reading on varying sizes of Post-it notes. They place the notes on the pages of their texts to help them remain actively engaged while reading. Props like sticky notes, as well as the sticky pictures I developed for primary readers (see Chapter 4 for the master), aid students in activating prior knowledge, clarifying confusion, and questioning the text as they read.

Study Skills Are *Not* Cognitive Strategies

When I ask middle school teachers in my cognitive strategy workshop to enumerate the strategies they are currently "teaching" their students, the room occasionally gets quiet. Then someone will cautiously mention SQ3R (Survey, Question, Read, Recite, Review). This old-timer has been around since World War II when it was developed to help U.S. troops master vast quantities of new technical information very quickly (Manzo, Manzo, & Estes, 2001, p. 266). Its relative success at that time fostered a healthy interest in the use of study skills to increase the efficiency of learners. I hesitate to squash *any* interest in strategy instruction, but study skills are not cognitive strategies.

Study skills are taught as formulas or systems that are imposed by teachers on learners. Study skills give learners specific methods to study for tests or memorize specific information or facts. Examples include various note-taking systems (e.g., Notetaking System for Learning [Palmatier, 1973]) and study methods (e.g., Predict, Organize, Rehearse, Practice, Evaluate [Simpson, 1986]).

Cognitive strategies, if taught appropriately, on the other hand, are *situational* in nature, to be used by students in response to the varying demands and challenges of reading different types and levels of text for different purposes. They are the "tools" in the tool belt analogy; skillful readers choose the right tool for the job rather than using the same tool for every cognitive assignment.

Reading Skills Are *Not* Cognitive Strategies

Last, the reading skills you may remember from years past are not cognitive strategies. Skills are repetitive in nature, learned through intense practice (e.g., multiplication facts, musical scales, or decoding), and produced unconsciously and almost instantaneously when needed. While skills are absolutely essential to automatic and accurate word identification, the cognitive strategies we will consider are situationally specific and highly flexible. That is, expert readers use specific strategies in response to the text, the purpose for reading, and their own experience and prior knowledge. They may use several strategies simultaneously and no doubt even develop their own approaches to a strategy as they become more expert readers. Any prompts, props, or procedures that teachers use to scaffold the learning of a specific strategy can be modified, enhanced, or dropped altogether as students grow more confident in their strategy usage. Just as teachers feel the freedom to refine and modify lesson plans once they become more confident teachers, maturing readers adapt cognitive strategies to express their own unique ways of extracting and constructing meaning from text.

When *Is* a Strategy a Cognitive Strategy?

A strategy *is* a cognitive strategy when it is a conscious thought or behavior used by a reader to process text. Strategies have the power to enhance and enlarge the scope of learning by making it more efficient. Strategic students learn and remember more in shorter periods of time with far less frustration. They are able to tackle challenging assignments with a higher degree of organizational skill, and more important, they can face difficult assessments with confidence. A strategy is a *cognitive strategy* when teachers are teaching readers how and when to use it independently, confidently, and strategically.

WHAT'S AHEAD?

To this point, we have identified the seven strategies of highly effective readers, capsulized the research that supports their instruction, and explained how cognitive strategies differ from skills and instructional activities. Just ahead in Chapter 2, we will explain how you can increases the likelihood that all of your students will become strategic readers by providing direct and explicit cognitive strategy instruction to them on a daily basis.

NOTES

1. The ten traits of highly effective teachers include: (1) mission-driven and passionate; (2) positive and real; (3) a teacher-leader; (4) with-it-ness; (5) style; (6) motivational expertise; (7) instructional effectiveness; (8) book learning; (9) street smarts; and (10) a mental life (McEwan, 2002c).

2. I call this "the guessing syndrome" and list the following telltale student behaviors of this serious and widespread problem: reads a word one day, but "forgets" it the next; misses details and even main ideas when reading; frequently misreads simple words; frequently mispronounces two-syllable words; and has serious problems with spelling.

3. The minimum words correct per minute for comprehension is 85. Students reading below 85 need to engage in repeated oral reading of text at their independent level to increase fluency rates.

4. I first encountered the terms *procedures* and *prompts* in Rosenshine (1997b). I added the alliterative terms *posters* and *props* to describe the variety of physical aids, charts, and objects that teachers use in the course of cognitive strategy instruction to make it more meaningful and thus more memorable.

Becoming a Strategic Teacher
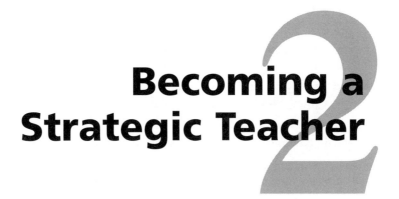

Good strategy use is complex and thus calls for prolonged and detailed instruction

Pressley, Goodchild, et al. (1989, p. 301)

What can educators do with or for the increasing numbers of students who read it but don't seem to get it? Show them how! In my early days of middle-grade teaching, I often thought that when students failed to do assignments or study for tests that it was a lack of motivation or bad attitude that kept them from being productive students. I totally missed the point: "The essence of good teaching is to show students how to do what is required to be successful" (Herber & Herber, 1993, p. 12), not telling them to concentrate or try harder. Showing students *how* skilled readers extract and construct meaning from text (understand and remember what they read) is the essence of becoming a strategic teacher.

WHAT DOES A STRATEGIC TEACHER LOOK LIKE?

Strategic teachers may "look" like other teachers physically, but they "walk" and "talk" very differently from nonstrategic teachers (Pressley, El-Dinary, Gaskins, et al., 1992). Strategic teachers are focused on showing students *how* to do the things they cannot as yet do independently. Let's listen in as one strategic teacher, Roger Craig (a composite of the many strategic teachers with whom I have worked), introduces the summarizing strategy to his fifth graders. The following script is drawn from several classroom observations, and after you have looked at these "snapshots" of Roger's lesson, we will examine the approaches that cognitive science research shows are effective in helping students acquire the seven strategies of highly effective readers.

Although Roger's stated instructional objective is teaching his students how to summarize and their voices are always an important part of classroom observations, the primary focus of *our* observation is on the things that Roger says and does. Come back to Roger's script when you are ready to teach summarizing to your students and reread it from that perspective.

Prior to beginning his several-week series of lessons, Roger carefully reviewed all of the district and state standards related to summarizing. He also looked at some sample assessments to determine how his students would be expected to produce a summary when test-taking time rolled around in the spring, and he considered what assignments and special projects he would be assigning to students during the school year. He then precisely defined to his own satisfaction what a summary is (in the light of the standards and assessments) and enumerated the critical attributes of the summarizing process. He also reviewed some nonexamples so he could show his students what a summary *wasn't*. Roger also thought of as many different circumstances and situations (both in and out of school) in which summary writing would be useful for his students and considered a variety of instructional activities that are known to be effective in *showing students how to summarize.* He then chose the prompts and props that seemed most useful for his purpose. He also selected text from which to read aloud and model summary writing for his students. Here is how Roger introduced the lesson:

"Class, during the next few weeks, I am going to teach you how to summarize. I promise you that if you are here every day and turn on your cognitive processing units (CPUs), you will be able to summarize just about anything when we finish—a basketball game, your summer vacation, or most important for this class, anything that you read.

A summary is one or two sentences (or sometimes a very short paragraph) that give the main idea or, as some people call it, "the gist" of a story, book, chapter, movie, or article. Summarizing is restating in your own words the meaning of something you have read—using different words from those in the story or article that you read. If you look around, you'll find summaries everywhere. There are even summaries of people's lives written after they die: obituaries. [Roger shows his students a transparency of Figure 2.1, Summary Examples, and reads the examples aloud to his students. Some of the students are eager to share examples of summaries they have noticed, and Roger asks them to bring their examples to class the next day.]

Summarizing is the ability to read, or hear, or experience something complicated and reduce it to one or two sentences. I think it's important to know what a good summary looks like. I know what the characteristics of a good chocolate cake are. I know how I want my eggs to look in the morning, and I know what the characteristics of a good summary are. It's short, to the point, contains the "big idea" of the text, omits trivial and unimportant information, collapses lists of information into one word or phrase, and is not a retelling of a story or text.

You will hear me use a number of different words when I talk about summaries, so I've put together a chart of important definitions. [Roger shows a transparency of Figure 2.2, Summarizing Definitions, pointing out the definition of a summary.] *We'll be going over these definitions later. Summarizing is one of the most useful strategies you will ever learn. If you can write (or orally give) a summary, you'll be able to take notes in your own words from a book or encyclopedia for a research report. You can tell a friend about a book you read or a movie you watched and actually have more to*

Summary Examples

Type	Summary	Length
	Kirk Hinrich wasn't clicking offensively, but Nick Collison contributed 33 points, going 14-for-22 from the field, and grabbed 18 rebounds to lead the Jayhawks past the Blue Devils after the score was tied at 35 at the half. Duke sharpshooter J. J. Redick was ice-cold, going 1-for-11 from a three-point range. Dahntay Jones led Duke with 23 points. Keith Langford was the only other Jayhawk in double figures with 13 points (*USA Today*, April 8, 2003, p. 7C).	40 Minutes
Book Review	In this persuasive and gently humorous novel, the discovery of a newborn baby girl left in a cardboard box creates opportunities for redemption and renewal for the handyman who finds her and for the dowager on whose estate she was abandoned (*Blessings* by Anna Quindlen, *New York Times* Notable Books 2002).	250 pages
	Stephen E. Ambrose, the military historian and biographer whose books recounting the combat feats of American soldiers and airmen fueled a national fascination with the generation that fought World War II, died yesterday at a hospital in Bay St. Louis, Miss. Mr. Ambrose, who lived in Bay St. Louis and Helena, Mont., was 66 (Goldstein, 2002).	66 years

Figure 2.1. Copyright © 2004 Corwin Press. All rights reserved. Reprinted from *Seven Strategies of Highly Effective Readers*, by E. K. McEwan. Thousand Oaks, CA: Corwin Press, www.corwinpress.com. Reproduction authorized only for the local school site that has purchased this book.

say than "It was really awesome." You'll be able to write a short answer on a test and know that you have included the most important ideas. Learning to summarize is like learning to ride a bicycle: Once you know how to do it, you'll never forget it. But just like riding a bicycle, learning how to summarize takes lots of practice.

Class, most students (and adults) have problems with summarizing because no one has ever shown them how to do it. I remember being asked in school to read something and then summarize it, but no one showed me how to do it. I wasn't summarizing, I was actually "paralyzing," if you know what I mean. It took me a long time to figure out that it wasn't my problem—it was the teacher's problem. He didn't know how to summarize either. But I am going to show you how and then give you lots of opportunities to practice before I give you any assignments to do on your own. The whole process will take several weeks, but when we finish, you will know how to summarize. Summarizing is especially helpful when you want to understand and remember what you read, so it's worth spending time on. Right now, I'm going to model one approach to summarizing for you. Then I'm going to explain the five rules [procedures and prompts] of summarizing that I've posted on the bulletin board

Summarizing Definitions

Term	Definition
Summary	One or two sentences in your own words that convey the main idea of a larger section of text
Gist	Synonymous with *summary*; comes from a British legal expression meaning the summed-up criminal charges being made against an individual
Key word	A word that conceptualizes or captures an important concept or main idea of a paragraph, section of text, article, or book
Paraphrase	Much shorter than the original text but longer than a summary
Retelling	Shorter than the original text but longer than either a summary or a paraphrasing; summarizes narrative text but contains more details as well as relating the sequence of events in order
Theme	A generalization, big idea, concept, lesson, or moral about life, human nature, or the world that is developed through the central event or outcome of a story; often stated in just one word but also described as a lesson that has been learned
Chunk	To divide a larger piece of text into smaller parts
Compact	To make a chunk even smaller by deleting unimportant information or collapsing lists into a word or phrase
Conceptualize	To think of one word that sums up a chunk of text
Connect	To combine several key words with connecting words to generate a summary sentence
Main Idea	The "big" or most important idea of a section of text, article, or book

Figure 2.2. This chart and some of its definitions were informed by Cunningham & More, 1986.

The Five C's of Summarizing

Comprehend		Read and understand the text.
Chunk		Divide the text into parts.
Compact	Make each chunk smaller.	
Conceptualize	Think of a key word for each chunk.	
Connect	Combine the key words into a summary sentence.	

[Roger displays transparency of Figure 2.3, The Five C's of Summarizing.] *Then later this week, I'll model several other approaches to writing summaries. After that, we'll practice writing some summaries together, and then we're actually going to write some summaries of picture books for the librarian, so if you have a favorite childhood book to nominate for summarizing, just let me know. Once we've written some summaries together, then you will work in small groups and write a group summary together. I'll be around to help you whenever you have a question. In a few weeks, every person in this class will be writing spectacular summaries.*

Class, remember that what we are doing today is just the beginning of learning to summarize. I know you want to start writing immediately, but in the beginning, it's important to learn each step well. I noticed that many of you did a great job of collapsing long lists of items and coming up with a word or two that "conceptualized" the list. I also noticed that some of you thought you didn't need to collapse the list and come up with a key word. You thought you could get away with skipping that step. Remember—be kind to your working memory. It cannot handle too much at once!

Class, this was a very productive session today. We made real progress toward our goal of learning to summarize. What did you learn today that you didn't know how to do yesterday? Turn to your neighbor and summarize what you learned how to do today. You will be able to use your ability to summarize when we begin our research report writing unit next month. You are going to breeze through taking notes. You won't have to copy down everything in the encyclopedia—you'll be able to write a sentence or two that summarizes what an article or book says. Can you think of some other ways you'll be able to use what you learned today? [Teacher gives students opportunity to respond.]

One of the reasons you were so productive was that you were willing to work hard on coming up with just the right key words. I heard some of the groups debating about which word best conceptualized a section. You didn't take shortcuts; you remembered the essence of summarizing—extracting and constructing the meaning of the text before you write or give your summary orally. Remember, if you can't tell somebody about what you've read in your own words, you're not ready to summarize it. You don't understand it yet. Read it again. Chunk it. Compact it. Get rid of the stuff that isn't important. Collapse the long lists and delete the unimportant information. Conceptualize it. Think of one key word that sums up each chunk. Then you'll be ready to write your summary. Good work, class.

THE TEACHING MOVES OF A STRATEGIC TEACHER

Roger Craig's words and actions in the preceding teaching script illustrate only a few of the varied instructional approaches or methodologies that are essential to the effectiveness of SRI: (1) direct instructing and explaining, (2) modeling, (3) giving directions, (4) scaffolding, (5) coaching, (6) attributing, and (7) constructing meaning. The term *teaching moves* captures the essence of what strategic teachers do. They are constantly on the move—physically, emotionally, and intellectually (both cognitively and metacognitively)—making adjustments to meet the challenges of teaching cognitive processes that are situational in nature to students who are often looking for easy and immediate answers. The effectiveness of these seven moves as shown by scientific research is impressive, and they range in style and philosophy from *direct instructing and explaining* on one end of the instructional methodology continuum to *jointly constructing meaning with students* on the other. On any given day in any given classroom, the strategic teacher employs all of these moves—whether with the whole class, a small group, or just one student. Five complementary teaching moves enhance and support the major teaching moves: (1) motivating-connecting, (2) recapping, (3) annotating, (4) assessing-evaluating, and (5) facilitating. Figure 2.4, Strategic Teaching Moves, lists and defines all twelve moves. You will no doubt add some of your own moves to this list as you begin integrating SRI into your classroom. When working with cognitive novices, always begin with direct instructing and explaining for the best results. The ultimate goal is to jointly extract and construct meaning with your students—the essence of SRI.

The brief quotations introducing each of the following teaching-moves sections are drawn from a list of frequently observed instructional approaches in classrooms of strategic teachers (Pressley, El-Dinary, Gaskins, et al., 1992, p. 528).

Strategic Teaching Moves

Option	Description
Direct instructing and explaining	Verbal input about what will happen in a lesson, what the goals are, why it's being done, how it will help students, and what the roles of teachers and students will be during the lesson
Modeling	The act of thinking aloud regarding cognitive processing as well as engaging in observable behaviors, such as note taking, producing a graphic organizer, writing a summary, or looking up something in a book or on the Internet
Giving directions	Unambiguous and concise verbal input that seeks to give students a way to get from where they are at the beginning of a lesson, task, or unit to the achievement of a specific task or outcome; provides wait time for students to process directions, time for students to respond, and opportunities to ask clarifying questions
Scaffolding	A process that enables students to solve problems, carry out tasks, or achieve goals that would otherwise be impossible without teacher modeling, prompting, and support
Coaching	Asking students to think aloud, cueing them to choose a strategy that has been taught thus far to solve a reading problem, delivering mini-lessons where needed, and giving feedback to students
Attributing	Communicating to students that their accomplishments are the result of their strategic approach to reading rather than their intelligence or ability
Constructing meaning	Working collaboratively with students to extract and construct multiple meanings from text
Motivating-connecting	The component of instruction that seeks to generate interest, activate prior knowledge, and connect instruction to the real world or the solution of real problems
Recapping	The act of summarizing what has been concluded, learned, or constructed during a given discussion or class period as well as a statement of why it is important and where it can be applied or connected in the future
Annotating	The act of adding additional information during the course of reading or discussion—information that students do not have but need in order to make sense of the text
Assessing-evaluating	Determining what students have learned and where instruction needs to be adjusted and adapted by assessing, both formally and informally
Facilitating	Thinking along with students and helping them develop their own ideas, rather than managing their thinking, explaining ideas, and telling them what and how to do something

Direct Instructing and Explaining

"Teachers explained one or more strategies in every class, sometimes new strategies, sometimes ones covered previously."

The first and most essential aspect of effective strategy instruction is *direct instructing and explaining* (Duffy, 2002; Duffy et al., 1987). Direct instructing and explaining is explicit in nature: *plain in language, distinctly expressed, clearly stated, and not merely implied.* Explaining conveys the sense of "making clear or intelligible something that is not known or understood" (Guralnik, 1980, p. 493). The kind of explaining needed for explicit cognitive strategy instruction involves telling students precisely what strategy they will be learning, why learning a particular strategy is valuable, under what circumstances they will find the strategy to be useful, and showing them what the critical attributes of the strategy look like in both thought and word. Explicit instruction means helping students to understand a complex task (e.g., writing a summary, making an inference) one step at a time. Students should never have to guess regarding the objectives, tasks, or rationale of lessons. A variety of experimental research studies have investigated and shown the efficacy of direct explanations by teachers to students regarding the exact nature of the strategy, reasons for using cognitive strategies, and the kinds of situations in which different cognitive strategies are most effective (Rosenshine, 1979). Recall Figure 1.1 in Chapter 1.

Modeling

"Most lessons included teacher modeling of one or more strategies, typically by teachers thinking aloud as they performed a task."

Whether this aspect of cognitive strategy instruction is called *mental modeling, simulation,* or *thinking aloud,* it consists of "showing students exactly how a good reader would apply [a particular] strategy" (Bereiter & Bird, 1985; Pressley, El-Dinary, & Brown, 1992, p. 112). If you have never engaged in thinking aloud for students, your initial attempts may seem awkward and artificial to you, but with practice, you can become a strategic teacher who routinely thinks aloud (Davey, 1983).

Thinking aloud means different things to different folks depending on who is describing it. For example, thinking aloud has been suggested as the perfect alternative assessment to the typical read-and-question format of many standardized and criterion-referenced tests (Wade, 1990), and indeed it is (in another context). Think-alouds have also been recommended as a way to teach students how to monitor and assess their own reading comprehension (Afflerbach, 2002), and think-alouds used in this context are a superb way for students to interact with their classmates as well.

In this discussion, however, *thinking aloud* refers to the "artificial representation of a real experience; a contrived series of activities which, when taken together, approximate[s] the experience of the process that ultimately is to be applied independently" (Herber & Nelson as quoted in Herber & Herber, 1993, p. 140). Figure 2.5, The Think-Aloud Process, illustrates what happens in your brain (or the brain of any highly effective reader) during the reading process combined with a description of how the "raw material" of a teacher

The Think-Aloud Process

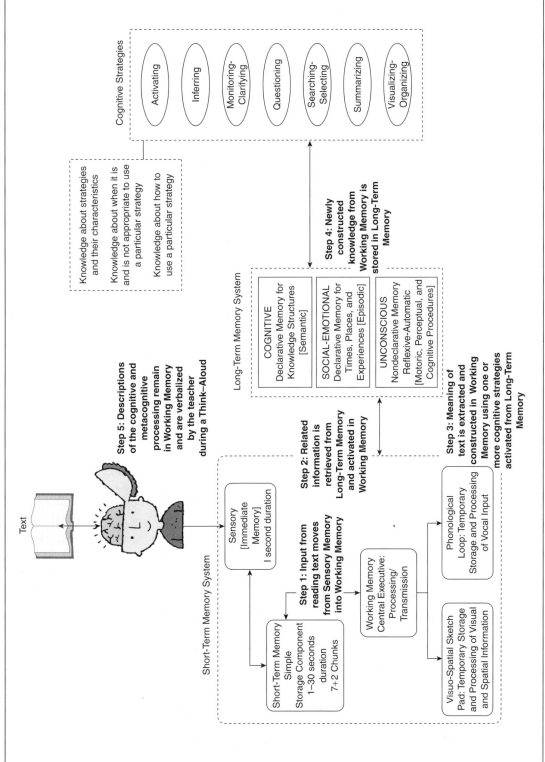

Figure 2.5. This figure was developed using Inspiration® Software and is based on the author's interpretation of the discussions, theories, and research found in the following: Baddeley, 1997; Baddeley & Logie, 1999; Beatty, 2001; Engle, Cantor, & Carullo, 1999; Engle, Kane & Tuholski, 1999; Engle, Tuholski, Laughlin, & Conway, 1999; Miyake & Shah, 1999; Novak, 1998; Pressley & Afflerbach, 1995; Squire & Kandel, 1999; Towse & Houstan-Price, 1999; van den Broek, Young, Tzeng, & Lindholm, 1999; van Someren, Barnard, & Sandberg, 1994; and Weinstein & Hume, 1998. Copyright © 2004 Corwin Press. All rights reserved. Reprinted from *Seven Strategies of Highly Effective Readers*, by E. K. McEwan. Thousand Oaks, CA: Corwin Press. www.corwinpress.com. Reproduction authorized only for the local school site that has purchased this book.

23

think-aloud is generated from this processing. The five explanatory steps are adapted from Van Someren, Barnard, and Sandberg (1994, p. 20). The steps are described here and numbered correspondingly in the figure.

Figure 2.5 illustrates the two memory systems, long-term and short-term, found in the human brain. Regrettably, a one-dimensional figure cannot do justice to the complexity of the brain. Some parts of the brain (e.g., working memory) are theorized to have both processing and storage capacities, and most of the boxes that seem to represent specific locations are, in reality, functions of the brain. For example, a specific part of the brain may process one type of information and store it in the same "location." Another limitation of Figure 2.5 is its simplicity. In the interests of clarity and brevity, only one two-way arrow is drawn between the various systems and the text input. However, cognitive processing during highly effective reading resembles a freeway system during rush hour in Los Angeles more than a single roadway through an uncluttered countryside.

As you (or any other reader) read a piece of text, whether easy or difficult, the content is perceived in your sensory (immediate) memory and is transmitted in milliseconds through your short-term memory to working memory (Step 1 on Figure 2.5). The text input activates information, concepts, ideas, and feelings in your three long-term memory stores (cognitive, social-emotional, and unconscious), and the data are immediately transmitted to your working memory (see Step 2). There, in the central executive section of your working memory, one or more of your cognitive strategies processes the text; connects it to the applicable information, concepts, ideas, or feelings retrieved from long-term memory; and constructs new meaning (Step 3), which will ultimately make its way back into your long-term memory stores (Step 4) if sufficient processing takes place and strong connections are made. Your cognitive processes may have included clarifying confusion by fixing up a mix-up, inferring the author's meaning by making a prediction or developing a hypothesis, visualizing a particularly vivid scene in the text, or formulating a question to ask an expert.

The gist of the text you read and precisely how you processed it remain active for a short while in your working memory (particularly if you continue to reflect on it after reading), and with practice, your thought processes can be verbalized (Step 5). You will then be able to think aloud about your thinking (processing). Cognitive scientists call "thinking about one's thinking" *metacognition*. The more metacognitive you are, the more readily you will be able to articulate your thinking processes for students. The more metacognitive your students become, the more easily they will be able to monitor and clarify as they read, think aloud to demonstrate their personal use of cognitive strategies, and extract and construct meaning that is long-term. As you become more adept at thinking aloud, students will follow your lead. Initially, facilitate thinking aloud with a script that contains a draft of your thoughts (cognitive processes) during reading.

Although you may feel that this kind of verbalizing is unnecessary, even a waste of time, consider the fact that many students (particularly low-achieving or reluctant readers) will never just pick up strategies or catch on to reading-to-learn with implicit instruction. All students, even the gifted ones, will benefit from daily opportunities, irrespective of grade level or content area, to hear a skilled reader think aloud. The most at-risk students *must* have these opportunities before they will be able to use cognitive strategies personally *or* engage in thinking aloud themselves. Some authors suggest modeling multiple strategies during a think-aloud, but introducing more than one strategy simultaneously may overload the working memories of first-time strategy learners. Unless students are in the upper grades or have had prior exposure to and explanations of the strategies being modeled, less is better. Because thinking aloud *is* both contrived and artificial, take care to make it as realistic and meaningful as possible. Do explain how you figured out the words you did not know, what connections you made to prior knowledge, and how you made sense of unfamiliar concepts and "inconsiderate" text. At first you may feel uncomfortable about sharing your reading "problems," but be assured, your students will pay close attention and take comfort in the fact that you are able to fix up your mix-ups without losing your way. Practice, no matter what the endeavor, produces automaticity and ease. Take all the time you need to become confident before articulating your thoughts to students. The Teacher Think-Alouds found in Chapter 3 model each of the seven strategies.

Giving Directions

"Students were presented an advanced vocabulary for talking about their new thinking. Teachers explicitly defined strategies in terms of their component processes."

You might think it unusual to find a section on *giving directions* in a discussion of the components of cognitive strategy instruction, but this essential aspect of SRI is frequently given short shrift in the interests of time. Giving directions to students is one of the more important teaching moves on the continuum of SRI methodologies, and in the absence of clear and precise directions from their teachers, many students (especially those at risk of academic failure) shut down and tune out. Their experiences remind me of the countless directionless directions I get when looking for workshop locations in unfamiliar cities. Many of the trying-to-be-helpful folks that give me directions make the same mistakes that some experts (teachers) make when giving directions to novices (students). First, they don't provide enough wait time for processing new information. They spout interstate numbers as if they are trying to beat the clock on a quiz show and then look at me in wonderment when I ask if US 14 is the same as Center Street. I can easily forgive *these* direction givers. After all, they didn't volunteer to help me. I buttonholed them behind the counter of a fast-food restaurant or pumping gas at QuikTrip.

My direction givers frequently also violate the second commandment of giving directions: Keep it simple and direct. Rather than telling me to turn left at Maple Avenue, then right at Stone, these helpful souls share six ways to know if I've gone too far. By the time they've finished their litany, I can't remember whether I was turning at Maple, Oak, or Elm. I only know it was a tree. But I'm terrified to ask any questions for fear of further confusion and usually leave in bewilderment, trying in vain to find someone else who can give me what I need: clear, unambiguous directions, time for processing what I've heard, and the opportunity to ask clarifying questions. Students need the same kind of directions from their teachers, particularly when it comes to cognitive strategy instruction.

Scaffolding

"Teachers emphasized the utility of the strategies being taught. Teachers offered information about when to use and when not to use particular strategies . . . [and s]tudents were prompted to model and explain the strategies they were learning, with the precise vocabulary provided in class included in these student commentaries."

When I am explaining the concept of *scaffolding* to teachers, I use the term *supportive.* It means *to keep students from failing or declining.* The educational concept of scaffolding is analogous to the scaffolds that workers install to keep themselves from falling when they are washing windows, painting, or framing. In the instructional realm, scaffolding is in place when the tasks that students are asked to complete (or master) are graduated in difficulty, with each new one being only slightly more difficult than the last. Scaffolded instruction ensures success and keeps students confident and motivated to learn.

Scaffolding can take place in any of four different instructional areas: (1) people, (2) text, (3) tasks, and (4) materials (Dickson, Collins, Simmons, & Kameenui, 1998). Teachers or instructional aides usually provide the "people scaffolds," but peers can also provide instructional support for their classmates if they are taught to do so and then affirmed by adults for their encouraging attitudes. This process also coincidentally aids the understanding, retention, and achievement of more able students (Johnson & Johnson, 1990). The most common kind of teacher scaffolding takes place through the modeling of specific cognitive strategies. Less common, although extremely important, is metacognitive modeling that articulates the rationale for why and how a certain strategy is chosen for a specific reading task. As teachers fade out their thinking aloud (modeling) during cognitive strategy usage, they should always be ready to step in as needed when students are having difficulty with a piece of text or are struggling with finding a key word to use in a summary. Students need encouragement, instruction, and ongoing opportunities to model their own thinking for one another. Then as teachers reduce the amount of modeling, responsibility can be transferred to students for this task.

Content (i.e., the text to be read or the subject to learned) can also be scaffolded to make cognitive strategy instruction less threatening and confusing for students. Use easy, high-interest reading material during the initial phases of cognitive strategy instruction. To choose challenging text for students to read during initial SRI is a surefire way to frustrate them and fail in your own attempts to teach cognitive strategy usage.

A third kind of scaffolding involves the *tasks* that students are expected to master. For example, to write or give a summary, students first need to know how to chunk text: to divide it up into smaller manageable pieces. They also need to know how to collapse lists and delete trivial and unimportant information. The ultimate cognitive challenge of summarizing is conceptualizing key words for each chunk and connecting them into a summary sentence. Only when students have reasonably mastered the preliminary cognitive processes of summarizing will they be able to produce a summary, in writing or orally.

A fourth kind of scaffolding is provided by a variety of *instructional materials* (the procedures, prompts, and props) that support students throughout initial cognitive strategy instruction. Ideally, students won't have to look at the "Five C's of Summarizing" chart forever. They will have internalized the steps, added some new twists of their own, and begun to use them independently. But until that moment, leave the scaffolding in place.

Coaching

"Teacher coaching was the most prominent mode of instruction throughout the program. Coaching included hints, cues, and elaborations of student responses."

In the context of SRI, *coaching* refers to the things that teachers do to foster students' independence in learning. As described in Chapter 1, coaching occurs in the context of a cognitive apprenticeship (Collins, 1991; Collins et al., 1990; Collins et al., 1991; Schoenbach, Greenleaf, Cziko, & Hurwitz, 1999). In a cognitive apprenticeship environment, students observe and emulate their master teachers who regularly think aloud regarding their thought processes, not only during reading and writing but also during other classroom activities. This running commentary by teachers helps students to gradually become self- regulated and cognitively competent. At the same time, strategic teachers are engaging in coaching by way of encouraging, cueing, and prompting (Pressley et al., 2001; Taylor, Pearson, Clark, & Walpole, 2000).

Coaching includes the concept of stretching students a bit farther during each succeeding guided practice while still maintaining the instructional level within their zones of proximal development (Mason et al., 1984; Vygotsky, 1979), where expectations are higher than students can handle independently but not so high as to frustrate their efforts. The following behaviors are just a few of the ways that teachers engage in coaching during strategy instruction:

- Asking students to think aloud as they use cognitive strategies to extract and construct meaning from text
- Cueing students to choose one of the strategies that have been taught thus far to solve a reading problem
- Delivering mini-lessons whenever appropriate during the reading of text, to demonstrate how strategic readers decide which strategy to use in a particular instance
- Giving feedback to their students regarding their progress
- Modeling thinking or offering prompts to remind students of possible thoughts or actions they might take

Coaching usually occurs during the portion of the reading lesson designated as guided practice, in which students are in various stages of assuming increasing responsibility for independent strategy usage and the teacher is gradually releasing responsibility to students as they gain expertise. Pearson and Gallagher (1983) refer to this as a model of "planned obsolescence" in which teachers work themselves out of their explicit instruction and detailed modeling roles and into the instructional components of attributing and constructing.

Attributing

"Teachers frequently attributed student success to the strategies students used."

Strategic reading is challenging mental work, as we pointed out in Chapter 1. Strategic teachers are constantly promoting and "selling" the worth of complex cognition to students. They take every opportunity for pointing out to students that their success in understanding and remembering difficult concepts and ideas was directly related to their cognitive strategy usage. When strategic teachers receive excellent written summaries from their students or overhear a student making a spectacular inference, they are quick to attribute the quality of written work and cognitive processing to their students' resourceful use of cognitive strategies. That is, strategic teachers communicate to students that their thinking is not the result of how smart they are or aren't but is instead the result of their successful application of cognitive strategies. Strategic teachers continually emphasize the importance of the process (cognition), as opposed to the product (the assignment).

Constructing Meaning

"Teachers discussed and modeled flexibility, including discussions about how students might differ in their use of strategies. Students were often reassured that it was all right if their images, predictions, and so on, varied from ones modeled by the teacher or offered by other students. Students learned that, in fact, they should expect and value individual differences."

Constructing meaning is the most energizing and rewarding aspect of SRI. It is tempting for educators to bypass the more mundane teaching moves, such as explaining and giving directions, preferring to fast-forward to the construction of meaning. That is not to say that strategic teachers do not emphasize extracting and constructing meaning whenever students are processing real text (Brown & Campione, 1994). However, strategic teachers know that they will be unable to enjoy the delights of constructing meaning at increasingly more challenging levels of text with their students if they have not laid an instructional foundation of explaining, modeling, and coaching during SRI. As individual group members (students with their teacher) discuss their reactions to their reading, they are in turn influenced by the opinions, experiences, and feelings of other group members. The final meaning of the text that emerges is the product of the group's interaction (Pressley et al., 1995). This more inclusive definition of comprehension not only permits more diverse individual response and interpretation, but it also allows for the consideration of multiple avenues of meaning (Borokowski & Muthukrishna, 1992; Fielding & Pearson, 1994).

THE CHALLENGES OF STRATEGIC READING INSTRUCTION

As appealing as the notion of making learning more meaningful and lasting for students may be to teachers, no one is eager to add more responsibilities to their teaching load. Even though the pressure of high-stakes tests keeps some teachers awake into the wee hours of the morning, there is no groundswell of interest in implementing schoolwide strategy programs. The very idea that an entirely "new" set of instructional activities must take place *before* students can even begin reading their textbooks or novels, or *before* their teachers can begin teaching the assigned curricula, is not a popular one. Teachers are frequently skeptical regarding the benefits of SRI—as well they might be, given the constant onslaught of innovations and expectations that assail the average teacher. They need to view any research with a critical eye to determine if what works on the printed page has the potential to work in their classrooms and schools. Along with the good news, there are significant challenges, frustrations, and obstacles to implementing cognitive strategy instruction in your classroom, school, or district.

Time

One major obstacle to implementing SRI is the time commitment—from everyone. "Becoming an effective . . . strategies instruction teacher takes several years" (Brown, Pressley, Van Meter, & Schuder, 1996, p. 20; Marks et al., 1993). Training, developing, and becoming strategic teachers require a hefty investment of human and monetary resources. Teaching students how and when to use cognitive strategies is a vastly different enterprise than drilling students on a discrete skill or serving up a smorgasbord of literature or content and expecting students to discover what it means on their own.

Staff Development

To teach, coach, and mentor strategic teachers takes a devotion to professional development that is seldom seen in most school districts. Duffy (1993) points out that "helping teachers [become good strategy teachers] will require a significant change in how teacher educators and staff developers work with teachers and what they count as important about learning to be a teacher" (pp. 244–245). The process will take far more than a day or two of casual staff development, because most teachers did not experience this kind of instruction as students themselves. Irene Gaskins, the founder and director of The Benchmark School (Gaskins & Elliott, 1991), advises that it takes teachers at least three years to become strategic teachers (I. Gaskins, personal communication, July 5, 2000).

Also, the typical approach to strategy instruction in most schools is haphazard. Someone, typically an administrator or the reading teacher, becomes aware of the power of cognitive strategies to improve student achievement and convenes a committee to design a staff development program. The "strategies" (usually instructional activities) chosen for implementation are often selected at random, based on the preferences of the teacher who will be doing the training. Teachers may not see the relevance of a particular instructional activity to their grade level or content area or appreciate the importance of modeling their use of strategies to students and emphasizing the motivational aspects of effective strategy instruction. The critical attributes of the strategies as used by skilled readers are often obscured by the instructional activity, and some teachers throw out the strategy (baby) with the activity (dirty bath water). Furthermore, implementation schedules are often too ambitious, leaving teachers undertrained and overwhelmed.

Or teachers may go to a one-day workshop or a convention breakout session and buy into the concept of "reading strategies" based on what they experienced. From my perspective as a staff developer, this approach presents four major problems: (1) The activities are presented as "the strategies" and are often taught with little or no connection to teachers' content specialty or curriculum; (2) a few activities are introduced in isolation, and the notion of a well-conceived multiple-strategy school model is seldom introduced; (3) teachers are led to believe that students will acquire cognitive strategies without explicit instruction; and (4) teachers fail to understand that cognitive strategy instruction is a rigorous, lengthy, and ongoing process—one that requires a major commitment of time and intellectual energy by both teachers and students.

The National Reading Panel (2000) warned that "in spite of heavy emphasis on modeling and metacognitive instruction, even very good teachers may have trouble implementing, and may even omit, crucial aspects of strategic reasoning. The research suggests that when [metacognitive instruction is only] partially implemented, students of strategic teachers will still improve. But it is not easy for teachers to develop readers' conceptions about what it means to be strategic. It takes time, coaching, and careful monitoring to help both teachers and students to be successful" (pp. 4–49).

Ambiguity

A major challenge for administrators and staff developers with regard to strategy instruction is that "being strategic" is much more than knowing a few or even a great many individual strategies. Strategy usage is not a "paint by the numbers" activity. "When faced with a comprehension problem, strategic readers coordinate and shift strategies as appropriate. They constantly alter, adjust, modify, and test until they construct meaning and the problem is solved" (National Reading Panel, 2000, pp. 4–47). What is needed is a model that (1) allows for the ambiguity and messiness that occurs during "real reading," (2) helps teachers deal with constant decision making and unanticipated actions and reactions, (3) encourages teachers to become strategic readers themselves in the "each one teach one" tradition, and (4) allows time for teachers to become expert (Gaskins & Elliot, 1991; Pressley et al., 1995).

THE BENEFITS OF STRATEGIC READING INSTRUCTION

While the challenges of SRI are enormous, the benefits outweigh them. When cognitive strategy instruction begins with listening comprehension activities in kindergarten and is thereafter embedded in content-area instruction at every level, cognitive strategies can be developed to a high level of competence Guthrie et al., 1998), thereby increasing not only the ability of students to learn but also their depth of knowledge. What can we conclude from our examination of cognitive strategy instruction?

"The integration of metacognitive instruction with discipline-based learning can enhance student achievement and develop in students the ability to learn independently. It should be consciously incorporated into curricula across disciplines and age levels." (Bransford, Brown, & Cocking, 2000, p. 21)

WHAT'S AHEAD?

Just ahead, we will examine each of the seven strategies of highly effective readers in depth, as well as "listen" to teachers model the strategies as they read text (narrative and expository) at various levels of difficulty. The next step to becoming a strategic teacher is to determine the critical attributes of the seven strategies of highly effective readers.

Understanding the
Seven Strategies

3

To assume that one can simply have students memorize and routinely execute a set of strategies is to misconceive the nature of strategic processing or executive control. Such rote applications of these procedures represents, in essence, a true oxymoron—nonstrategic strategic processing.

Alexander and Murphy (1998, p. 33)

When I first began to present SRI workshops to educators, my biggest stumbling block was nonspecific definitions and fuzzy objectives. When someone pinned me down regarding just what a summary was, I waffled. Or if a teacher asked me to define *inferring,* the best I could do was "reading between the lines." "Reading between the lines" is a wonderful figure of speech, but it tells students nothing about what is happening in the minds of skilled readers while they are engaging in this mysterious process. The more specific and definitive I became in my instruction about precisely what a strategy "looked like" operationally during the act of skilled reading, and the more explicitly I could model the thoughts and behaviors that demonstrated that strategy, the more readily I could show my students (whether teachers, administrators, or actual students) how to do it for themselves.

The goal of this chapter is to bring more clarity and specificity into your understanding of the seven strategies of highly skilled readers. The strategies are arranged in alphabetical order in the chapter, and each one is illustrated with a teacher think-aloud: (1) activating, (2) inferring, (3) monitoring-clarifying, (4) questioning, (5) searching-selecting, (6) summarizing, and (7) visualizing-organizing. Remember as you read the think-alouds following each strategy explanation that they are intended as examples to show you how one teacher processed a specific piece of text. Your own thinking aloud, even for the same text, will be entirely different because your experiences, background knowledge, and strategic processing are unique. In your classroom, thinking aloud should be a natural act that occurs daily as you describe your thought processes while reading text, either a selection you have chosen specifically for modeling or a classroom text you are reading together with students.

COGNITIVE STRATEGY 1: ACTIVATING

At the root of our ability to learn is our ability to find the experience we have in our memory that is most like the experience we are currently processing.

Schank (1999, p. 41)

The activation of prior knowledge, both before *and* during reading, is a way that effective readers prime their cognitive pumps, so to speak. Whether the knowledge stored in long-term memory is factual, conceptual, or experiential, recalling what is already known about a subject and then connecting it to what is being read greatly increases the likelihood, if not the certainty, that readers will understand and remember what is read while also generating increased levels of motivation and attention. Schank (1999) calls this process *reminding* and explains, "Far from being an irrelevant aspect of memory, reminding is at the heart of how we understand and how we learn" (p. 21).

Activating and retrieving what is known about a specific subject or knowledge domain from the long-term memory system for use in working memory gives readers more information with which to make predictions and generate hypotheses. Activating your students' prior knowledge is not only about asking them what they already know about a specific subject, but it also involves helping them figure out the connections between what they know and what they are reading. One very popular instructional activity designed specifically for achieving this goal is K-W-L (Ogle, 1986), but two cautions are necessary if you wish to use K-W-L as a way to help students activate prior knowledge.[1]

First, K-W-L is an instructional activity, not a strategy, and merely going through the motions of asking students what they know and recording it on a chart may or may not give students the kind of background knowledge they will need to understand a piece of informational text or a story. I have observed lessons in which students knew very little or had mistaken ideas about the concepts in the text. Activating erroneous information is beneficial to learners only if the teacher gently guides them in the correction of any errors of fact, concept, principle, or proposition by showing them what misconceptions they hold. Many students come to school with "faulty mental models" (Pellegrino, 2002, p. 2), making it difficult, if not impossible, to integrate new information and concepts, thus putting up a barrier to deep and meaningful learning. Teachers also have an obligation to readily admit to their own knowledge gaps or mistakes, to model the searching and selecting strategy to find answers, and to demonstrate intellectual honesty for their students. They will soon find students following their lead.

A second important caution when using an activity like K-W-L is that "activity" won't ensure "achievement." Students must individually process the text for themselves, extracting and constructing their own meaning. Carr and Ogle

(1987), in a study of another version of K-W-L called KWL-Plus, found that it was only when students were expected to individually summarize their understanding of what they had read at the end of the lesson that they made the connections needed to gain meaning from the text.

The Teacher Think-Aloud on page 36 presents a teacher modeling the activating strategy while reading *Old Man Rabbit's Dinner Party* (Bailey, 1949). Also, look for an instructional activity in Chapter 4 called *Turn On Your CPU (Central Processing Unit)* that provides prompts and props to help students activate prior knowledge and make connections while they are independently reading text.

COGNITIVE STRATEGY 2: INFERRING

A fully explicit text would not only be very long and boring, but it would destroy the reader's pleasure in imposing meaning on the text—making it their own.

Oakhill et al. (1998, p. 347)

I vividly remember my introduction to the intimidating world of writing fiction. I was working on the first book in a series for reluctant readers ages 10–12. My biggest problem as an author: talking too much. Or in this case, making my characters talk too much. My initial attempts at creating believable dialogue were clumsy and boring. "Leave something to the reader's imagination," my editor advised. She could well have said, "Let your readers infer."

Figuring out what an author has left *unsaid* in the text is usually thought to be the essence of inferring. I call it "reading the author's mind." Some call it "reading between the lines." But inferring is actually putting together and reconciling four different sources of information or knowledge for the purpose of extracting and constructing meaning from the text: (1) what is written in the text, (2) what is unwritten in the text, (3) what is already known by the reader in the form of background knowledge from prior learning, and (4) what is known from readers' personal experiences. An inference can pop into the minds of readers in several different forms: (1) as a prediction of what might happen later on in the text based on what they have read so far; (2) as a conclusion regarding a concept, proposition, or principle in expository text; or (3) as a brand-new idea formed by combining the readers' prior knowledge with the meaning they have extracted from the text (Anderson & Pearson, 1984).

Inference is defined by van den Broek (1994) as "information that is activated during reading yet not explicitly stated in the text" (p. 556). Many teachers describe inferring to their students as a combination of "reading between the lines" (what is unwritten) and "reading outside the lines" (what is known *only* by the reader). While these phrases are certainly among the most popular definitions of inferring, the expressions are far too figurative to use with students unless the lesson also includes ample amounts of teacher modeling (thinking aloud) *and* direct explanation. Most students need to "see" the "invisible" writing between the lines that their teachers (or other skilled readers) see in their minds' eyes as they read. They also need to hear what kind of prior knowledge and experiences their teachers are combining with the text to construct meaning.

Teacher Think-Aloud for Activating

Think-Aloud Script	**Read-Aloud Text:** *Old Man Rabbit's Dinner Party*
When I read a story, I make as many connections as I can between the things I already know and the things I read in the story. I am using a cognitive strategy called activating prior knowledge. *The more I already know about something I am reading, the easier it is to understand and remember what I read. Sometimes I know things because I've learned about them in school. Sometimes I know things because I've actually experienced them in my own life. Sometimes I know things because I've read about them in other books. But, every connection I can make when I'm reading helps me to understand and remember what I read.*	Old Man Rabbit sat at the door of his little house, eating a nice, ripe, juicy turnip. It was a cold frosty day, but Old Man Rabbit was all wrapped up, round and round, with yards and yards of his best red wool muffler, so he didn't care if the wind whistled through his whiskers and blew his ears up straight. Old Man Rabbit had been exercising, too, and that was another reason why he was so nice and warm.

TEACHER READS ALOUD TO FIRST DOTTED LINE.

I can tell right away that this is a just-pretend, fairy-tale kind of story because rabbits don't live in houses with doors or sit in chairs. That's something that I know. The first connection I can make is with the word "turnip". I know that turnips are purple vegetables with leafy green tops like carrots. In my opinion, turnips don't taste as good as carrots but they are very healthy. I also know that rabbits love them. I remember another story I once read where Peter Rabbit was in Mr. MacGregor's garden eating his vegetables. In this story, Old Man Rabbit is in Farmer Dwyer's corn patch. I wonder if the author of this story ever read the Peter Rabbit story. I would ask her that question if she were here.

Early in the morning he had started off, lippity, clippity, down the little brown path that lay in front of his house and led to Farmer Dwyer's corn patch. The path was all covered with shiny red leaves. Old Man Rabbit scuffled through them and he carried a great big bag over his back. In the corn patch he found two or three fat, red ears of corn that Farmer Dwyer had missed, so he dropped them into his bag. A little farther along he found some purple turnips and some yellow carrots and quite a few russet apples that Farmer Dwyer had arranged in little piles in the orchard. Old Man Rabbit went in the barn, squeezing under the big front door by making himself very flat, and he filled all the chinks in his bag with potatoes, and he took a couple of eggs in his paws, for he thought he might want to stir up a little pudding for himself before the day was over.

TEACHER READS ALOUD TO SECOND DOTTED LINE.

Thinking about the Peter Rabbit story reminds me of another reason this is a make-believe story, just like the Peter Rabbit story. In stories like these, animals act like people, but they also act like animals. Old Man Rabbit is eating turnips like rabbits do, but he also has a red wool muffler wrapped around him like a person would. I know what a muffler is. It's a long scarf. My daughter once knit a muffler that was six feet long. She could wrap it around and around herself too. I do know that a muffler is also a part that cars and trucks need to keep their engines from making too much noise. But, I know that lots of words have many meanings and so I know that the muffler in this story is a scarf— not a part of a car or truck.

Then Old Man Rabbit started off home again down the little brown path, his mouth watering every time his bag bumped against his back, and not meeting anyone on the way because it was so very, very early in the morning.

When he came to the little house he emptied his bag and arranged all his harvest in piles in his front room—the corn in one pile, the carrots in one pile, the turnips in another pile, and the apples and potatoes in the last pile. He beat up his eggs and stirred some flour with them and filled it full of currants to make a pudding. And, when he had put his pudding in a bag and set it boiling on the stove, he went outside to sit a while and eat a turnip, thinking all the time what a mighty fine old rabbit he was, and so clever, too. Well, while Old Man Rabbit was sitting there in front of his little house, wrapped up in his red muffler and munching the turnip, he heard a little noise in the leaves.

TEACHER READS ALOUD TO END OF TEXT.

I know from reading books and also from living in states where there are four seasons that in the fall farmers harvest their crops and animals gather up food for the long winter months when snow covers the ground and they can't find any. I know about something else that happens in the fall—the leaves turn brilliant colors and drop off the trees to the ground.

There are lots of hints in the story that it's fall: Farmer Dwyer has harvested his corn; he's picked apples from the orchard, and there are shiny red leaves on the ground that Old Man Rabbit is walking through. I wonder why it says that Old Man Rabbit was clever. Maybe he was collecting food. I've read some other stories about animals getting ready for winter. I also wonder what the little noise in the leaves was. Could be a mouse. I'll read on to find out.

Inferring is one of the most essential cognitive strategies that skilled readers use. It is frequently employed in combination with other strategies, but its complexity and sophistication, as well as its heavy dependence on background knowledge and vocabulary, often make it a challenge to teach to students (Hirsch, 2003). Based on their extensive interviews with expert readers, Pressley and Afflerbach (1995) identified the following higher-level inferences that skilled readers are constantly making:

- Referents of pronouns (i.e., determining the person to whom a pronoun is referring)
- Meanings of unknown vocabulary
- Subtle connotations in text
- Elaborations of ideas based on knowledge of the text or author or subject area
- How ideas in a text relate to one's own opinions and theories
- The author's purposes in writing the text
- The author's assumptions about the world
- The author's sources and strategies in writing the text
- The text characters' intentions and characteristics
- The nature of the world in which the written text takes place
- The conclusions suggested by the text

The Teacher Think-Aloud on pages 38–41 contains an example of the inferring strategy using an excerpt from *Tom Sawyer* (Twain, 1876), while Chapter 4 contains three instructional activities designed to facilitate the acquisition of inferring by your students: *Add It Up, A Dozen Ways to Infer,* and *A Dozen Ways to Say "Infer."*

COGNITIVE STRATEGY 3: MONITORING-CLARIFYING

Readers can interpret and evaluate an author's message from the print on the page only to the extent that they possess and call forth the vocabulary, syntactic, rhetorical, topical, analytic, and social knowledge and sensitivities on which the meaning of the text depends.

Adams (1998, p. 73)

Monitoring is thinking about how and what one is reading, both during and after the act of reading, for purposes of determining if one is comprehending the text. Its cognitive partner, *clarifying,* consists of fixing up the mix-ups that interfere with comprehension. Monitoring and clarifying function as a team. Monitoring is evaluative; clarifying is regulatory (Baker, 2002). Readers who are monitoring "address text ideas immediately while they are reading . . . try to develop and grapple with ideas, and try to construct meaning" (Beck, McKeown, Hamilton, & Kucan, 1997, p. 6). Clarifying (clearing up confusion) consists of drawing on appropriate fix-up actions based on knowledge (cues) about six different language systems: (1) graphophonic, (2) semantic, (3) pragmatic, (4) syntactic, (5) schematic, and (6) lexical (Collins et al., 1990).

Teacher Think-Aloud for Inferring: Part 1

Think-Aloud Script	**Read-Aloud Text:** *The Adventures of Tom Sawyer*

There are many important ideas and meanings in a story that aren't written down in actual words. I have to figure them out using clues, just like a detective solves a mystery. I do this by using a cognitive strategy called inferring. *Inferring is putting together the actual words in the text with what the author means (but doesn't always put into words) along with what I know from my experience and what I've learned in school. I use the poster on the bulletin board to remind me to "add up" everything I know with what's in the text so I can figure out what it means.*

TEACHER DISPLAYS ADD IT UP POSTER.

I'm going to infer out loud for you so you can "see" or "hear" what's going on in my brain while I'm reading the first few paragraphs of a book.

Inferring is a kind of thinking or processing that readers do, and when I say "I infer" it means that "I think" a certain way about something; I have drawn a conclusion or made a judgment.

There are many different ways that I can say "I infer," and if you listen to people you will often hear them say, "I think," or "I deduct," or "I believe." What I mean when I say think, deduct, *or* believe *is that I've added up what I've read, what the author means but hasn't put into words, what I know from experience, and what I know from learning in school, and I've come up with an inference. I use the poster I've put up on the bulletin board to remind me of all of the different ways I can say "infer."*

TEACHER DISPLAYS WAYS TO SAY INFER GRAPHIC ORGANIZER.

TEACHER READS ALOUD TO FIRST DOTTED LINE.

Whoever is talking in these first few lines is pretty upset. I don't know who is speaking these words, but the capital letters and exclamation points let me know how that person feels. I believe that Tom must be in trouble or maybe even hiding from the person who's calling his name. I don't understand the question "What's gone with that boy, I wonder?" I will have to read between the lines right here. To do that I figure out something the person might have said that would make sense here and then decide if that's what this person means but isn't saying it the same way I would. I'm going to try: I wonder what that boy is up to now? That makes sense to me. Or it could mean, I wonder where that boy is hiding now? That makes sense, too. I'm going to go with my first sentence. I think that's what the author means even though he wrote something else.

"TOM!" No answer.

"Tom!" No answer. "What's gone with that boy, I wonder? You, TOM!"
No answer.

The old lady pulled her spectacles down and looked over them about the room; then she put them up and looked out under them. She seldom or never looked through them for so small a thing as a boy; they were her state pair, the pride of her heart, and were built for "style," not service—she could have seen through a pair of stove lids just as well. She looked perplexed for a moment, and then said, not fiercely, but still loud enough for the furniture to hear:

"Well, I lay, if I get hold of you I'll—"

She did not finish, for by this time she was bending down and punching under the bed with the broom, and so she needed breath to punctuate the punches with. She resurrected nothing but the cat. "I never did see the beat of that boy!"

She went to the open door and stood in it and looked out among the tomato vines and "jimpson" weeds that constituted the garden. No Tom. So she lifted up her voice at an angle calculated for distance, and shouted:

"Y-o-u-u, Tom."

There was a slight noise behind her and she turned just in time to seize a small boy by the slack of his roundabout and arrest his flight.

Read-Aloud Text from the public domain (Twain, 1876).

Teacher Think-Aloud for Inferring: Part 2

Think-Aloud Script

TEACHER READS ALOUD TO SECOND
DOTTED LINE.

I infer from the language of the story that the historical period or "time" of the story is at least a hundred years ago. I think that the story takes place (setting) in the southern part of the United States because of the expressions that are used ("Well, I lay"). I think that the author of this story has a sense of humor because he says things like "she could have seen through a pair of stove lids just as well," and "loud enough for the furniture to hear." He uses a lot of figurative language.

I think that the old woman is somewhat vain because she wears glasses that look good but are totally useless for seeing anything. I suspect Tom is naughty and often hides from the old lady because she is looking for him under the bed. I also guess that Tom will be getting a spanking.

TEACHER READS ALOUD TO END OF TEXT.

I think that Tom and the woman live in a small town where everybody knows and trusts everybody else because the door is standing open—something you wouldn't find in the city. I think that the house is run-down because the garden only has tomato vines and weeds.

I think that Tom is big enough to think of doing naughty things, but small enough to be caught by the seat of his pants. I think Tom knows he is in trouble because he is hiding.

I've made some notes about what the author wrote and what I read "between the lines" to help me keep track of the inferences Mark Twain expects his readers to make.

TEACHER DISPLAYS INFERENCES FROM *TOM SAWYER.*

Add It Up

What You Read	![book image] xxxxxxxxxx xxxxxxxxxx	This is what the author wrote and is printed on the page.
What's "Between the Lines"	This is what the author means but didn't put into words.	xxxxxxxxxxx xxxxxxxxx xxxxxxxxxxx
What You Know	This is what you know based on your personal experiences.	
What You've Learned	This is knowledge that you have gained from learning in school and reading books.	

Ways to Say I Infer

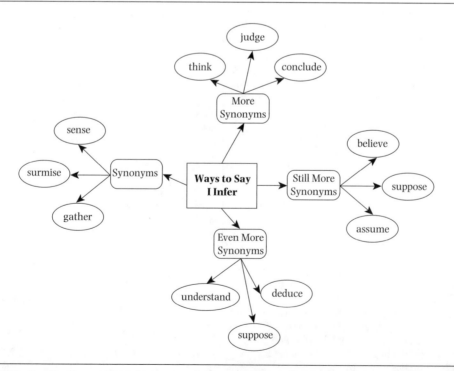

Teacher's Inferences from *Tom Sawyer*

What the *Author* (Mark Twain) Wrote	What the *Teacher* Reads Between the Lines
"What's gone with that boy, I wonder?"	Where did that boy go? Where is that boy? What's that boy up to?
". . . they were her state pair . . ."	They were her good glasses and only for "show."
"she could have seen through a pair of stove lids just as well"	She couldn't see through them at all. She was blind as a bat with her glasses on.
"but loud enough for the furniture to hear"	She didn't shout but her voice could probably be heard all over the house.
"Well, I lay, if I get a hold you I'll—"	If I catch you, you're going to get a spanking.
"I never did see the beat of that boy."	I haven't seen hide nor hair of Tom. I haven't seen Tom at all.
"She lifted up her voice at an angle calculated for distance . . ."	She lifted up her head so her voice would carry and Tom would hear her no matter where he was hiding.
". . . she turned just in time to seize a small boy by the slack of his roundabout and arrest his flight."	She grabbed Tom by the back of his pants and in doing so lifted him right off the ground so that it looked like she had stopped him while he was flying through the air.

Highly effective readers fix up their mix-ups in routine and automatic ways, much like skilled drivers adapt to changes in road conditions, detours, or the sense that they are lost. *Cues* are signals or hints about the way the English language works that are communicated to skilled readers through the printed word. To notice those cues, readers have to draw on their background knowledge about language. Consider the variety of cues that children from linguistically rich environments pick up naturally and that voracious readers easily learn in school.

For example, as you processed the preceding text, you may have slowed down or even stopped at the word *graphophonic*. You detected a slight mix-up, something that slowed down your reading and raised a question in your mind. *Graphophonic* is a tongue-twister of a word, and to pronounce it, you likely used your graphophonic knowledge to decode it. Once you "heard" the word in your mind or even said it aloud to practice it, you were able to move on.

At the same time you were decoding *graphophonic*, you were also using *semantic cues* to infer the meaning of *graphophonic*—having to do with both written language (graph) and spoken words (phon). Without any conscious awareness of doing so, you no doubt used *pragmatic cues* to enlarge the word's dictionary meaning based on your personal experiences with phonics instruction. You also recognized from the *syntactic cues* that *graphophonic* was an adjective, describing the word *cues*.

Since you already have a well-developed knowledge structure surrounding this word, you drew from *schematic cues* to fit in what you were reading with what you already know. Last, you used *lexical cues* to think of all of the words you know that are related to *graphophonic*—phonics, phonemic, phonological, telephone, phonograph, and so on. And you did all of this processing in a fraction of second—in the blink of an eye. As Moats (1999) says, "Teaching reading is rocket science" (n.p.). In addition to using cues from the various language systems (i.e., the text's linguistic characteristics), highly effective readers also monitor their reading on several other levels by asking and answering questions for themselves. "Self questioners know what they know and, as importantly, know what they don't know" (King, 1989, p. 367). Here are some of the questions that highly effective readers use to monitor and clarify their reading: (1) Does this text satisfy my purpose for reading? (2) Is the text too difficult for me to understand? (3) What is the style of the text? (4) Does the author of the text have any biases? (5) Why am I having such a hard time concentrating on the text? (6) What should I do about the fact that the text is poorly written? (7) Do I have enough background knowledge to understand this text? (8) Where could I find more information to help me? (9) Shall I look up this word I don't know, or shall I keep reading? (9) Should I read faster? Or more slowly? (10) Do I need to reread this to increase my understanding?

The Teacher Think-Aloud on page 43 illustrates the cognitive strategy of monitoring-clarifying using a historical document: a letter from President Thomas Jefferson to Captain Meriwether Lewis containing instructions regarding his exploration of the Louisiana Territory. Chapter 4 contains two instructional activities to facilitate the development of monitoring-clarifying: *Turn On Your CPU (Central Processing Unit)* and *Fix Up Your Mix-Ups*.

Teacher Think-Aloud for Monitoring-Clarifying

Think-Aloud Script	**Read-Aloud Text:** Letter From Jefferson to Lewis

When I read difficult text or text about an unfamiliar subject, I use a cognitive strategy called monitoring-clarifying. *When I use this strategy, I pay close attention to what I am reading and remain aware of how well I understand it and then clarify or fix up any of my misunderstandings or mix-ups. Sometimes I use a Checklist like the one I have put up on the overhead.*

TEACHER DISPLAYS CLARIFYING CHECKLIST (pg. 44).

The text that I am reading is an excerpt of a letter that Thomas Jefferson, the third president of the United States, wrote to Meriwether Lewis, an army officer, who was engaged along with Lieutenant William Clark to explore parts of the Louisiana Purchase. I don't know a lot about this topic, but I know that when I am traveling by car west of the Mississippi River, I see quite a few signs about Lewis and Clark. They covered a lot of territory in their travels.

TEACHER READS TO FIRST DOTTED LINE.

As soon as I begin reading, I get a little confused by Jefferson's use of the word "objects." He says that Lewis is well acquainted with the objects of his confidential message. Does he mean the contents or subjects of the message? I'm not sure. Perhaps Jefferson is talking about objectives or goals that Lewis will have for his exploratory mission since he talks about carrying them to execution much as one would set about carrying out a plan.

It appears from this text that Lewis is to have whatever he needs to get the job done.

Obviously, punctuation and grammar have changed since Thomas Jefferson's day. I notice that rather than using the form "its" to show a possessive, Jefferson uses "it's." I wonder when that usage changed. These little things slow down my reading.

Jefferson uses the word "communicated" in the first line in the way that we use it today, but then he says that the Missouri River communicates with the Pacific Ocean. Now, he can't mean that the river and the ocean talk to each other. So he must have some other meaning in mind. I'm going to assume (or infer) that he means they just flow into or out of each other, that there is no land interrupting the flow of the water.

TEACHER READS TO END OF TEXT.

I ran into another phrase I don't understand—"characters of a durable kind." I know the dictionary meaning of character: someone who plays a role in a play or the kind of person someone is (honest, kind), as in a character trait. But neither of those meanings makes sense in this context. I'm going to reread this to myself again and see if I can make sense of it. I think maybe I get it now. Character in this context seems to be just like the word "characteristic" in our language today. So Jefferson is talking about places along the river with characteristics. I think the word "mark" means "landmark" here: a place you could identify if you went back again.

June 20, 1803

To Meriwether Lewis esquire, Captain of the 1st regiment of infantry of the United States of America.

Your situation as Secretary of the President of the United States has made you acquainted with the objects of my confidential message of Jan. 18, 1803 to the legislature: you have seen the act they passed, which, tho' expressed in general terms, was meant to sanction those objects, and you are appointed to carry them into execution.

Instruments for ascertaining by celestial observations the geography of the country, thro' which you will pass, have been already provided. light articles for barter, & presents among the Indians, arms for your attendants, say for from 10 to 12 men, boats, tents, & other traveling apparatus, with ammunition, medicine, surgical instruments & provisions you will have prepared with such aids as the Secretary at War can yield in his department; & from him also you will receive authority to engage among our troops, by voluntary agreement, the number of attendants abovementioned, over whom you, as their commanding officer, are invested with all the powers the laws give in such a case.

As your movements while within the limits of the US will be better directed by occasional communications, adapted to circumstances as they arise, they will not be noticed here. what follows will respect your proceedings after your departure from the US.

Your mission has been communicated to the Ministers here from France, Spain, & Great Britain, and through them to their governments; and such assurances given them as to it's objects, as we trust will satisfy them, the country of Louisiana having been ceded by Spain to France, the passport you have from the Minister of France, the representative of the present sovereign of the country, will be a protection with all it's subjects: and that from the Minister of England will entitle you to the friendly aid of any traders of that allegiance with whom you may happen to meet.

The object of your mission is to explore the Missouri river; & such principal stream of it, as by it's course & communication with the waters of the Pacific ocean, may offer the most direct & practicable water communication across this continent, for the purpose of commerce.

Beginning at the mouth of the Missouri, you will take observations of latitude & longitude, at all remarkable points on the river, & especially at the mouths of rivers, at rapids, at islands & other places & objects distinguished by such natural marks & characters of a durable kind, as that they may with certainty be recognized hereafter the courses of the river between these points of observation may be supplied by the compass, the log-line & by time, corrected by the observations themselves, the variations of the compass too, in different places, should be noticed.

The interesting points of the portage between the heads of the Missouri & the water offering the best communication with the Pacific ocean, should also be fixed by observation, & the course of that water to the ocean, in the same manner as that of the Missouri.

Read-Aloud Text from the public domain (Jefferson, 1803).

Clarifying Checklist
_____

Is there something specific you don't understand? A word, phrase, concept, idea?

☐ Ask someone, e.g., an adult, an expert, a classmate, the author, or your teacher.

☐ Look it up: in the dictionary, an encyclopedia, the index, the glossary, or on the Internet.

☐ Make a prediction: "This must be what the author means. I'm going to keep on reading and see if I'm right."

☐ Predict word meaning based on context or word structure.

Is the text poorly written, disorganized, or very long?

☐ Chunk it, i.e., divide the text into smaller sections and work on one section at a time.

☐ Draw a picture or diagram, i.e., make a graphic organizer.

☐ Outline it.

Are you confused about the meaning of the text?

☐ Read the back cover copy, the blurb, the preface, a chapter summary, the introduction, a review, or critique for more clues about the meaning.

☐ Connect what you have read to your experience: "This reminds me of the time that. . . ."

☐ Read the text again or even once more, if necessary.

☐ Read the text more slowly.

☐ Stop and think out loud to yourself about what you have read.

☐ Talk to someone, i.e., think aloud to a friend, family member, or classmate.

☐ Ignore the parts you don't understand temporarily and keep reading.

Do you need to remember what you are reading for a test or to write a summary?

☐ Form a study group and talk about the text with your classmates.

☐ Make a mental picture, i.e., imagine what the text is describing.

☐ Write it down, i.e., take notes.

COGNITIVE STRATEGY 4: QUESTIONING

Asking one's own questions is a form of making predictions and is essential to comprehension—it forces one to construct meaning rather than passively accept text as it is encountered.

Cecil (1995, p. 3)

Questioning is as common in schools as homework and tests, and often it is just as ineffective in promoting meaningful learning. That's because the wrong individuals, in my opinion, are asking the questions: the teachers. Students are supposed to come up with correct answers as evidence of their comprehension, but teachers usually end up answering their own questions. Beck et al. (1997) suggest that the typical initiate, respond, and evaluate (IRE) questioning model (Dillon, 1988; Mehan, 1979) leaves much to be desired when it comes to uncovering students' comprehension breakdowns. Furthermore, hearing classmates (or the teacher) give *correct* answers to questions usually does nothing for the student who may have no clue as to why the answer *is* an appropriate one. It is the generation *and* answering of higher-level questions by students that "encourage[s] deeper processing and more thorough organization" (Just & Carpenter, 1987, p. 422).

Questioning, whether in the asking or answering mode, is a powerful strategy for processing text, but students need explicit instruction regarding various types of questions combined with daily opportunities for hearing teachers think aloud about how they self-question, generate questions, and find answers to questions asked by others. The cognitive benefits of teaching a variety of questioning approaches to students include improved memory for text, the ability to answer questions with more accuracy, and the ability to more easily find answers to questions as well as to discriminate between types of questions and how to access answers to them (Trabasso & Bouchard, 2002, pp. 180–181).

The questioning strategy is multifaceted and is generally used in tandem with the inferring, summarizing, and searching-selecting strategies. Consider the many ways that your students can use questions in the classroom and in their recreational and academic reading: (1) to ask the author (in a figurative sense), (2) to quiz themselves to make sure they are getting the main idea and important details, (3) to generate questions to ask classmates as part of homework assignments, (4) to figure out which questions the teacher will use on the quiz this Friday, (5) to quiz members of their cooperative group about something they have been reading together, or (6) to ask the teacher about something that is confusing or unknown in the text. Teaching your students how to use the questioning strategy in all of its combinations and permutations goes far beyond just asking higher-level questions after students have read a text selection. They need explicit instruction regarding the critical attributes of the various types of questions, prompts to help them generate their own questions, and ample teacher modeling to show them how it's done. If your students never ask you or each other any questions, they are missing out on an entire dimension of learning: finding answers to the questions that puzzle them.

The Teacher Think-Aloud on pages 46–50 models the questioning strategy, while Chapter 4 contains posters illustrating prompts for four types of questions: recall, compare/contrast, cause/effect, and evaluation (Posters 4.6 through 4.9) as well as an instructional activity, *Do You Have Any Questions?*

Teacher Think-Aloud for Questioning: Part 1

Think-Aloud Script	**Read-Aloud Text:** *The Emperor's New Clothes*

Think-Aloud Script

When I read text (whether a story or nonfiction), I constantly ask questions. Sometimes I ask myself questions to make sure I'm paying attention and understanding while I'm reading. Or I might be asking the author a question because there's something in the text that I don't quite understand. I know that the author of what I'm reading isn't really here, but questioning is a way of getting into authors' minds and figuring out what they mean. Questioning is a very important cognitive strategy, and when I am in a questioning mode, I always understand and remember what I read more completely.

There are several different approaches I can take to questioning while I'm reading, but today, I'm going to make up some questions that can be answered by reading this story. When I make up questions to ask someone else, I have to know the answers or have an idea of what a good answer would be. Making up questions is different from self-questioning or questioning the author. When I question myself or question the author, I am trying to find answers. Right now, I'm making up questions to which I will have to know the answers. When I make up questions, I read and think differently than when I'm looking for answers in the text. I use the Question-Answer Quadrant to help me keep track of the kinds of questions I need to ask and where the answers to these questions will be found.

TEACHER DISPLAYS QUESTION-ANSWER QUADRANT (pg. 50).

I am going to make up four kinds of questions to ask someone who has read this story, one for each of the quadrants on the chart.

The answer to the first question I come up with has to be stated exactly in one place in the book. I remind myself of that by looking at the picture prompt in the upper left-hand quadrant of the Question-Answer Quadrant. It's a book with a single arrow pointing to one place.

The answer to the second question I'm going to make up has to be found in several different places in the text. The picture prompt for that kind of question is the book in the top right-hand quadrant. There are arrows pointing to several places. So, I have to ask a question that will require putting together information from several different places to answer it.

The answer to the third question I will make up has to be in the book, but it won't be written down. I'll have to use my brain and the inferring strategy to think of this question and so will the person who answers it.

Read-Aloud Text: *The Emperor's New Clothes*

Many years ago there was an Emperor who was so fond of new clothes that he spent all of his money on them. He never went to the theater or hunted wild boar in the forest unless he could show off a new outfit. He had a different one for every hour of the day. Although one might describe an emperor by saying, "He is in his council chamber deliberating on affairs of state," it was said of this Emperor, "He is in his wardrobe room deciding what to wear."

Strangers arrived daily in the city to pay their respects to the Emperor, and one day, two swindlers, pretending to be weavers, made their appearance. They told everyone that the fabrics they wove were not only exceptionally beautiful, but also possessed the unique quality of being invisible to those individuals who were either simpletons or unfit for their jobs.

#1

"This must be splendid cloth," thought the Emperor. "If I had a suit made from such cloth, I could easily determine which individuals in my kingdom are unfit for their offices and could distinguish the wise from the foolish. I must have this fabric woven for me at once." The Emperor directed his treasurer to give large sums of money to the weavers in order that they might begin working immediately.

So the two swindlers set up their looms, and pretended to work very busily, though in reality they did nothing at all. They asked for the most delicate silk and the purest gold thread; put both into their own knapsacks, and then pretended to be weaving at the empty looms until late at night.

"I should like to know how the weavers are getting on with my cloth," said the Emperor to himself, after some little time had elapsed. He was, however, somewhat hesitant, when he remembered that a simpleton or one unfit for his office, would be unable to see the weavers' handiwork. "Surely," he thought, "I have nothing to risk." However, just to be sure, he sent a faithful old minister to observe the weavers. "He will be able to see how the cloth looks for he is a man of sense," thought the Emperor. "No one could be more suitable for his office than he is."

Text adapted from the original work in the public domain by E. K. McEwan (Andersen, 1875).

Teacher Think-Aloud for Questioning: Part 2

Think-Aloud Script	**Read-Aloud Text:** *The Emperor's New Clothes*
The answer to the fourth question I'm going to make up comes from my own experiences and how they relate to something I read in the book. Notice on the chart there's a picture of a brain for the fourth question.	So the faithful old minister went into the hall where the swindlers were working diligently at their empty looms. "What can be the meaning of this?" thought the old man, opening his eyes very wide. "There's not the least bit of thread on the looms." However, he did not express his thoughts aloud. The swindlers courteously invited him to come closer to their looms and then asked whether he found the design pleasing. The poor old minister looked and looked, but he could not see anything on the looms, and for a very good reason—there was nothing there.
TEACHER READS ALOUD TO FIRST DOTTED LINE.	
The first kind of question is easy to ask and answer because the answer is always right there in the text. In the section I just read, there is a good In the Book Question: Why did the Emperor decide to hire the swindlers? The answer is given right there: so he could tell if his employees were fit for their jobs. I've highlighted the section in the third paragraph where the answer can be found and labeled it with a #1.	"What!" thought the minister again. "Is it possible that I am a simpleton? I have never thought so myself, and no one must discover it now. Can it be that I am unfit for my office? No, that must not be said either. I will never admit that I cannot see the cloth."
TEACHER READS ALOUD TO SECOND DOTTED LINE.	"Well, Sir Minister," said one of the swindlers, still pretending to work. "What do you think?" #2
While I read, part of my working memory is thinking about the second kind of question I want to ask, a Throughout the Book Question. An answer to that kind of question is found in several different places in the story (or book), and I have to combine information to summarize it: What things did the swindlers do and say to give the impression that they were actually making clothes for the Emperor?	"Oh, it is excellent," replied the minister, looking at the loom through his spectacles. "I will tell the Emperor without delay how very beautiful your handiwork is." #2
I've highlighted two places that contain information that can be combined to answer that question and labeled them with #2.	"We shall be much obliged to you," said the swindlers, and then they named the different colors and described the patterns of the imaginary cloth. The old minister listened attentively to their words so that he might repeat them to the Emperor. Then the swindlers asked for more silk and gold, saying that it was necessary to complete what they had begun. However, they put all that was given them into their knapsacks; and continued to work diligently at the empty looms.
I skimmed ahead in my reading to see if there were any other places that mention things the swindlers did and said, and I found quite a few. Searching-Selecting is another cognitive strategy that I use a lot when I'm making up questions. I need to be able to look for words or phrases that tell me what I want to know. In this case, I was looking for places where I saw the word "swindlers" because those places might have a part of the answer I needed. I'm going to highlight and write #2 near all of the different sections of the text where parts of the answer to the second question can be found.	The Emperor shortly sent another ambassador of his court to find out when the cloth would be completed. The second observer surveyed the looms on all sides, and like the old minister saw nothing at all but the empty frames.
	"Does not the fabric appear as beautiful to you, as it did to my lord the minister?" asked the impostors.
Notice as I'm reading that I'm highlighting the sections of the text that have the words "the swindlers" in them. Each section mentions something the swindlers are doing or saying.	"I certainly am not a simpleton," thought the ambassador. "It must be that I am not fit for my job. That is very strange, but no one shall know anything about it." He praised the fabric he could not see and declared that he was delighted with both colors and patterns. "Indeed," he reported to the Emperor, "the cloth which the weavers are preparing is extraordinarily magnificent." Of course the whole city was talking of the splendid cloth which the Emperor had ordered to be woven at his own expense.
TEACHER READS ALOUD TO END OF STORY.	

Text adapted from the original work in the public domain by E. K. McEwan (Andersen, 1875).

Teacher Think-Aloud for Questioning: Part 3

Think-Aloud Script	**Read-Aloud Text:** *The Emperor's New Clothes*

Think-Aloud Script

Now that I've finished reading the story, I am ready to write the other two kinds of questions: an In the Book question and an In Your Brain question.

To ask an In the Book and an In Your Brain Question, I have to come up with a question that can be answered from reading the story, but the answer is not actually spelled out in words in the text. To ask and answer this kind of question, I have to use all of my cognitive processing powers to figure it out—I have to infer.

Here's the question I came up with: What do you think is the moral or theme of this story? Hans Christian Andersen doesn't state exactly what the moral or theme of the story is. I have to dig a little deeper and ask myself what lesson this story teaches. What application of this story can I make in my own life? I used the words, "What do you think?" in this question, because different readers will no doubt come up with different morals or themes. That's OK because when we read a story like this, we can think about it in lots of different ways. There's no one right answer.

Good stories are like that. Since I can't find the answer right in the text, I underlined some places where there are clues to figuring out the moral or the theme of the story. The theme will no doubt have something to do with honesty, but the moral might be a little more difficult to actually state. It might be that "Being vain makes people ignore the truth," or it could be that "Only those with nothing to lose can afford to be honest." Or, the moral could be "If you want your friends to tell you the truth, don't get mad at them when they do".

The fourth kind of question is the easiest kind to ask and answer. It's an In Your Brain Question. I have to use the activating strategy to activate some knowledge that I have in my brain—knowledge that only I have. Here's my question: Have you ever known anyone like one of the characters in the story? To review, here are the four questions I generated and the kinds of answers I would expect to receive to my questions.

Read-Aloud Text: *The Emperor's New Clothes*

And now the Emperor himself wished to see the stunning creation of the weavers while it was still on the loom. Accompanied by the officers of his court, the Emperor visited the swindlers at work. As soon as they became aware of his presence, they worked more diligently than ever—although they still did not pass a single thread through the looms. #2

"Is not the workmanship absolutely magnificent?" pointed out the minister and the ambassador who had earlier reported to the Emperor. "Notice the splendid design and the glorious colors." Meanwhile, they pointed to the empty frames, for they imagined that everyone else could see the exquisite piece of workmanship.

"How is this?" said the Emperor to himself. "I can see nothing. This is terrible. Am I a simpleton, or am I unfit to be an Emperor? That would be the worst thing that could happen."

But, to the swindlers he said, "Oh, the cloth is charming. It has my full approval." And he smiled most graciously while closely inspecting the empty looms, for on no account would he say that he could not see what two officers of his court had praised so highly. All those assembled strained their eyes, hoping to discover something on the looms, but they could see no more than the others. Nevertheless, they all exclaimed, "Oh, how beautiful," and advised his majesty to have some new clothes made from this splendid material for the approaching procession. #2

The swindlers sat up the whole night before the day on which the procession was to take place. They had sixteen candles burning so that everyone might see how anxious they were to finish the Emperor's new suit. They pretended to roll the cloth off the looms, cut the air with their scissors, and sewed with needles that contained no thread. At last they announced, "The Emperor's new clothes are ready!"

As the Emperor, with all the officers of his court looking on, arrived for his fitting, the swindlers raised their arms as if they were holding something up and said, "Here are your Majesty's trousers! Here is the coat! Here is the cape! The whole suit is as light as a cobweb. In fact one might actually think one has nothing at all on, when dressed in it. That, however, is the great virtue of this delicate cloth." #2

Text adapted from the original work in the public domain by E. K. McEwan (Andersen, 1875).

Teacher Think-Aloud for Questioning: Part 4

Think-Aloud Script

- *First, there's the In the Book Question*: Why did the Emperor decide to hire the swindlers to weave his clothes? *I highlighted the answer near #1. The Emperor decided to hire the swindlers because he wanted to find out if the people who were working for him were fit for their jobs. With these special clothes, he could tell the clever employees from the stupid ones.*

- *Second, there's the All Over the Book Question. I had to make up a question for which I had to look in several different places in the story to find the answer:* What things did the swindlers do and say to give the impression they were actually making clothes for the Emperor? *To answer this question I have to use my summarizing strategy because I need to collapse (or make smaller) the long list of words and actions so I can answer the question in one sentence. I think the answer to this question is, The swindlers pretended to be weaving, holding and sewing the cloth, helping the Emperor put on the imaginary outfit and they gave the Emperor all kinds of compliments about how wonderful his new clothes looked.*

- *Third, there's the In the Book and In Your Brain Question, the kind of question for which I need to use the inferring strategy both to make it up and to answer it. The question is,* What do you think is the moral or theme of this story? *I suggested several possibilities, and you can probably think of several more.*

- *Last, there's the In Your Brain Question that is based on my own experiences and the subject of the text. The question is,* Have you ever known anyone like one of the characters of the story? Describe how the person you know is similar to the character. *When I asked that question, I was thinking of a boss I once had who was like the emperor. My boss never wanted to hear the truth, either.*

Read-Aloud Text: *The Emperor's New Clothes*

"Yes indeed!" said all the courtiers, although not one of them could see anything.

"If your Imperial Majesty will be so gracious as to take off your clothes, we will fit your new suit in front of the mirror," said the swindlers. #2

The Emperor was accordingly undressed, and the swindlers pretended to dress him in his new suit. The Emperor meanwhile turned round from side to side in front of the mirror.

"How splendid his Majesty looks in his new clothes and how well they fit," everyone cried out. "What a design! What colors! These are indeed royal robes!"

"The canopy which is to be carried over your Majesty in the procession, is waiting," announced the master of the ceremonies.

"I am quite ready," answered the Emperor. "Do my new clothes fit well?" he asked. The lords of the bedchamber who were to carry his Majesty's train felt about on the ground as if they were lifting up the folds of actual cloth. The Emperor walked under his high canopy in the midst of the procession, through the streets of his capital. All of the bystanders and those at the windows cried out, "Oh, how beautiful are the Emperor's new clothes." No one would admit that he could not see these much-admired clothes, because, in doing so, he would have declared himself either a simpleton or unfit for his office.

Certainly, none of the Emperor's outfits had ever made so great an impression, as these invisible ones.

"But the Emperor has nothing at all on!" said a little child.

"Listen to the voice of innocence," exclaimed his father, and what the child had said was whispered from one to another.

"But he has nothing at all on," at last cried out all the people. The Emperor was very irritated, for he knew that the people were right. But he thought, "the procession must go on." And the lords of the bedchamber took greater pains than ever to appear to be holding up a train, although, in reality, there was no train to hold.

Text adapted from the original work in the public domain by E. K. McEwan (Andersen, 1875).

Question-Answer Quadrant

Why did the Emperor decide
to hire the swindlers?

What things did the swindlers
do and say to give the impression
that they were actually making
clothes for the Emperor?

 and

What do you think
is the moral or theme
of this story?

Have you ever known anyone
like one of the characters in the
story? Describe how the person
you know is similar to the character.

Adapted from Raphael (1984).

COGNITIVE STRATEGY 5: SEARCHING-SELECTING

While the literacy needs of the adult center primarily on obtaining information from nonfictional texts, literacy instruction in the schools concentrates almost exclusively on fictional texts and literary appreciation.

Venezky (2000, p. 22)

The foregoing statement highlights a critical problem in many elementary schools (and even middle schools): an overly rich diet of fiction. Expository or informational text is not widely used in elementary classrooms (Hirsch, 2003; Hoffman et al., 1994; Kamberelis, 1998; Pressley, Rankin, & Yokoi, 1996). Expository text is seldom read aloud in primary grades, despite the fact that students engage in more meaning-seeking and meaning-making efforts during informational book read-alouds then when hearing fiction read-alouds (Smolkin & Donovan, 2000). I often remind workshop participants that there are only two possible careers for someone who wants to read fiction full-time:

writing book reviews or teaching comparative literature. Both are worthy callings, but there aren't nearly enough openings for all of the students who are currently reading fiction exclusively. As a former media specialist who was trained as a reference librarian, I have a healthy, if not reverential, respect for information and for those individuals who can find it in a timely way and then use it to solve problems.

Although the searching-selecting strategy is not mentioned widely in the major reviews of the literature that helped to inform my choice of the six strategies included in this chapter (National Reading Panel, 2000; Pressley, Johnson, et al., 1989; Trabasso & Bouchard, 2000), I believe that it is an essential strategy for all readers to have, given the glut of information on the Internet, not all of it accurate. Guthrie and Kirsch (1987) describe searching and selecting as "the finding of text, browsing through information, or collecting resources for the purposes of answering questions, solving problems, or gathering information" (p. 220). Although searching-selecting is widely cited as both an essential workplace skill (Dreher, 1993; Mikulecky, 1982; Secretary's Commission on Achieving Necessary Skills, 1992; Venezky, 2000) and a vital academic strategy (California Department of Education, 2001; New Jersey Department of Education, 2002; Wisconsin Department of Public Instruction, 2003)[2], most teachers do not feel called to teach it. They defer to the librarian or media specialist and believe that students *must* certainly have adequate searching and selecting skills since they spend so much time surfing the Internet.

We cannot, however, expect students to "pick up" the searching-selecting strategy by osmosis, nor does instruction designed to teach the other cognitive strategies contribute specifically to the ability of students to search and select (Guthrie & Kirsch, 1987). Students need explicit instruction in how to search for and then select the information they need to accomplish an academic task or a personal information quest. Dreher (2002) suggests a model of locating information that includes the following five steps: (1) Formulate a goal or plan of action, (2) select appropriate categories of documents or text for inspection, (3) extract relevant information from the inspected categories, (4) integrate extracted information with prior knowledge, and (5) monitor the completeness of the answer, recycling through the component processes until the task is complete (p. 295).

Be sure to review Poster 4.10, How to Search and Select, and the accompanying instructional activity named The Prospector found in Chapter 4. The Teacher Think-Aloud on page 52 focuses on the searching-selecting cognitive strategy.

COGNITIVE STRATEGY 6: SUMMARIZING

> *[Summarizing:] the ability to recursively work on information to render it as succinctly as possible, requires judgment and effort, knowledge and strategies.*

> Brown & Day (1983, p. 1)

Summarizing is one of the more challenging cognitive processes that readers and writers are called upon to execute. When the eminent historians Doris

Teacher Think-Aloud for Searching-Selecting

Think-Aloud Script	**Read-Aloud Text:** *D-Day*

Think-Aloud Script

TEACHER READS ALOUD TO THE FIRST DOTTED LINE.

Recently during my reading of the book, D-Day, by Stephen Ambrose, I came across the paragraph I just read.

If I am reading about an unfamiliar subject, I often encounter words, phrases, ideas, or concepts that I don't know. If I'm going to understand and learn from what I read, I need to find out what these unfamiliar words mean. That's when I use the Searching-Selecting cognitive strategy. This is one of my favorite strategies because it's like being a prospector mining for gold or silver. When I read the section from Ambrose's book, I didn't know what Eureka sets were. I am going to search for this information because knowing the meanings will improve my comprehension and will also add to my store of knowledge about WW II.

I use a plan when I search and select. At this point, I use it so often I don't have to think about it. It's automatic for me. Here are the steps: (1) Reflect, (2) Prospect, (3) Detect, (4) Select, and (5) Connect. I call it "The Prospector."

I've never heard of Pathfinders before, but I can tell from their name that they must be some kind of advance group of soldiers. They are finding the way or the path and probably leading other soldiers to where they should go. I put "Eureka sets" into the Google search engine and retrieved several sites. But I need to do some selecting and choose one that makes sense.

TEACHER READS ALOUD TO THE SECOND DOTTED LINE.

As I scan the list, I immediately know that the first four have nothing to do with D-Day or World War II. I see that the first Web site listed has only the word "Eureka" in it. The reason it's here, I think, is that the Eureka Vacuum Cleaner Company probably pays Google for advertising so that whenever anyone puts anything into the search engine with the word "Eureka" in it, vacuum cleaners come up as the first choice. The others are listed because they have the two words "Eureka sets" in them. As I scan through those, I can quickly figure out that I don't need a consulting firm, a florist, or computer search software company. The link "Independent Company" looks very promising because it has the words "paratrooper" and "Eureka sets" in it.

TEACHER READS ALOUD TO END.

When I clicked on this link, I found the paragraph I just read. It explained that Pathfinders were responsible for landing with the Eureka sets strapped to their legs. They would set them up so that planes flying overhead would know where and when to tell the paratroopers to land. As I reread the section from Ambrose, I can see that perhaps Ambrose was describing Eureka sets in the phrase "automatic direction-finder radios," but he confused me instead. Searching-Selecting helped me clarify my confusion.

Read-Aloud Text: *D-Day*

"The Pathfinders went in first. They preceded the main troops by an hour or so. Their mission was to mark the drop zones with automatic direction-finder radios, Eureka sets, and Holophane lights formed into Ts on the ground" (Ambrose, 1994, p. 196).

EUREKA Vacuum Cleaner Bags, Filters and Parts
www.TotalVac.com EUREKA Vacuum Supplies & Part—Free Shipping

Eureka Promoting Well-Being
...as improving, it will be. **Eureka sets** out to create the right and appropriate environment for each client. As each and every one ...
www.cottagewebs.co.uk/eureka/ - 16k - Cached - Similar pages

Eureka
A 2003 AARS winner, **Eureka sets** loads of old-fashioned looking blossoms that hold their hue to the end in large clusters of apricot warmed by copper. ...
www.brackengardens.com/store/ moreinfo.cfm? Product_ID = 277 - 15k - Cached - Similar pages

JEP: Delivery Mechanisms
To manage the user's interaction with the service, **Eureka sets** a maximum number of records that can be returned to the browser at any one time, and includes ...
www.press.umich.edu/jep/04-01/arcolio.html - 22k - Cached - Similar pages

Independent Company
Up until this time the method of deploying all of the paratrooper's heavier equipment, the **Eureka sets** in the case of the Independent Company, was to drop a ...
www.extraplan.demon.co.uk/batt_ind_coy.htm - 14k - Cached -

"The beacon the pathfinders used was the Eureka radio marker, a remarkably accurate system used in conjunction with the Rebecca system in the aircraft. There was an instance of a Eureka set undergoing repair in a Signals hut and it had accidentally been left switched on, and before long a stick of parachutists came crashing down onto the roof. Up until this time the method of deploying all of the paratrooper's heavier equipment, the Eureka sets in the case of the Independent Company, was to drop a container from the aircraft's bomb bay, however this was a most awkward and unsatisfactory technique of delivery" (Twenty-First Independent Parachute Company, 2003).

Kearns Goodwin (1987) and Stephen Ambrose (1994) were taken to task by their literary peers for failing to summarize the ideas of others in their own words and then forgetting to cite the sources from which they inadvertently "borrowed" the information (Goldstein, 2002; Kirkpatrick, 2002), I thought of many of my former students. Despite my seemingly clear instructions and warnings, they persistently copied paragraphs from the *World Book Encyclopedia* onto their note cards and then diligently copied the same paragraphs into their final research reports. Even more disheartening was my inability to show them how to do it differently. Today's students are still cutting and pasting, only now it's from the Internet.

Restating the meaning of what one reads in one's own words—different words from those used in the original text—is a daunting task for all readers and writers. Whether we're famous historians, educational authors, teachers, or a class of fourth graders preparing for the high-stakes Communication Arts assessment, we share a common problem: shortcutting the comprehension step in the summarizing process. We don't want to invest the time and cognitive effort that is essential, no matter how smart we are, to struggle with extracting and constructing meaning from text. The University of Washington Psychology Writing Center (2003) gives this advice to its students regarding the summarizing of text: "If you can't put the information into your own words, you aren't ready to write about it [or talk about it]. To learn how to paraphrase what you want to write, try to explain it to someone else without referring to your source" (p. 2).

Summarizing has its roots in a time-honored tradition of reading comprehension instruction: finding the main idea. In days gone by, main idea instruction consisted of little more than reading short selections and circling the best title for the selection. That was then. This is now. Today's high-stakes assessments demand that students engage in strategic reading. For example, in Texas, K–3 students are expected to retell [or act out the order of] important events in stories, while second- and third-grade students are expected to produce summaries of text selections. In the upper grades, fourth and fifth graders are expected to determine the main idea and how it is supported with details, and fourth through eighth graders are expected to paraphrase and summarize text to recall, inform, or organize ideas (Texas Education Agency, 2002).

The first step in preparing to teach your students *how* to summarize either narrative or expository text is to settle on the definitions that you will use. (Recall the list of definitions related to summarizing that Roger Craig used in Chapter 2.) Make sure that *you* can explain, describe, defend, *and* model the critical attributes of summarizing as defined by the content standards of your district or state. Summarizing is a complex cognitive process, but once your students know the kind of thinking that is required for summarizing, you can then guide them to the specifics of your particular summarization definition.

The Teacher Think-Aloud on pages 54–58 presents a summarizing think-aloud in which the teacher models *The Five C's of Summarizing* introduced by Roger Craig in Chapter 3 and explained in more detail in Chapter 4.

Teacher Think-Aloud for Summarizing: Part 1

Think-Aloud Script	**Read-Aloud Text:** *The Emperor's New Clothes*

Think-Aloud Script

One of the things I often have to do as an author is to summarize something I've read. Sometimes it's a book, sometimes an article, and sometimes a story. Today I'm going to think aloud for you as I write a summary of a fairy tale: The Emperor's New Clothes *by Hans Christian Andersen. A summary is a one-sentence version of what the story is about, written in my own words. Sometimes people call it the gist of the story or a thumbnail sketch.*

I'm going to use five steps that make summarizing easier. They are shown in the chart I've posted, The Five C's of Summarizing. Each step has a picture prompt and a word prompt to help me remember the key words of the steps:

> *Comprehend it.*
> *Chunk it (topics, characters, scenes, or story elements).*
> *Compact it.*
> *Conceptualize it.*
> *Connect it.*

TEACHER DISPLAYS THE FIVE C'S OF SUMMARIZING (pg. 58).

The first C stands for Comprehend. This reminds me that if I'm going to write a summary, I need to understand what the story is about. I can't tell somebody else what it's about unless I really get it myself. Then I need to Chunk the story. To chunk a book, article, or story means to divide it into smaller parts or chunks (just like you would cut up a big hunk of cheese into smaller pieces or chunks). There are no hard-and-fast rules for chunking. It's up to the reader to decide which chunking method will work best.

If I'm reading nonfiction, I might chunk it according to topics or subjects. But if I am reading fiction, I think about dividing it by characters, story scenes, or story elements.

I've skimmed the story (scanned it quickly) to see if I can decide ahead of time which way to chunk it. Now if it were a book, I couldn't really decide on how to chunk ahead of time. I would have to chunk it after I had finished reading it. After skimming the story, I've decided to chunk by characters. Here's why. If I chunked it by story elements (main character, setting, problem, resolution), I would have a hard time focusing on just one character. If I decided to chunk it by scenes, I would have a hard time also. The scenes happen so quickly and are so short it would be hard to work with that many chunks.

Read-Aloud Text: *The Emperor's New Clothes*

Many years ago there was an Emperor who was so fond of new clothes that he spent all of his money on them. He never went to the theater or hunted wild boar in the forest unless he could show off a new outfit. He had a different one for every hour of the day. Although one might describe an emperor by saying, "He is in his council chamber deliberating on affairs of state," it was said of this Emperor, "He is in his wardrobe room deciding what to wear."

Strangers arrived daily in the city to pay their respects to the Emperor, and one day, two swindlers, pretending to be weavers, made their appearance. They told everyone that the fabrics they wove were not only exceptionally beautiful, but also possessed the unique quality of being invisible to those individuals who were either simpletons or unfit for their jobs.

"This must be splendid cloth," thought the Emperor. "If I had a suit made from such cloth, I could easily determine which individuals in my kingdom are unfit for their offices and could distinguish the wise from the foolish. I must have this fabric woven for me at once." The Emperor directed his treasurer to give large sums of money to the weavers in order that they might begin working immediately.

So the two swindlers set up their looms, and pretended to work very busily, though in reality they did nothing at all. They asked for the most delicate silk and the purest gold thread; put both into their own knapsacks, and then pretended to be weaving at the empty looms until late at night.

"I should like to know how the weavers are getting on with my cloth," said the Emperor to himself, after some little time had elapsed. He was, however, somewhat hesitant, when he remembered that a simpleton or one unfit for his office would be unable to see the weavers' handiwork. "Surely," he thought, "I have nothing to risk." However, just to be sure, he sent a faithful old minister to observe the weavers. "He will be able to see how the cloth looks for he is a man of sense," thought the Emperor. "No one could be more suitable for his office than he is."

So the faithful old minister went into the hall where the swindlers were working diligently at their empty looms. "What can be the meaning of this?" thought the old man, opening his eyes very wide. "There's not the least bit of thread on the looms." However, he did not express his thoughts aloud. The swindlers courteously invited him to come closer to their looms and then asked whether he found the design pleasing. The poor old minister looked and looked, but he could not see anything on the looms, and for a very good reason—there was nothing there.

Read-Aloud Text adapted from the original work in the public domain by E. K. McEwan (Andersen, 1875).

Teacher Think-Aloud for Summarizing: Part 2

Think-Aloud Script	**Read-Aloud Text:** *The Emperor's New Clothes*

Think-Aloud Script

Because there are so many interesting characters in this story, I've decided to chunk by characters. So while I read the story I'm going to highlight the names of the characters. I'm also going to think about what the various characters are like as I read. That will help me understand the story and give me some ideas of character traits or adjectives I could use for conceptualizing key words.

TEACHER READS ALOUD TO THE FIRST DOTTED LINE, HIGHLIGHTING REFERENCES TO CHARACTERS IN THE STORY.

I'm feeling good about the way I decided to chunk the story. When I chunk by character, I have to combine the chunks from various parts of the story in my mind. Sometimes when I chunk, I can physically divide the text by drawing lines or boxes around sections, but that doesn't work when I'm chunking characters. So far, I'm getting the idea that nobody is able to tell the truth in this story. Only the swindlers are having a good time. The Emperor and all of the men who work for him are very worried.

So far, I've highlighted the Emperor (not a very nice person), the swindlers (not very nice people either), and the honest old minister (he's worried about keeping his job). Sometimes I have to change my mind from what I originally thought about the chunking because it just doesn't work, but this time the character chunking is working out quite well for me.

TEACHER KEEPS READING TO THE SECOND DOTTED LINE, HIGHLIGHTING REFERENCES TO CHARACTERS.

Of course, the weavers and swindlers are one and the same men. The Emperor we recognize. And then there are all of the officials who work for the Emperor (statesmen, courtiers, councilors, attendants).

Everybody is pretending there is cloth on the loom, including the swindlers. But only the swindlers know the truth. The others think there must be something wrong with them. They think that they must be unfit for their jobs.

Read-Aloud Text: *The Emperor's New Clothes*

"What!" thought the minister again. "Is it possible that I am a simpleton? I have never thought so myself, and no one must discover it now. Can it be that I am unfit for my office? No, that must not be said either. I will never admit that I cannot see the cloth."

"Well, Sir Minister," said one of the swindlers, still pretending to work. "What do you think?"

"Oh, it is excellent," replied the minister, looking at the loom through his spectacles. "I will tell the Emperor without delay how very beautiful your handiwork is."

"We shall be much obliged to you," said the swindlers, and then they named the different colors and described the patterns of the imaginary cloth. The old minister listened attentively to their words so that he might repeat them to the Emperor. Then the swindlers asked for more silk and gold, saying that it was necessary to complete what they had begun. However, they put all that was given them into their knapsacks; and continued to work diligently at the empty looms.

The Emperor shortly sent another ambassador of his court to find out when the cloth would be completed. The second observer surveyed the looms on all sides, and like the old minister saw nothing at all but the empty frames.

"Does not the fabric appear as beautiful to you, as it did to my lord the minister?" asked the impostors. "I certainly am not a simpleton," thought the ambassador. "It must be that I am not fit for my job. That is very strange, but no one shall know anything about it." He praised the fabric he could not see and declared that he was delighted with both colors and patterns. "Indeed," he reported to the Emperor, "the cloth which the weavers are preparing is extraordinarily magnificent." Of course the whole city was talking of the splendid cloth which the Emperor had ordered to be woven at his own expense.

And now the Emperor himself wished to see the stunning creation of the weavers while it was still on the loom. Accompanied by the officers of his court, the Emperor visited the swindlers at work. As soon as they became aware of his presence, they worked more diligently than ever—although they still did not pass a single thread through the looms.

"Is not the workmanship absolutely magnificent?" pointed out the minister and the ambassador who had earlier reported to the Emperor. "Notice the splendid design and the glorious colors." Meanwhile they pointed to the empty frames, for they imagined that everyone else could see the exquisite piece of workmanship.

Read-Aloud Text adapted from the original work in the public domain by E. K. McEwan (Andersen, 1875).

Teacher Think-Aloud for Summarizing: Part 3

Think-Aloud Script	Read-Aloud Text: *The Emperor's New Clothes*
TEACHER READS ALOUD TO END OF THE STORY, HIGHLIGHTING REFERENCES TO CHARACTERS. *As I look back through the story and notice all of the places I highlighted, I'm getting some good ideas.* *As I skim the story, I am Compacting it, ignoring the parts that are unnecessary for my summary.* *Now I have to take each of these chunks (or descriptions about characters) and Conceptualize them—think of one word (concept) that sums up each chunk. I need four words, one key word for each of my chunks—the four characters I picked. I'm going to put these key words on a graphic organizer so I can look at them all together while I write my summary.* TEACHER DISPLAYS GRAPHIC ORGANIZER (pg. 58). *My first chunk is the Emperor. I need to think of a word (one that isn't related to any other word in the story) that describes the Emperor and the kind of person he is: OBSESSED. I'm going to write that in a circle on the organizer. The Emperor was so obsessed about clothes that he let himself get swindled.* *My second chunk is all about the employees who go to see the empty loom and say they can see cloth when they can't. I've got just the word to describe them: FEARFUL.* *Then I have a third chunk—it's a big one— for the swindlers. There is a great word to describe them— CUNNING (it means clever or sneaky).* *And then we have the last chunk for the only character in the whole story who tells the truth—the little child. There is no other word but HONEST for the child.* *Now that I comprehend (understand) the story, I could retell it to you just like it happened. But that would be too long. A summary is very short. It tells the important parts of the story in my own words and does it in just one sentence.*	"How is this?" thought the Emperor. "I can see nothing. This is terrible. Am I a simpleton, or am I unfit to be an Emperor? That would be the worst thing that could happen." But, to the swindlers he said, "Oh, the cloth is charming. It has my full approval." And he smiled most graciously while closely inspecting the empty looms, for on no account would he say that he could not see what two officers of his court had praised so highly. All those assembled strained their eyes, hoping to discover something on the looms, but they could see no more than the others. Nevertheless, they all exclaimed, "Oh, how beautiful," and advised his majesty to have some new clothes made from this splendid material for the approaching procession. --- "The swindlers sat up the whole night before the day on which the procession was to take place. They had sixteen candles burning so that everyone might see how anxious they were to finish the Emperor's new suit. They pretended to roll the cloth off the looms, cut the air with their scissors, and sewed with needles that contained no thread. At last they announced, "The Emperor's new clothes are ready!" As the Emperor, with all the officers of his court looking on, arrived for his fitting, the swindlers raised their arms as if they were holding something up and said, "Here are your Majesty's trousers! Here is the coat! Here is the cape! The whole suit is as light as a cobweb. In fact one might actually think one has nothing at all on, when dressed in it. That, however, is the great virtue of this delicate cloth." "Yes indeed!" said all the courtiers, although not one of them could see anything. "If your Imperial Majesty will be so gracious as to take off your clothes, we will fit your new suit in front of the mirror," said the swindlers. The Emperor was accordingly undressed, and the swindlers pretended to dress him in his new suit. The Emperor meanwhile turned round from side to side in front of the mirror. "How splendid his Majesty looks in his new clothes and how well they fit," everyone cried out. "What a design! What colors! These are indeed royal robes!" "The canopy which is to be carried over your Majesty in the procession, is waiting," announced the master of the ceremonies.

Read-Aloud Text adapted from the original work in the public domain by E. K. McEwan (Andersen, 1875).

Teacher Think-Aloud for Summarizing: Part 4

Think-Aloud Script	**Read-Aloud Text:** *The Emperor's New Clothes*
There is nothing left but the easy part: Connecting the words (concepts) I have chosen to make a sentence. Of course, I have to add some connecting words to the four words and do some experimenting with several different versions of the sentence until it "reads" right to me. This is the one that I finally decided was right.	"I am quite ready," answered the Emperor. "Do my new clothes fit well?" he asked. The lords of the bedchamber who were to carry his Majesty's train felt about on the ground as if they were lifting up the folds of actual cloth.
There once was an emperor who was so <u>obsessed</u> with beautiful clothes that he allowed some <u>cunning</u> thieves to spin lies rather than cloth, making fools of his <u>fearful</u> subjects until an <u>honest</u> child proclaimed the Emperor's nakedness.	The Emperor walked under his high canopy in the midst of the procession, through the streets of his capital. All of the bystanders and those at the windows cried out, "Oh, how beautiful are the Emperor's new clothes."
Now if I were writing a paraphrase or a retelling of the story, which are both longer than a summary, I could write a sentence containing each key word. Here's my example of a paraphrase using the same key words.	No one would admit that he could not see these much-admired clothes, because, in doing so, he would have declared himself either a simpleton or unfit for his office. Certainly, none of the Emperor's outfits had ever made so great an impression, as these invisible ones.
There once was an emperor who was so <u>obsessed</u> with beautiful clothes that he was fooled by some swindlers who promised that only those who were fit for their jobs would be able to see the beautiful cloth they were weaving. <u>Fearful</u> of looking stupid and losing their jobs, the emperor's officials pretended to see the beautiful fabric, even though the looms were empty. The <u>cunning</u> swindlers pretended to be working hard on the outfit, confident that no one would risk telling the truth and thus appear unfit for their jobs. The swindlers would have fooled everyone except for an <u>honest</u> child.	"But the Emperor has nothing at all on!" said a little child. "Listen to the voice of innocence," exclaimed his father, and what the child had said was whispered from one to another.
	"But he has nothing at all on," at last cried out all the people. The Emperor was very irritated, for he knew that the people were right. But he thought, "the procession must go on." And the lords of the bedchamber took greater pains than ever to appear to be holding up a train, although, in reality, there was no train to hold.

Read-Aloud Text adapted from the original work in the public domain by E. K. McEwan (Andersen, 1875).

The Five C's of Summarizing

Comprehend	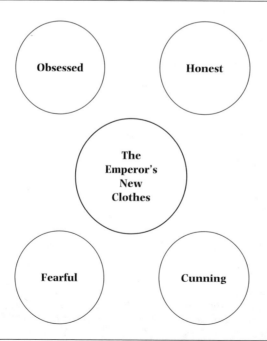 Read and understand the text.
Chunk	Divide the text into parts.
Compact	Make each chunk smaller.
Conceptualize	Think of a key word for each chunk.
Connect	Combine the key words into a summary sentence.

Graphic Organizer

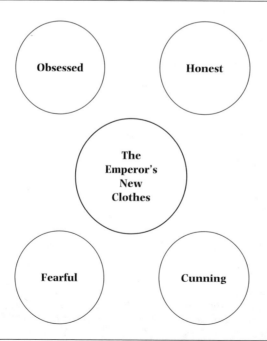

Obsessed

Honest

The Emperor's New Clothes

Fearful

Cunning

COGNITIVE STRATEGY 7: VISUALIZING-ORGANIZING

Any sort of systematic attention to clues that reveal how authors attempt to relate ideas to one another or any sort of systematic attempt to impose structure upon a text, especially in some sort of visual representation of the relationships among key ideas, facilitates comprehension as well as both short-term and long-term memory for the text.

Pearson & Fielding (1991, p. 832)

Visualizing-organizing gets my vote for the most misused, underappreciated, and untapped treasure among the seven strategies featured in this chapter. Oh, make no mistake, there are dozens of stunning graphic organizers and hundreds of beautiful illustrations and photos in every published basal reading series and content-area textbook on the market. Pretty pictures and glitzy organizers do not necessarily contribute to students' understanding and retention of text. Visual images and organizers are of little value to students unless they have personally unleashed their own cognitive powers on visualizing and organizing what they read. It is only when students develop their own personal concept maps that the structure of a discipline or the complexity of an idea or proposition sticks with them. In fact, one of the biggest pluses of graphic organizers is the way in which they can reduce cognitive overload by keeping concepts both abbreviated and visible.

A graphic organizer, graphic representation, or "nonlinguistic representation" (Marzano, Pickering, & Pollock, 2001, p. 72) is a visual illustration of a verbal statement (Jones et al., 1988/1989, p. 20) and involves the following tasks or abilities: (1) to read text, (2) to determine which type of graphic organizer would be best suited for constructing a personal schema to better understand and remember large bodies of information, (3) to choose the frames or labels for the parts of the organizer, and (4) to construct the organizer by drawing it, either manually or using a software program designed for that purpose.

A second way to tap into the visual aspects of processing is through representational mental imagery (Borduin et al., 1994; Pressley, 1976) in which readers paint a picture, take a snapshot, or make a video in their minds of the scene or action taking place in the story. Students who have difficulty with mental images should be encouraged to act out scenes or make a story board to help them "see" exactly what is happening in the story. The process of mental imaging can take place while reading is going on, but most students should be encouraged to stop after they have read a particularly well-described scene, action, or location, and envision exactly what happened or what a place looks like before they continue reading.

In their summary conclusion to *How People Learn: Brain, Mind, Experience, and School*, Bransford et al. (2000) make a strong case for the role of organizing in meaningful learning (the italics are mine):

> Effective comprehension and thinking require a coherent understanding of the *organizing* principles in any subject matter; understanding the essential features of the problems of various school subjects will lead to better reasoning and problem-solving.

Transfer and wide application of learning are most likely to occur when learners achieve an *organized* and coherent understanding of the material.

Learning and understanding can be facilitated in learning by emphasizing *organized*, coherent bodies of knowledge (in which specific facts and details are embedded).

In-depth understanding requires detailed knowledge of the facts within a domain. The key attribute of expertise is a detailed and *organized* understanding of the important facts within a specific domain. (pp. 238–239)

The Teacher Think-Alouds on pages 61–63 demonstrate visualizing and organizing, respectively, while Chapter 4 provides two instructional activities for the visualizing-organizing cognitive strategy—*Visualize a Video* and *Organize It!*

WHAT'S AHEAD?

I hope that your excitement regarding SRI is building. If you are eager to begin using and teaching some of the cognitive strategies you have read about in this chapter, begin Chapter 4 immediately. It includes a variety of instructional activities along with posters, props, and prompts to scaffold your students' learning that you can adopt or adapt for your own classroom.

Teacher Think-Aloud for Visualizing

Think-Aloud Script	**Read-Aloud Text:** *The Adventures of Tom Sawyer*
This short excerpt from The Adventures of Tom Sawyer *brings all sorts of wonderful mental images into my mind. Twain uses lots of figurative language. I love it when Aunt Polly (I know it's Aunt Polly because I read the blurb on the inside front cover) pulls her spectacles down and looks over them around the room (I can just see her doing it). I can't tell whether she's upset or amused or if she's putting on a show for someone she thinks might be watching her (like Tom, from wherever he's hiding). I can see her putting them up over her eyes to look out under them. I even tried it with my own glasses just to see how it felt when I did it. Of course, I can see out of my glasses. But I know just how Aunt Polly feels. There are some things I wear that aren't comfortable (like a pair of shoes I have) that I wear anyhow because I think they make me look good. I'm just like Aunt Polly.*	"TOM!" No answer. "Tom!" No answer. "What's gone with that boy, I wonder? You, TOM!" No answer. The old lady pulled her spectacles down and looked over them about the room; then she put them up and looked out under them. She seldom or never looked through them for so small a thing as a boy; they were her state pair, the pride of her heart, and were built for "style," not service—she could have seen through a pair of stove lids just as well. She looked perplexed for a moment, and then said, not fiercely, but still loud enough for the furniture to hear:
I think it's funny when she bends down and punches under the bed with her broom. I imagine she has quite an ample posterior and seeing it up in the air is very amusing. I can hear her breathing out and making noises while she waves her broom around under the bed. Again I think she's doing this to show off for Tom, wherever he is hiding.	"Well, I lay, if I get hold of you I'll—" She did not finish, for by this time she was bending down and punching under the bed with the broom, and so she needed breath to punctuate the punches with. She resurrected nothing but the cat. "I never did see the beat of that boy!"
I can see the backyard with the vines and weeds. It feels like summer. I can smell the fresh tomatoes on the vines and imagine the juice dripping down Tom's chin while he bites into one. Maybe that is where he's hiding. Or I can see the cat peeking out from behind the weeds. I think it looks like a jungle back there. There probably isn't anyone to do the yard work because Tom is hiding or off having fun.	She went to the open door and stood in it and looked out among the tomato vines and "jimpson" weeds that constituted the garden. No Tom. So she lifted up her voice at an angle calculated for distance, and shouted:
I get a wonderful picture in my mind when Aunt Polly picks Tom up by the seat of his pants. He wasn't flying, but when Aunt Polly picked him up, she probably lifted him off the ground.	"Y-o-u-u, Tom." There was a slight noise behind her and she turned just in time to seize a small boy by the slack of his roundabout and arrest his flight.

Read-Aloud Text from the public domain (Twain, 1876).

Teacher Think-Aloud for Organizing: Part 1

Think-Aloud Script	**Read-Aloud Text:** *Reptiles Do the Strangest Things*

When I read nonfiction, I often make a graphic organizer to help me understand and remember what I read. The graphic organizer I'm going to make while I read aloud to you is called a concept map. A concept is an idea or the picture we get in our minds when we hear a certain word. For example, when I hear the word "dog," I get lots of pictures in my mind—my cousin Carlene's English shepherd who herds her sheep, our son's poodle, and the German shepherd that my husband used to have. Although these dogs are all very different looking, they have some very important things in common that make them dogs.

Making a concept map is a way to show how ideas or concepts connect with each other. I'm going to make a concept map as I read Reptiles Do the Strangest Things *[The numbers in this think-aloud correspond to numbers on the map.]*

TEACHER DISPLAYS CONCEPT MAP (pg. 64).

TEACHER READS ALOUD TO FIRST DOTTED LINE.

The first important concept is Brontosaurus (1). I'm a little confused right now because I thought this book was about reptiles, and I thought reptiles were snakes, and now the authors are writing about the Brontosaurus, but I'm going to keep reading and see what happens. I'm putting the first oval on my concept map and I'll write the word "Brontosaurus" in it.

TEACHER READS ALOUD TO SECOND DOTTED LINE.

Now my confusion is cleared up because the authors told me that dinosaurs were reptiles. So I'm adding two more concepts to my map—Dinosaurs (2) and Reptiles (3). Now I have to figure out how the concepts or ideas of Brontosaurus, Dinosaurs, and Reptiles are related. This is the hard part of making a concept map because I need to think of the linking words to describe the relationships between these three concepts. I know they are all different concepts, but the authors of this book must have thought they were related because they put them all together in the same book.

The book says that dinosaurs were reptiles that ruled the earth for millions of years. That would make them the ancestors of reptiles today. If I want the concepts to be connected in the right order, I have to watch the direction of my arrow. So to have the sentence read "Dinosaurs are ancestors of reptiles," I have to make the arrow go from "dinosaurs" to "reptiles" rather than the other direction. Another rule I follow when I make a concept map is to use the abbreviation "e.g.," which means "for example." The Brontosaurus is an example of a dinosaur. I see an example of another dinosaur that I can put on my concept map: Tyrannosaurus Rex (4).

Millions and millions of years ago there lived a huge animal called a Brontosaurus. He was as long as a line of elephants and weighed over 75,000 pounds. He was so big he could hardly move around on land. He spent his days wading in the water, eating green plants.

The Brontosaurus was a dinosaur. Dinosaurs were reptiles. They ruled the earth for millions of years.

There were dinosaurs as small as rabbits. There were dinosaurs as tall as a four-story building. A terrible kind of dinosaur called the Tyrannosaurus Rex had a huge head and a thousand teeth. He could kill and eat a Brontosaurus. Tyrannosaurus Rex means "king of the lizard tyrants." Brontosaurus means "thunder lizard." Dinosaur means "terrible lizard."

These fantastic reptiles all died a long time before there were any people on earth. So no one ever saw a dinosaur. But today we know about them from their bones.

Dinosaur bones have been found buried in rocks in many parts of the world. You can see these bones in museums. In one, there is a giant skeleton of a Tyrannosaurus Rex. Even without his skin he is scary.

Today there are only five kinds of reptiles. They are the Lizards, the Turtles, the Snakes, the Crocodilians, and an odd animal called the Tuatara.

Read-Aloud Text from *Reptiles Do the Strangest Things* by Leonora Hornblow and Arthur Hornblow, Jr., copyright © 1970 by Random House, Inc. Used by permission of Random House Children's Books, a division of Random House Corporation, Inc.

Teacher Think-Aloud for Organizing: Part 2

Think-Aloud Script

I'm going to add some more concepts to my map—the meanings of the names of the various dinosaurs. Tyrannosaurus Rex means "king of the lizard tyrants." That's going to be (5) on the map. The meaning of Brontosaurus is going to be (6) and the meaning of dinosaur, "terrible lizard," is (7). Choosing the connecting word for these new concepts is easy. I will use the word "means."

TEACHER READS ALOUD TO THIRD DOTTED LINE.

This paragraph tells me something else that's very important about dinosaurs. They aren't around anymore. I know a word (concept) that sums up that idea: extinct (8). The text also tells me another important concept about dinosaurs. Their bones are on exhibit in museums (9). I'll add it to the map. And, since I've been to a museum and seen a Tyrannosaurus Rex with all of its bones put together, I'm putting that on my concept map also (10).

TEACHER READS ALOUD TO END OF TEXT.

I'm going to add five more concepts to my map right now: Lizards (11), Snakes (12), Turtles (13), Crocodilians (14), and Tuatara (15). Those are the reptiles that are still living today. When I finish reading this book, I'll have a concept map of the whole book on one page.

The last thing I do when I'm finished with my map is read it in the direction the arrows are going on my map and put the connecting words in between the words in the ovals.

I'm going to do that right now. Dinosaurs are the ancestors of reptiles. Dinosaur means terrible lizard. Some examples of dinosaurs are Brontosaurus, which means thunder lizard, and Tyrannosaurus Rex, which means king of the lizard tyrants. Dinosaurs are now extinct, and their bones are displayed in museums.

There are five kinds of reptiles living today: lizards, snakes, crocodilians, turtles, and tuatara. I could summarize the first chapter just from reading my concept map. That's a good way to review what I learned.

Concept Map: *Reptiles Do the Strangest Things*

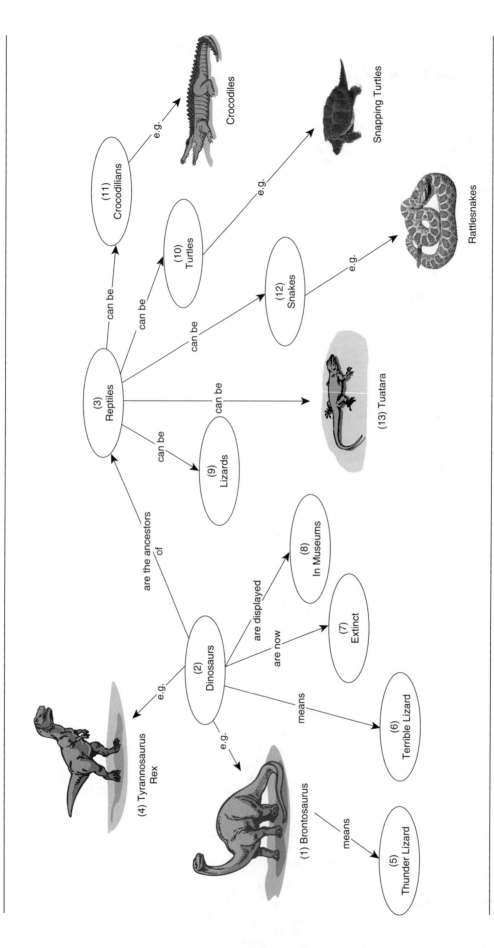

Instructional Activities to Engage Your Students

Teachers' lesson plans are temporary documents that must be modified as the dynamic and responsive instructional exchange unfolds.

Duffy and Roehler (1989, p. 27)

The twelve instructional activities in this chapter are "temporary documents" like the ones described by Duffy and Roehler in the opening epigraph. They are not recipes or prescriptions as much as suggestions and possibilities. They are not *the* strategies or *the* definitive activities but rather launching pads and works-in-progress to help you become more skilled at SRI. Some of them are my own inventions with contributions from teachers across the country; some have been adopted and adapted from instructional activities developed by other professionals. Where I have used the ideas or terminology of others, I have made every attempt to accurately describe the original work and provide citations. Figure 4.1 summarizes the instructional activities, including recommended grade levels as well as individual cognitive strategies used during the activity.

Each instructional activity is presented in the following format:

- Description of the activity
- Background information
- Anticipatory set
- I Do It: Modeling and explaining the strategy (activity) for students
- We Do It: Further explaining and guided practice
- You Do It: Students working in small groups or individually

The figures, forms, handouts, posters, and think-alouds found in this chapter are numbered in sequence within their respective categories and

Instructional Activity Options

Instructional Activity	Activating-Predicting	Inferring	Monitoring-Clarifying	Questioning	Searching-Selecting	Summarizing	Visualizing-Organizing	Notes
Turn On Your CPU: Grades 1–8	X		X				X	
Turn On Your Math CPU: Grades 4–8	X	X	X				X	
Add It Up: Grades 1–8	X	X					X	
A Dozen Ways to Infer: Grades 3–8		X		X				
A Dozen Ways to Say "Infer": Grades 3–8		X		X	X		X	
Fix Up Your Mix-Ups: Grades 1–8			X	X	X		X	
Do You Have Any Questions?: Grades 1–8		X		X		X		
The Prospector: Grades 4–8		X		X	X	X		
The Summarizer's Five C's: Grades 3–8		X		X	X	X	X	
Visualize a Video: Grades K–2	X					X	X	
It Pays to Increase Your Word Power: Grades 4–8				X		X	X	
Organize It: Grades 3–8		X		X	X	X	X	

Figure 4.1. Copyright © 2004 Corwin Press. All rights reserved. Reprinted from *Seven Strategies of Highly Effective Readers*, by E. K. McEwan. Thousand Oaks, CA: Corwin Press, www.corwinpress.com. Reproduction authorized only for the local school site that has purchased this book.

grouped with their applicable instructional activity. They are labeled in two places for your convenience: (1) with a title at the top of the page and (2) with a numerical label and name of the activity in the footer. There are five categories of instructional aids, but not every activity contains every type of aid.

- Figures (charts that provide information intended only for the teachers' use)
- Forms (materials for teachers to duplicate for students' use [e.g., sticky pictures, bookmarks])
- Handouts (charts and worksheets for students to either place in their strategy notebooks or to use as a fill-in form for thinking aloud)
- Posters (8½ × 11 reproducible and enlargeable learning aids for use either in lesson presentation or as handouts for students)
- Teacher Think-Alouds (scripts showing how a teacher might think aloud to model a specific activity)

Full-color masters of all of the posters, bookmarks, handouts, and forms found in the book are available in a downloadable PDF format from www. elainemcewan.com for a modest sum.

There are two ways to approach the reading of this chapter:

- Read it straight through as you would an ordinary book chapter, although be forewarned that it is a *long* chapter containing twelve instructional activities with more than forty instructional aids.
- Skim the text, placing sticky notes or arrows on an activity you would like to consider more thoughtfully later on.

This chapter is designed as an instructional resource—a place to which you will turn when you are looking for ideas about how to integrate strategy instruction into your lesson plans.

TURN ON YOUR CPU (CENTRAL PROCESSING UNIT): GRADES 1–8

Description

Turn On Your CPU is designed to help distractible and daydreaming readers activate prior knowledge, monitor and clarify their comprehension, and visualize or organize parts of the text as they read. It is suitable for Grades K–8 and uses highly engaging posters, prompts, and props (e.g., sticky pictures, sticky arrows, and bookmarks) to help students read, understand, and remember.

Background Information

I was introduced to sticky arrows when a friend gave me a small, leather-bound case containing slender sticky notes of the Post-it variety. I did not know at the time what a valuable comprehension tool they would prove to be. Later at the urging of a first-grade teacher, I developed a sticky-pictures counterpart to the arrows for primary readers, and a math teacher suggested math stickies for reading math text (see the following activity, Turn On Your Math CPU). Reprographic masters and directions to make both kinds of sticky pictures are included.

I model and explain Turn On Your CPU whenever I am working with a new group of students or teachers because it is an activity I use with great success in my own reading and writing. While highly effective readers generally use the seven cognitive strategies regularly and without prompting, less-skilled readers or those who are reading difficult or unfamiliar text benefit from having procedures, prompts, posters, or props to activate and motivate their CPUs. The very act of admitting total bewilderment as a reader and then taking appropriate steps to clarify the confusion improves reading comprehension. Ignoring one's mix-ups or blaming the author for being disorganized or using big words is a waste of valuable reading time.

The prompts found on the posters and student handouts, as well as the suggested props (sticky arrows, flags, pictures, and bookmarks) provide scaffolding to support students' initial attempts to use their full range of cognitive powers. This instructional activity specifically demonstrates and scaffolds three of the seven cognitive strategies: activating, monitoring-clarifying, and visualizing-organizing.

Anticipatory Set

Most students and teachers are computer savvy and familiar with terms like *word processing* and *information processing*. They may not be as familiar with the term *central processing unit* (CPU), but a computer's CPU is very similar to the crucial processing component in the brain's working memory called the *central executive*. Use a desktop or laptop computer to show your students what it means to "turn on a CPU" and then compare that to how your students must intentionally "turn on" their own thinking processes before they can comprehend what they hear and read. When they are daydreaming or off-task, their CPUs are, in a sense, turned off or at least in standby mode. Your students will not learn or remember what they read or hear unless they are cognitively processing new information.

Demonstrate for students that when you turn on a classroom computer, it powers up and begins running several tests to make sure everything is working properly. Unfortunately there are no switches to turn on your students' cognitive processing abilities *and* activate their concentration, motivation, and commitment. There are, however, props and prompts that can motivate students and keep them engaged. Explain to your students that you will be using an activity to help them turn on their CPUs and then keep them turned on and tuned it to what they are reading. The activity involves putting down sticky pictures, arrows, or flags on the text they are reading and then thinking aloud about *why* they put down the arrows they did and what their responses and reactions are.

I Do It: Modeling and Explaining the Strategy (Activity) for Students

One of the most important components of any instructional activity is demonstrating by thinking aloud regarding your personal use of a strategy. Choose text that offers maximum opportunities for modeling each of the CPU prompts listed on Posters 4.1 (prompts for primary students) and 4.2 (prompts for upper-grade and middle school students). If you need help in preparing your think-aloud, reread the section in Chapter 2 that describes the critical attributes of thinking aloud and also review the Teacher Think-Alouds for activating, monitoring-clarifying, and visualizing-organizing found in Chapter 3.

The purpose of a think-aloud (in this context) is to model *your* thinking about the text that you are reading aloud using the Turn On Your CPU prompts and props. If you teach Grades K–2, choose text in which you can use each of the six primary word and picture prompts found on Poster 4.1, the sticky pictures created from Form 4.1, and the bookmarks created using Form 4.2. If you are working with students in Grades 3–8, choose text in which you can use the four word and picture prompts for sticky arrows found on Poster 4.2 and the bookmarks created using Form 4.3.

Give copies of your think-aloud text to students or prepare a transparency or PowerPoint slide for projection. Rehearse thinking aloud using the various prompts and props. Read the text aloud two to three sentences at a time and then stop momentarily to "think aloud" about the strategies (cognitive processing) you are using. Remember not to lapse into *explaining* or *giving directions.* There will be plenty of time for that when you begin teaching the strategy. As you think aloud regarding the various processes going on in your mind while you are reading the text, match them (if possible) to one of the prompts on the Sticky Picture Prompts or Sticky Arrow Prompts posters and then either physically put down an arrow on the text or transparency or use the animation feature on your PowerPoint program to place the sticky picture or arrow on the text. See the example in Teacher Think-Aloud 4.1.

Whenever you put down a sticky arrow or picture to indicate your confusion during reading, model looking up a word in the dictionary, find information about a subject or person in the encyclopedia, or enter a word or phrase into a search engine to see if a short explanation is available on the Internet (if you have a connection in your classroom). As you put down a sticky picture of a camera, describe the images that the text generated in your mind while you read. When you put down a book-and-brain sticky picture, explain to students how you connected prior knowledge and experiences with new information in the text. Articulate a feeling or emotion that the text evoked as you put down a sad or smiley sticky picture. Practice thinking aloud on several occasions before you take your thinking show "on the road."

We Do It: Further Explaining and Guided Practice

Guided practice consists of walking your students step-by-step through Turn On Your CPU. Prior to beginning, prepare enough sticky arrows or pictures for your students. Use Form 4.1 to create sticky pictures for primary

Sticky Picture Prompts

If you can connect  to something you have read or experienced, put down this sticky picture.

If you want to remember 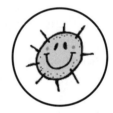 (pack it up and take it with you), put down this sticky picture.

If  makes you feel happy, put down this sticky picture.

If  helps you imagine a picture or video in your mind, put down this sticky picture.

If  makes you feel sad, put down this sticky picture.

If you are mixed up about , put down this sticky picture.

Sticky Arrow Prompts

**If you don't understand it,
put down a sticky arrow.**

**If you can make a connection to it,
put down a sticky arrow.**

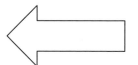 

**If you feel happy, sad, angry, or
even bored about it, put down
a sticky arrow.**

**If you can visualize or organize it,
put down a sticky arrow.**

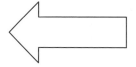 

Sticky Pictures Master

I can connect it.	I can connect it.	I can connect it.	I can connect it.
I want to remember it.	I want to remember it.	I want to remember it.	I want to remember it.
I feel sad about it.	I feel sad about it.	I feel sad about it.	I feel sad about it.
I feel happy about it.	I feel happy about it.	I feel happy about it.	I feel happy about it.
I can picture it.	I can picture it.	I can picture it.	I can picture it.
I don't understand it.	I don't understand it.	I don't understand it.	I don't understand it.

Sticky Pictures Bookmark Master

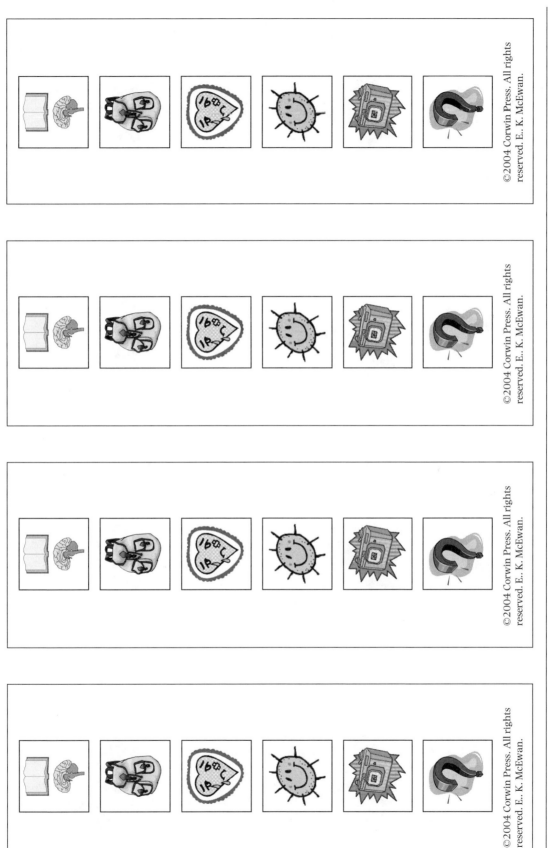

Sticky Arrows Bookmark Master

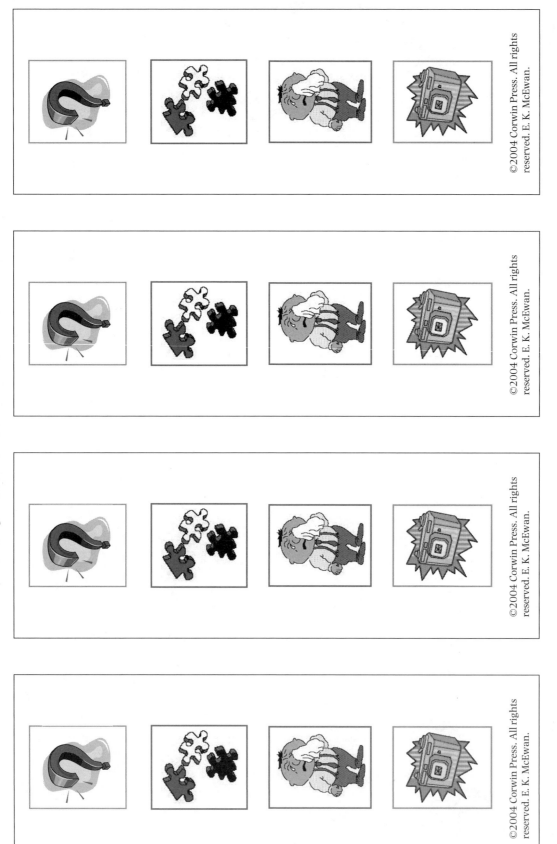

Teacher Think-Aloud: Turn On Your CPU

Think-Aloud Script	Read-Aloud Text: *Old Man Rabbit's Dinner Party*
 *I can make a connection to something I have experienced. My sister knit a muffler that was so long she could wrap it around herself three times.*	Old Man Rabbit sat at the door of his little house, eating a nice, ripe, juicy turnip. It was a cold frosty day, but Old Man Rabbit was all wrapped up, round and round, with yards and yards of his best red wool muffler, so he didn't care if the wind whistled through his whiskers and blew his ears up straight. Old Man Rabbit had been exercising, too, and that was another reason why he was so nice and warm.
 *I can make a connection to something I have read. This story reminds me of the Peter Rabbit stories. There's a farmer in those stories also.*	Early in the morning he had started off, lippity, clippity, down the little brown path that lay in front of his house and led to Farmer Dwyer's corn patch. The path was all covered with shiny red leaves. Old Man Rabbit scuffled through them and he carried a great big bag over his back. In the corn patch he found two or three fat, red ears of corn that Farmer Dwyer had missed, so he dropped them into his bag. A little farther along he found some purple turnips and some yellow carrots and quite a few russet apples that Farmer Dwyer had arranged in little piles in the orchard. Old Man Rabbit went in the barn, squeezing under the big front door by making himself very flat, and he filled all the chinks in his bag with potatoes, and he took a couple of eggs in his paws, for he thought he might want to stir up a little pudding for himself before the day was over.
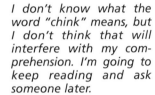 I don't understand it. *I don't know what the word "chink" means, but I don't think that will interfere with my comprehension. I'm going to keep reading and ask someone later.*	Then Old Man Rabbit started off home again down the little brown path, his mouth watering every time his bag bumped against his back, and not meeting anyone on the way because it was so very, very early in the morning.
 I can picture it. *I can picture a beautiful fall day. I can hear the leaves crunching and rustling as Old Man Rabbit walks through them. I smell the dirt on the vegetables and I can see the eggs golden yellow, all beaten up in Old Man Rabbit's bowl.*	When he came to the little house he emptied his bag and arranged all his harvest in piles in his front room—the corn in one pile, the carrots in one pile, the turnips in another pile, and the apples and potatoes in the last pile. He beat up his eggs and stirred some flour with them and filled it full of currants to make a pudding. And, when he had put his pudding in a bag and set it boiling on the stove, he went outside to sit a while and eat a turnip, thinking all the time what a mighty fine old rabbit he was, and so clever, too. Well, while Old Man Rabbit was sitting there in front of his little house, wrapped up in his red muffler and munching the turnip, he heard a little noise in the leaves.

Fringed Sticky Flags

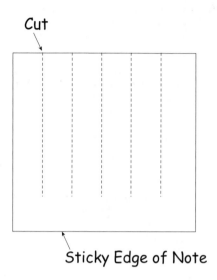

students.[1] Determine which four colors of sticky arrows or flags you will use with older students. The choice of colors is up to you. Be sure to color in the arrows on the poster or transparency to correspond with your chosen colors. If the name brand arrows are too expensive, give each student several 3" × 3" Post-it notes to create Fringed Sticky Flags. See the figure above for directions.

Used sensibly, a set of eight arrows per student (two of each color) will last through several readings, although many teachers tell me that their students are so eager to use the arrows while they read, they bring their own supply to school. Establish your ground rules in advance. For example, students who lose or misuse their arrows will have to wait until the next lesson to get more.

As you begin the guided practice session, remind students of the think-aloud you did earlier and continue to think aloud as needed during it. Explain to students that they will use sticky pictures, arrows, or flags during their silent or shared reading in the same way that you used them when you read and thought aloud for them. The desired outcome of this activity is increased student processing of text through the use of sticky pictures or arrows to motivate the articulation (whether aloud or silently) of reactions to and interactions with the text. Explain to students that in deciding to put down a certain color of sticky arrow or a specific picture to mark text while they are reading, they are reminding themselves to use three of the seven cognitive strategies: one to activate their prior knowledge and motivate them to make connections between what they know or have experienced and the text they are reading, one to monitor their comprehension and fix up any reading mix-ups, and a third to visualize (make mental pictures) or organize (construct an organizer like a chart, Venn diagram, or web) what they are reading. Explain the meaning of each of the sticky pictures or arrows and the accompanying prompts. Clarify any words that are confusing to your students, and once again briefly model what the process will look like when students are using it.

Pass out copies of text that students will read during guided practice, text that is easier than the usual instructional text, and give each student a small number of sticky pictures or arrows (in four different colors). At the beginning of guided practice, read the text aloud while students put down the arrows that indicate the kind of processing they are doing. Then ask students to share how they processed (connected, monitored, visualized, or organized). If your students are embarrassed to talk about their processing in a large group, pair your students and instruct them to share after reading each small chunk of text. As *you* increase your thinking aloud, your students will follow your example

Once you have read a few paragraphs with the whole group, ask students to read a short section of text with a partner to practice using the props and prompts. Or you might chorally read the text and then ask students to put down their sticky arrows individually. If you are working with a small reading group, become a fellow reader by pointing out parts that created confusion for you during the reading. Read the text from your students' perspectives and predict where they will have difficulties, or prompt them to make connections from books you have read aloud to them or with them. In the beginning, provide as much support as you can. Before long they will be eager to share their feelings, connections, images, and confusion with you *and* their peers.

You Do It: Students Work in Small Groups or Individually

The ultimate instructional goal of Turn On Your CPU is that your students will become aware of the need for activating, monitoring-clarifying, and visualizing as they read and *do it on their own*. For that to happen, you must continually model your use of the cognitive strategies, point out to students where and how they could use these strategies in text you are reading together, and repeatedly remind them of the benefits of strategy usage, both now and in the future. Bring books that you are personally reading to class and show students how you have used sticky pictures or arrows to help you process text more effectively. Encourage students to do the same with their recreational reading and to think aloud with their classmates just as you have thought aloud for them. To encourage your students to habitually "turn on their CPUs," distribute individual bookmarks you have duplicated on card stock and laminated using Forms 4.2 and 4.3.

TURN ON YOUR MATH CPU (CENTRAL PROCESSING UNIT): GRADES 4–8

Description

Turn On Your Math CPU is a variation of the preceding activity designed for reading math text. It offers math teachers a way to keep distractible students focused on the reading and processing, not only of "story problems" but also on the growing quantity of narrative reading found in mathematics textbooks. Students are motivated by props and prompts to respond and think aloud (and increasingly quietly) about math.

Background Information

Math teachers don't typically think of themselves as reading teachers, but the amount of mathematics-related text that students are expected to read and understand increases with each successive textbook adoption. If you want your students to be successful on state mathematics assessments, they need reading skills that match or surpass their mathematical skills. The idea of math stickies was conceived by Kim Buck, a middle school math teacher in Stover, Missouri, after she attended one of my workshops and saw the sticky pictures for primary readers. Her students find them appealing, and the prompts and pictures motivate them to process text and talk about their processing in ways that simply telling them won't accomplish. If the sticky pictures Kim developed don't quite mesh with your teaching style, develop your own version.

Anticipatory Set

If you have already used Turn On Your CPU for reading narrative and expository text with your students, an introduction to sticky math pictures won't take long. If you are a math specialist and have turned directly to this page, please review the preceding instructional activity, Turn On Your CPU.

I Do It: Modeling and Explaining the Strategy (Activity) for Students

Choose several word problems or a section of narrative text from your math book to use for thinking aloud while using the math sticky pictures. Teacher Think-Aloud 4.2 is a brief example from a middle school math text in which Kim put down three different kinds of math sticky pictures to show her students how she would process the text. Here's how Kim explained the sticky pictures to the class:

• *I know this well enough to explain it to someone else.* Putting down this sticky picture means that you *really* understand what you are reading and could in fact, if asked, explain it to someone in your group.

• *This connects to something I know or have done.* Putting down this sticky picture means that you have some knowledge or experiences in your long-term memory that you can connect with what you are reading in your math book.

• *I need multiplication facts to work this problem.* Putting down this sticky picture means that you recognize you need to know a multiplication fact to work a problem. Give yourself a pat on the back if you know that fact. If you don't, how about asking for help in learning them.

Teacher Think-Aloud: Turn On Your Math CPU

Think-Aloud Script	Read-Aloud Math Text
	"A **circle** is the set of all points in a plane that are the same distance from a given point called the **center**. The **diameter** is the distance across the circles through its center. The **radius** is the distance from the center to any point on the circle. The **circumference** is the distance around the circle."

I need to put this in my math notebook.

I need to write these definitions in my own words into my math notebook.

(Collins et al., 2002, p. 297)

I can connect this to something I already know or have done.

"The Greek letter π is used to represent the circumference divided by the diameter. Approximations often used for π are 3.14 and 22/7." (p. 298)

So this is what π is for. I remember celebrating "pi day" on March 14 (3rd month, 14th day, ∞3.14) in fifth grade. We had oatmeal pies and sang songs.

Find the circumference of a circle with a radius of 14 meters.

$$C \approx 2\,\pi\,r$$

$$C \approx 2 \times \frac{22}{7} \times 14$$

$$C \approx 2 \times \frac{22}{\cancel{7}_1} \times \frac{\cancel{14}^2}{1}$$

I need to know my multiplication facts to work this problem.

$$C \approx 2 \times \frac{22}{1} \times \frac{2}{1}$$

$$C \approx 88$$

(p. 298)

I really need to learn my multiplication facts better. They crossed out the 7 and the 14 and put a 2 there because $2 \times 7 = 14$.

From Collins et al. (2002).

- *I need to copy this into my math notebook.* Putting down this sticky picture means I recognize an important formula or definition that I will need in the future. (Kim's students keep a math reference manual for important formulas and definitions. When they need the information to answer a question or work a problem, they know exactly where to find it.)

- *I know how I can use this.* Putting down this sticky picture means you realize that the information will be helpful to you in doing problems from the book or in solving a real-world math problem.

- *I don't understand it.* Putting down this sticky picture means that you are confused and need to ask someone (the teacher or a classmate) what it means.

We Do It: Further Explaining and Guided Practice

Choose several word problems or narrative text from your textbook and guide students step-by-step using the math sticky pictures. Create math sticky pictures using Form 4.4 as a master, following the directions found in the footnote on pg. 133.

You Do It: Students Work in Small Groups or Individually

Once your students have the idea, assign the next lesson to be read using math sticky pictures. Stop midway through the assignment to make sure students have the idea and are stopping to talk about where they placed their sticky pictures and what actions they intend to take to respond to their processing.

ADD IT UP: GRADES 3–8

Description

Add It Up is designed to help students understand the critical attributes of inferring—that is, figuring out exactly *where* an inference comes from and *how* to come up with one independently. The activity focuses students' attention on "trouble spots" in the text and shows them how to figuratively add up information from four sources to generate an inference: (1) what is written in the text (the actual words), (2) what is unwritten in the text (the author's intent or what is "written between the lines"), (3) what is known by the reader from life experiences, and (4) what is known by the reader from other books or school learning. Students will also need to activate prior knowledge as well as visualize or organize to make an inference. Inferring is highly text dependent and must be nurtured in your students through constant coaching, modeling, prompting, and cueing during all of their guided *and* independent reading.

Background Information

Many teachers define *inferring* as "reading between the lines," and while this phrase seems like a logical definition to adults who already *know* how to

Math Stickies Master

I know this well enough to explain it to someone else.	I know this well enough to explain it to someone else.	I know this well enough to explain it to someone else.	I know this well enough to explain it to someone else.
This connects to something I know or have done.	This connects to something I know or have done.	This connects to something I know or have done.	This connects to something I know or have done.
I need multiplication facts to work this problem.	I need multiplication facts to work this problem.	I need multiplication facts to work this problem.	I need multiplication facts to work this problem.
I need to put this in my math notebook.	I need to put this in my math notebook.	I need to put this in my math notebook.	I need to put this in my math notebook.
I have a bright idea about how to use this.	I have a bright idea about how to use this.	I have a bright idea about how to use this.	I have a bright idea about how to use this.
I don't understand it.	I don't understand it.	I don't understand it.	I don't understand it.

Form 4.4. Turn On Your Math CPU. Reprinted by permission of Kim Buck.

infer, students often find it incomprehensible. Inferring can be compared to an addition problem that adds up words and thoughts instead of numbers—a problem in which four different sets of ideas and words are combined to produce an inference. The meaning "between the lines" *is* important, no question about it, but your students will definitely need to add in some additional information to produce an inference. While research tells us that inferring is highly dependent on students' background and vocabulary knowledge, most students (and readers in general) *will* become far more inferential, whatever the text they are reading, when given some explicit instruction as to what constitutes an inference.

Anticipatory Set

If appropriate, ask your students if they have ever heard the expression "reading between the lines." Solicit some possible definitions for this expression from students, if any. For a time when I was younger, I thought "reading between the lines" actually meant that there were real words written in invisible ink between the lines and that everyone could see them but me. I eventually came to understand that this invisibility was figurative in nature, but your students may be as confused as I was. Tell them that you are going to help them learn how to read between the lines. In fact, you will actually *show* them how to do it. Then they will be able to read the text that is written and understand what is unwritten but inferred.

I Do It: Modeling and Explaining the Strategy (Activity) for Students

One of the most important components of any instructional activity is thinking aloud regarding your personal use of the applicable strategies during the I Do It instructional phase. Choose text that offers maximum opportunities for modeling the inferring strategy. Once you develop a successful think-aloud for introducing inferring, you will be able to use it again and again. Reread the section in Chapter 2 that describes thinking aloud as well as the Teacher Think-Aloud 3.2, for inferring, in Chapter 3. And see Teacher Think-Aloud 4.3.

As you model how you infer, use the language of the related posters and handouts. Keep your vocabulary as consistent as possible. Make sure to tell your students that there are at least a dozen synonyms for the word *infer* so that when they hear people say "I think" or "I assume," the statements they are hearing are usually inferences of one kind or another. See also the instructional activity coming later in this chapter, A Dozen Ways to Say "Infer."

There is sometimes a temptation to talk too much when explaining a concept as complex as inferring. Make sure that you have a clear grasp of the critical attributes of inferring before you explain it to students. If in doubt, first explain inferring to your spouse, children, or best friend. If you can't explain it with clarity and specificity to them, then you are probably not ready to explain it to your students. If your initial attempts confuse them, they will stay confused for a very long time—perhaps forever.

Teacher Think-Aloud: Add It Up

What you read	*xxxxxxxxxx* *xxxxxxxxxxx*	Hanging on to the gyrating handle was like riding a bucking bronco.
What's between the lines	Operating a jackhammer is pretty hard on a person's body.	*xxxxxxxxxxxx* *xxxxxxxxx* *xxxxxxxxxxxx*
What you know from experience	I've seen a jackhammer and I've been to a rodeo. I investigated buying a jackhammer once to dig holes in my rock-hard soil.	
What you learned in school	I know what the word "gyrating" means—swinging around and moving violently, and the word is a bit of an exaggeration in this context.	

The Teacher's Inference:
What it all adds up to for me is this: I think (or assume or deduce) that this sentence is about a construction worker who is breaking up old concrete in order to build a new highway. If I had more text I might discover that the person operating the jackhammer is a do-it-yourselfer who rented the jackhammer at Home Depot. I would guess that this individual is going to be very stiff when he or she finishes breaking up the front steps in order to build new ones.

We Do It: Further Explaining and Guided Practice

Display an enlarged copy or provide individual copies of Add It Up Poster 4.3. Remind students of your earlier think-aloud, and once again, use the prompts and illustrations on the poster defining *inferring*. Explain to students that when they do not understand what they are reading, they need to *infer* by adding up (or combining) four sources of information and knowledge: (1) what the text actually says in the words printed on the page, (2) the experience they have activated from the social-emotional (memories) part of their long-term memory, (3) the knowledge they have activated from cognitive long-term memory, and (4) what they think the author might have meant or intended but did not specifically state in words.

Add one or two examples of your own, drawn from prior class reading or experience, to illustrate that accurate decoding and knowledge of some dictionary definitions may not be enough to figure out an author's intended meaning. Highly effective readers activate all of their prior knowledge and experience and then combine that with the printed words and the author's intended meaning.

Choose text from which you and your class will infer together. Then put a transparency of Handout 4.1 on the overhead, and as you read the text with your students, choose a place to stop and infer together, filling in the four different parts of the "addition" problem. If your students have a hard time (and don't be discouraged if they do), stop, explain again, and model once again. Inferring is a difficult concept to understand, and the cognitive process of inferring requires putting a lot of information together in what is sometimes a very overcrowded working memory. You may have moved to the Guided Practice step too quickly. Help students understand that inferring is one of the most challenging cognitive strategies to use because it is so context dependent. The ability to infer depends on "word and world knowledge" (Hirsch, 2003).

Once you have successfully practiced inferring together in a piece of carefully selected text, engage in still more guided practice during classroom reading activities. When you encounter a particularly good example of text that requires inferring to understand, point to the A Dozen Ways to Say "Infer" Poster 4.4 and make an inference together. Encourage and affirm students who begin to think aloud regarding their own inferences. Every time one of your students infers, do what they do for first-time callers on some radio talk shows—ring a bell. Or pass out a sticker, hand out a free homework pass, or offer free computer or library time. Prompt students when you come to parts of the text in everyday assignments that you know contain opportunities for inferring. Don't tell them what you infer the meaning to be. Coach them through the "addition problem" step-by-step. The more attuned your students become to the importance of inferring to extract and construct meaning, the more readily they will begin to notice what they don't know and realize the importance of finding it out in order to make an inference. That will then motivate them to acquire new word meanings, look for explanations and information they don't have, and "chew" on text—complex cognition at its finest. You will be surprised to find your own reading becoming more strategic as you teach the cognitive strategies to your students. That is one of the added benefits of SRI.

Add It Up

What you read (what the author says)

"They were her state pair and she could have seen through a pair of stove lids as well."

+

What's written between the lines (what the author means but doesn't say)

She couldn't see through her glasses at all.

+

What you know from experience (you've been there and done that)

+

What you've learned in school (knowledge)

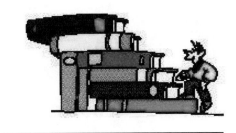

=   An Inference

Student Think-Aloud Form for Making an Inference

What you read	
What's between the lines	
What you know	
What you've learned	

You Do It: Students Work in Small Groups or Individually

You may be tempted to occasionally remark to yourself regarding your students, "One day they have it and the next day they don't." Do not become discouraged. Your students' abilities to infer will come and go with the difficulty level of the text, their relevant background knowledge, and their motivation and interest levels. Your role is to prompt, cue, coach, remind, and affirm whenever you see students struggling to develop an inference or coming up with spectacular inferences on their own without prompting.

A DOZEN WAYS TO INFER: GRADES 3–8

Description

A Dozen Ways to Infer is designed to introduce students in Grades 3–8 to a dozen categories of inferences that readers routinely encounter in their reading. This activity is based on Add It Up, the previous instructional activity for teaching inferring. The questioning strategy plays a major role in this activity, which uses a PowerPoint™ presentation (if you're feeling ambitious) to illustrate a dozen ways to infer, and then encourages students to engage in an ongoing treasure hunt to find examples of these types of inferences in their textbooks, newspapers, magazines, and library books.

Background Information

The typology of inferences found in this activity is adapted from Johnson and Johnson (1986). I have expanded their list somewhat and added *prompts* (questions to activate students' inferential thinking) and text examples to illustrate each one. Figure 4.3, Kinds of Inferences, shows the complete list. I first used this activity with third and fourth graders and developed a PowerPoint presentation with touches of animation here and there to make my lesson more motivating. The examples and graphics increase the likelihood that students will continue to think about inferring once the lesson is over. The effort it took to develop the PowerPoint is worthwhile since inferring is a difficult-to-teach strategy. If your classroom is not equipped with a projector and laptop, consider taking your class to the media center to introduce inferring. (My version of a Dozen Ways to Infer is available as a download from my Web site for a modest sum.)

When you find a piece of text (e.g., from your science or social studies textbooks, a read-aloud novel, or even a book you are personally reading) that offers varied opportunities to infer, drop it into your strategy file. If you develop a prompt or prop that is effective for scaffolding your students' development of strategy usage, refine, polish, and "publish" it. Teachers in Japan routinely work together in collaborative efforts called Lesson Study Groups (Yoshida, 1999) in which they fine-tune and perfect lessons by teaching both each other and their students.

I used the statements and questions from Figure 4.3 in my PowerPoint presentation. Students were given time to read the statement on the screen, and I read it aloud for slower readers. When introducing a cognitive strategy, provide a scaffold for struggling readers whenever you can. The students then huddled in their cooperative groups to come up with the best answer to the question shown in the third column. Once a team captain had given the group's agreed-upon answer, I clicked the mouse and an animated photo or graphic illustrated the answer I had chosen. In some instances, I got "wrong" answers, responses that answered a question other than the one I had asked.

In my efforts to keep everyone engaged and inferring for as long as possible, I try to turn off-center answers into another opportunity for inferring and questioning. Here's how it goes: For example, the question that goes with the second statement on Figure 4.3 (*She swirled the frosting around the cake and then placed it in the display case*) is, *What is this person's occupation or job?*

One answer that eager beavers (who haven't taken time to infer) frequently come up with is, "To advertise the cake."

I always respond, "That's a great inference. But it doesn't answer the question I asked. If your team can come up with the question that you *are* answering, I'll give you credit."

Kinds of Inferences

Kind of Inference	Text Statement	Question
Location or setting	The rider hung on tightly with both legs to avoid being tossed to the ground.	Where is this happening?
Career, occupation, or job	She swirled the frosting around the cake and then placed it in the display case.	What is this person's occupation?
Feeling	I won first prize in the science fair.	What is the feeling being described?
Time (clock or historical period)	The birds were singing and the sun was high in the sky.	What is the time of day?
Action	He ran the bases in record time but was called out at home plate.	What is the action being described?
Instrument, tool, or device	"You have a very high fever," she said.	What tool is being used?
Cause	My room had never looked so neat.	What is the cause?
Effect	I rode on the Ferris wheel three times.	What is the effect?
Object	There was something to please every shopper in the display window: beanbags, wingbacks, and even a rocking model.	What is the object?
Category	We've been to Disneyland, Sea World, and now we're heading off to Legoland.	What is the category?
Problem	I have to stop eating so many ice-cream sundaes.	What is the problem?
Solution	I need money to buy a birthday present for Mom.	What is the solution?

Figure 4.3. A Dozen Ways to Infer. Categories and questions adapted and expanded from Johnson and Johnson (1986). Text samples are from author.

After a few seconds of processing, the team usually figures out the question they answered: *"Why* did the baker put the cake on display?" If you can find ways to turn questioning inside out and upside down for your students, their abilities to infer will improve exponentially.

Anticipatory Set

The following is the script I use when working with third and fourth graders. You can adapt it to your specific grade level.

> I love to play games, and I especially like competitions where team members are required to put their brains together and combine what they know to answer questions. I have a great game for you to play today. In order to play, you first have to infer individually. Then you have to put together your inferences with those of your team members and figure out which one makes the most sense. But first I want to remind you about what inferring actually is. (Show Poster 4.3.)

I Do It: Modeling and Explaining the Strategy (Activity) for Students

Your think-aloud for this activity consists of choosing several examples from Figure 4.3, Kinds of Inferences, and see Teacher Think-Aloud 4.4. Display one of the sentences and its accompanying question and then think aloud as you add up an inference using the step-by-step approach suggested in the preceding activity.

We Do It: Further Explaining and Guided Practice

Tell students that you will be playing a game during guided practice that is similar to the think-aloud you did. This activity presupposes that your students have had an introduction to cooperative learning or teaming and will know the basic rules and expectations for working together as a group. Team members will read a sentence, be asked a question about the sentence, and then be expected to make an inference to answer the question appropriately. First, divide the class into heterogeneous teams of three to five students. Choose a captain for each team. Explain the rules of the game. The captain's job is to huddle with the group members, get their input regarding what the agreed-upon answer is, and then report it when called on. A team will be disqualified from a round if someone other than the captain gives an answer or if the captain is unable to wait until called on. Although the students' desks may be grouped in pods, students *must* stand up and lean into a huddle to confer. This practice is important for two reasons: (1) It encourages students to actually talk to one another (confer) and combine all of their knowledge and experiences in order to answer the questions, and (2) it keeps students from overhearing each other's inferences.

Teacher Think-Aloud: A Dozen Ways to Infer

What I read	The rider hung on tightly to avoid being tossed to the ground.
The question	Where is this happening?
What I know from experience	The first picture I get in my mind when I read this is one of those mechanical bulls you find in some country-western restaurants. But the rider wouldn't be tossed to the ground there. He or she would be tossed to the floor. I went horseback riding once and the horse was a little frisky, and I really had to hang on to avoid getting thrown off the horse, so this could be happening at a riding stable.
What I've learned (knowledge)	I read an article about cowboys lately and all of the injuries they get when they are thrown off bucking broncos and bulls, so this could be taking place at a rodeo.

The Teacher's Inference

To be absolutely certain of where this is taking place, I will need more information than this text gives me, but I'm going to assume that it's happening at a rodeo and that the rider is either on a bronco (horse) or a bull.

You Do It: Students Work in Small Groups or Individually

Choose text that most students can easily read independently. Divide the class into pairs or teams and then give copies of the Think-Aloud Form (Handout 4.2). Explain once again how to develop an inference and then read the text chorally, either with the whole group or as teams, to make sure that every student personally processes every word. Then ask students to figure out, according to the handout, what kinds of inferences they made. Ask them to fill in the blanks for those kinds of inferences in the center section. Move from group to group to monitor their progress, encourage their inferring, and affirm good inferences.

Inferring must be modeled, practiced, scaffolded, coached, and affirmed every day in the context of "real" reading to become a routine reading process. Your mission as the teacher is to be on the lookout constantly for text examples that provide opportunities for inferring so that you or your students can think aloud to each other about the inferences you've made. Give your students extra copies of the Kinds of Inferences and the Student Think-Aloud Form on which to record statements from textbooks or library books that contain examples of the categories and questions on the form. Give extra credit to students who share their inferences with the class.

A DOZEN WAYS TO SAY "INFER": GRADES 4–8

Description

A Dozen Ways to Say "Infer" is a follow-up activity to the previous inferring activities, Add It Up and A Dozen Ways to Infer. It introduces twelve synonyms for the word *infer* and uses visualizing and organizing to explore and expand their meanings.

Anticipatory Set

Here's one possible way to engage and motivate students for this activity:

I get bored using the same words over and over and look for different words to express similar ideas or meanings. For example, you have probably heard me use synonyms, words that mean the same thing, for the word *infer*, when I've been inferring out loud. Sometimes I might say, "I think" or "I assume" instead of saying "I infer." Even though *infer, think,* and *assume* mean about the same thing, someone who was really interested in words and their dictionary meanings might find some little differences between them. I had a lot of fun with my dictionary and thesaurus and discovered a dozen synonyms for the word *infer* (See Poster 4.4), and we're going to construct some graphic organizers together for our classroom wall (actually, twelve of them) to help us learn and use all of these synonyms in our think-alouds and conversation about reading.

Student Think-Aloud Form for Kinds of Inferences

Kind of Inference	Text Statement	Question
Location or setting		Where is this happening?
Career, occupation, or job		What is this person's occupation?
Feeling		What is the feeling being described?
Time (clock or historical)		What is the time of day? What is the period in history?
Action		What is the action being described?
Instrument, tool, or device		What tool is being used?
Cause		What is the cause?
Effect		What is the effect?
Object		What is the object?
Category		What is the category?
Problem		What is the problem?
Solution		What is the solution?

Handout 4.2. A Dozen Ways to Infer. Categories and questions adapted and enhanced from Johnson and Johnson (1986).

A Dozen Ways to Say "Infer"

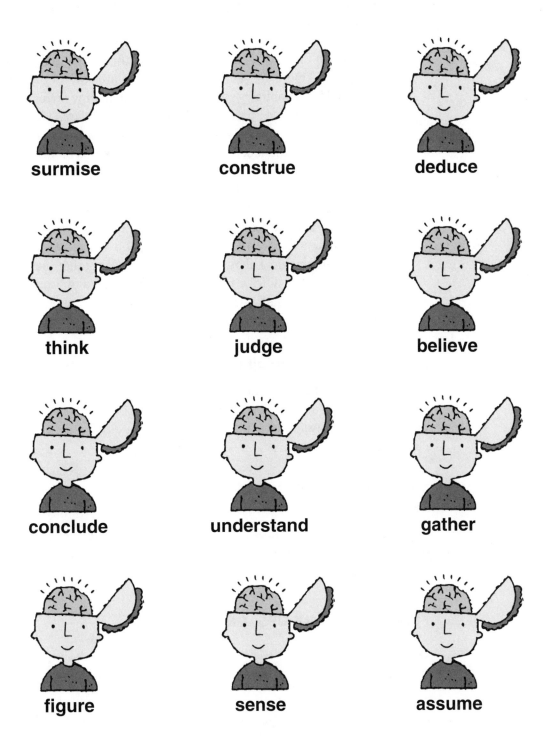

surmise   construe   deduce

think   judge   believe

conclude   understand   gather

figure   sense   assume

Poster 4.4. A Dozen Ways to Say "Infer." Copyright © 2004 Corwin Press. All rights reserved. Reprinted from *Seven Strategies of Highly Effective Readers*, by E. K. McEwan. Thousand Oaks, CA: Corwin Press, www.corwinpress.com. Reproduction authorized only for the local school site that has purchased this book.

I Do It: Modeling and Explaining the (Strategy) Activity for Students

Post or project the organizer found in Teacher Think-Aloud 4.5 where everyone can see it. Here is a sample script you might use to go with it, for modeling this activity:

> When I decide to make a graphic organizer, the first thing I have to decide is what kind of organizer to use. There are several organizers that are good for vocabulary studies. I'm going to use my own variation of one of the templates from the Inspiration® Software. The second thing I do when I'm making a graphic organizer is to figure out what the frames will be (the labels that describe what kinds of words go in the various shapes of the organizer. I going to put the word *think* in the center of my organizer. It's the key word of my organizer (i.e., all of the information we add to the organizer from now on will relate to the word *think*). I decided on four categories related to the word *think*: (1) definitions, (2) sentences, (3) reasons to think, and (4) places to think. There's nothing magical about those categories. You might have come up with one or two different ones. (Teacher thinks aloud during the generation of the ideas, sentences, and definitions, using a dictionary or other reference tools as needed.)

We Do It: Further Explaining and Guided Practice

After students have watched you think aloud while generating definitions, sentences, and ideas related to the word *think*, choose one of the other synonyms from the poster, and this time, develop the organizer with the whole class helping you.

You Do It: Students Work in Small Groups and Individually

After you and your students have developed an organizer together for one of the synonyms for *infer*, now divide students into teams with each team choosing a different synonym.

FIX UP YOUR MIX-UPS: GRADES 1–8

Description

Fix Up Your Mix-Ups is designed to introduce and facilitate usage of the monitoring-clarifying strategy. The activity systematically introduces students to the possible ways they can get confused when they are reading challenging text, helps them become attuned to comprehension breakdowns, and gives them the good news that *they* are quite capable of fixing up their mix-ups by engaging in Part 2 of the monitoring-clarifying strategy: clarifying or fixing up their mix-ups. Fixing up mix-ups requires that students engage in the searching-selecting

Teacher Think-Aloud: Developing a Graphic Organizer

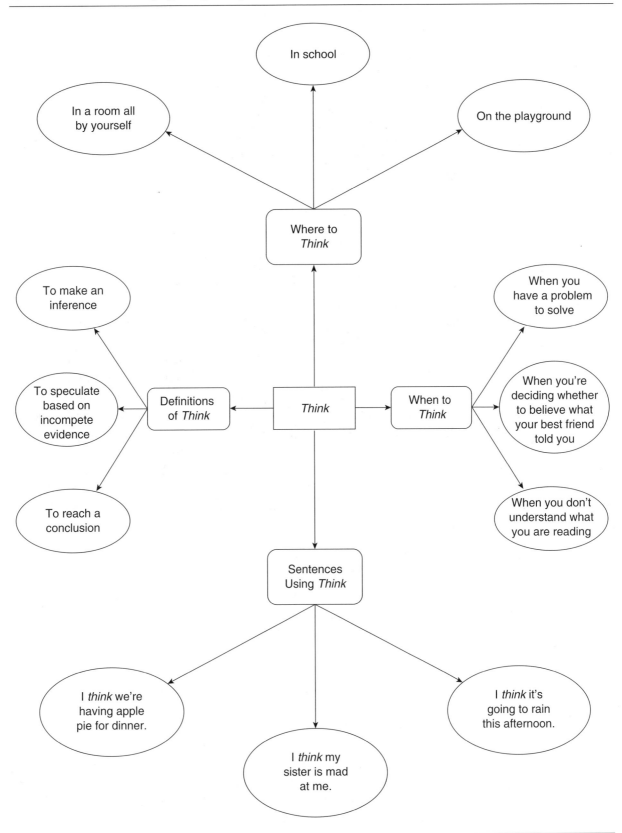

strategy to select appropriate information to answer questions, define words and terms, clarify misunderstandings, solve problems, or gather information.

Background Information

Monitoring one's reading comprehension and fixing up the mix-ups that inevitably occur is a habit—much like putting dirty dishes in the dishwasher or brushing one's teeth. These kinds of behaviors are performed both intentionally and consciously. The sooner that teachers can demonstrate the power of monitoring and clarifying to their students and then nurture these cognitive habits, the more expert students' reading will become.

Anticipatory Set

Ask your students if they have ever been driving with one or both of their parents when the driver got lost. Ask them to describe what happened. You will no doubt hear a variety of strategies (some effective and some a waste of travel time) to fix up the common mix-up of getting lost. Students may also be able to tell you stories of their own mix-ups while walking or riding their bikes in a new neighborhood. Write some of the strategies on the chalkboard, overhead, or dry-erase board and talk about which of the strategies are effective and which don't work. Share some personal examples of someone who, even though lost, won't stop and ask for directions. Explain that using fix-up strategies is a habit of the brain. Explain that the difference between highly effective and ineffective readers is *not* that effective readers *never* get lost or confused but that they always know when they *are* "lost," have no problem admitting it, and have a toolbox or belt of fix-up strategies (cognitive tools) available. Skilled readers are constantly asking the question, "Is it clicking or clunking?" (Klingner et al., 1998), and when it's clunking—they know exactly what to do to get it clicking again!

I Do It: Modeling and Explaining the Strategy (Activity) for Students

The best way to model fixing up your mix-ups is to curl up with a book: the course textbook, your basal reader, a novel your students are currently reading, or the Newbery Award winner you are reading aloud to the class. As you read, consider the ways in which your students could get mixed up while reading this specific piece of text. Is the textbook badly written, poorly organized, and inconsiderate of the needs of students? Does the novel have challenging vocabulary and require a wealth of background information to understand? Then choose a section of text and walk your students through it, thinking aloud about what you did to make sense of the book. Point out the mix-ups that occurred while you were reading it, even though you may have readily fixed them. Take time during every day (or class period) to model fixing up your mix-ups so that your students grow accustomed to the idea of looking up things they don't know, asking questions to clarify their confusion, and searching out answers with diligence and persistence. Use the Clarifying Checklist, Handout 4.3, to make sure you explain and repeatedly model every kind of mix-up that occurs.

Clarifying Checklist

Is there something specific you don't understand? A word, phrase, concept, idea?

☐ Ask someone: an adult, an expert, a classmate, the author, or your teacher.

☐ Look it up: in the dictionary, an encyclopedia, the index, the glossary, or on the Internet.

☐ Make a prediction: "This must be what the author means. I'm going to keep on reading and see if I'm right."

☐ Predict word meaning based on context or word structure.

Is the text poorly written, disorganized, or very long?

☐ Chunk it: Divide the text into smaller sections and work on one section at a time.

☐ Draw a picture or diagram: Make a graphic organizer.

☐ Outline it.

Are you confused about the meaning of the text?

☐ Read the back cover copy, the blurb, the preface, a chapter summary, the introduction, a review, or critique for more clues about the meaning.

☐ Connect what you have read to your experience: "This reminds me of the time that. . . ."

☐ Read the text again or even once more, if necessary.

☐ Read the text more slowly.

☐ Stop and think out loud to yourself about what you have read.

☐ Talk to someone: Think aloud to a friend, family member, or classmate.

☐ Ignore the parts you don't understand temporarily and keep reading.

Do you need to remember what you are reading for a test or to write a summary?

☐ Form a study group and talk about the text with your classmates.

☐ Make a mental picture: Imagine what the text is describing.

☐ Write it down: Take notes.

We Do It: Further Explaining
and Guided Practice: Grades K–2

Use *Fix Up Your Mix-Ups* with primary students during paired reading. Give each student a set of Fix-Up Stickies (Form 4.5). Explain what each of the fix-up stickies means and when it is appropriate to put one down on the page. Ask students to pair with a partner, take turns reading a section of text that you designate, and then put down the fix-up stickies that apply. Have them talk to each other about their mix-ups and then ask for volunteers to share how they clarified (or fixed up) their confusion.

We Do It: Further Explaining
and Guided Practice: Grades 3–8

Give each student a set of Fix-Up Stickies and remind students what each of the prompts and pictures means. Explain to students that this activity will give them a head start on their science (or math or social studies) assignment for tomorrow. Choose a particularly challenging section of text in tomorrow's reading assignment. Working step-by-step with your students, point out where you think their mix-ups might occur based on your reading of the text and show them once again what you would do to remedy the situation. This may require looking up some words, searching the Internet, talking to an expert, making a graphic organizer, chunking the text and getting rid of some unimportant information, or even writing a brief summary of each section. Then instruct students to use fix-up stickies for a second chunk of the assignment while you walk around the room to monitor. Debrief, asking students to share where they put down their stickies and what fix-up strategies they would use. Put a copy of the Clarifying Checklist on the overhead, and give copies to students to keep track of the fix-up strategies that are suggested.

You Do It: Students Work
in Small Groups or Independently

Once students have gained familiarity with this new set of prompts and pictures, assign this activity once or twice a week as a prereading activity.

DO YOU HAVE ANY QUESTIONS? GRADES 4–8

Description

Do You Have Any Questions? is an adaptation of the Question-Answer Relationship (QAR) activity, originally developed to teach students how to locate answers, particularly when those answers were not readily accessible in the text (Pearson & Johnson, 1978; Raphael, 1984; Raphael & Pearson, 1985; Raphael & Wonnacott, 1985). Rather than showing students where to look for *answers* to traditional end-of-chapter questions, my activity shows students how to *ask* specific types of questions, a far more challenging *and* productive cognitive assignment. *Do You Have Any Questions?* also uses and facilitates the development of summarizing and inferring.

Fix-Up Stickies Master

I don't know the word's meaning.	I don't know the word's meaning.	I don't know the word's meaning.
I don't know how to say the word.	I don't know how to say the word.	I don't know how to say the word.
I'm confused about what this means.	I'm confused about what this means.	I'm confused about what this means.
I don't know the word's meaning.	I don't know the word's meaning.	I don't know the word's meaning.
I don't know how to say the word.	I don't know how to say the word.	I don't know how to say the word.
I'm confused about what this means.	I'm confused about what this means.	I'm confused about what this means.

Background Information

How often, after summing up a lesson or reaching the end of a unit, have you asked your students if they have any questions? Usually you are greeted with silence. When I get silence after I ask that question during a workshop, I know exactly what it means: My students (teachers and principals) need additional opportunities to process what they have heard before they will be able to ask questions, or they don't know enough yet to know what they don't know. This instructional activity aims to change that state of affairs in your classroom. Some background information on QAR will put our revised version in context.

Although QAR has been around for what seems like forever, I did not encounter what I call the upside-down version of it until I read *Reading for Understanding* (Schoenbach et al., 1999). The authors describe its effectiveness with at-risk high school freshmen in a cognitive apprenticeship setting. I decided their approach was the perfect method for showing teachers how to unleash their students' processing powers to ask their own questions rather than answer the ones at the ends of the chapters.

Anticipatory Set

To introduce your students to this instructional activity, pose the question from which this activity gets its name: *Do you have any questions?* Your students will likely give you the same glazed looks you get from them when you ask the same question at the end of an explanation or lesson. Explain to students that you are worn out from being the only person in the class who ever asks any questions, and that you are also pretty tired of the fact that hardly anybody except the same faithful few answers your questions (if that is the case).

So tell your students that from now on, they will be asking all of the questions in your class. They will be asking the questions after reading the chapter, the questions to review for the midterm, and they will even be writing the questions that you will use on the final exam. These statements will no doubt surprise your students, and they will even momentarily consider them to be "good news." And they really will be good news for the development of their strategic reading abilities. The "bad news," which you will not share with them at this time, is that their central processing units (brains) will be working much harder than they ever have before, because asking questions—and coming up with defensible answers—is cognitively demanding. Just ask teachers!

I Do It: Modeling and Explaining the Strategy (Activity) for Students

One of the most important components of any instructional activity is thinking aloud regarding your personal use of the applicable strategies as you read aloud from the text you have chosen. Choose some fiction or nonfiction that offers maximum opportunities for modeling the strategies used in this activity. If you need help in preparing your questioning think-aloud, review the one in Chapter 3 (Think-Aloud 3.4). It models this activity and provides an extensive step-by-step lesson plan. Point out to students that although the focus of the activity is generating (developing, making up) questions, you are using five other cognitive strategies at the same time.

We Do It: Further Explaining and Guided Practice

Display the Question-Answer Quadrant Poster 4.5 and give copies of the Question-Answer Quadrant Handout 4.4 to students. Explain to students that the picture prompts are clues to help them know *where* the answers to questions will be found. They can serve as a double check for students. If they make up a question for Quadrant 3 and the answer can be found right on page 57, they have asked the wrong kind of question. Answers to Quadrant 1 questions are found in one specific place in the text. Note the picture prompt with a book and arrow. Answers to Quadrant 2 questions are found in several places in the text and will demand synthesizing and summarizing. Note the picture prompt of a book with several arrows, suggesting several different locations where a part of an answer can be found. Answers to Quadrant 3 questions are not located in a *specific place* in the book but rather are generated by combining background knowledge and inferences from the text. Note the picture prompts of a book and a brain. Answers to Quadrant 4 questions are not located in a *specific place* in the book, either. They are generated from readers' experiences as they relate to the topics of the text. Note the picture of the brain.

Remind students that this activity will require the use of six of the seven cognitive strategies. Even though the final product will be questions they make up and write down, they will have to activate prior knowledge, search for information and select the best option, make inferences about what an author means, summarize what they have found in their own words, and monitor-clarify to accomplish this difficult cognitive task.

Although you no doubt modeled the generation of all four types of questions during your earlier think-aloud, you may find it more productive to teach and practice only one question quadrant at a time or possibly pair the quadrants on the top half of the page (those in which the answers can be found in the text) before moving on to the questions on the bottom two quadrants that are more challenging to create because they require inferential thinking. This decision depends solely on the grade level and maturity of your students. Middle school students may be able to handle all four types of questions at once. Note that the following explanation covers all four quadrants.

Explain to students that the purpose of this activity is to teach them how to ask questions during their reading, research, and study. Tell them that in one sense they will be assuming the role of teacher as they read the text and write questions that teachers would generally ask students and expect them to be able to answer. Tell students that it does not matter how easy or difficult the questions are (as long as they follow the rules you explained) but that they *will* need to know the answers to any questions that they generate. Tell students that you will be talking about four different types of questions, and to help them remember and organize their questions, they can use the poster or the Question-Answer Quadrant Handout 4.4. To refresh your memory about the

Question-Answer Quadrant

(1)

Find it right
there in the

Search-Select
Monitor-Clarify

(2)

Find it
throughout
the

Search-Select
Monitor-Clarify
Summarize

(3)

Use your

and the

Activate
Infer
Monitor-Clarify

(4)

Use your

Activate
Infer
Monitor-Clarify

Poster 4.5. Do You Have Any Questions? Adapted from Raphael (1984).

Question-Answer Quadrant

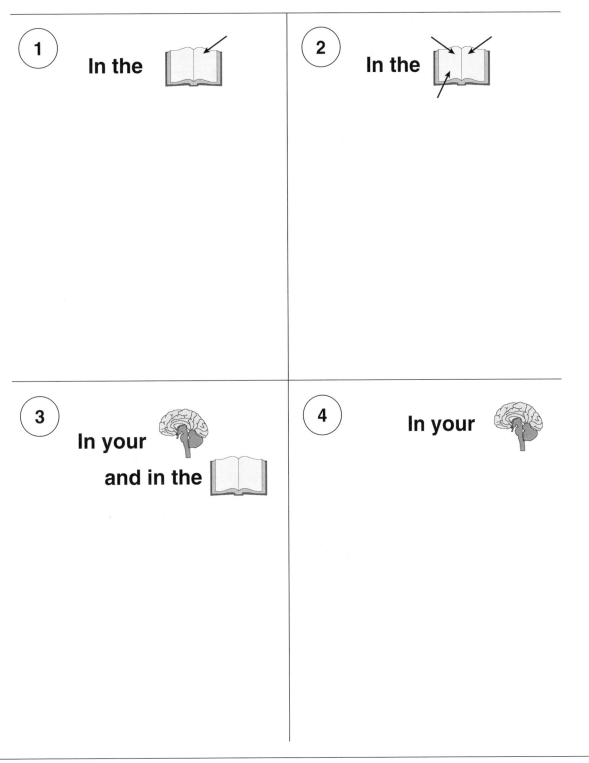

Handout 4.4. Do You Have Any Questions? Adapted from Raphael (1984).

four quadrants and how to generate questions for each one, review the Questioning Think-Aloud in Chapter 3.

Monitor your students' progress to determine when they are ready to begin working on their own to generate questions. The questioning strategy is an ideal way to uncover confusion and misunderstandings that students may have about the content. Encourage (or even require) students to use different wording in their questions than that used in the text to make their questions more challenging.

You Do It: Students Work in Small Groups or Individually

Once or twice a week, require that students write four questions, one from each of the categories introduced in this activity, after they have read an assignment. In addition to writing the questions, they must be prepared to answer them or make a judgment regarding the defensibility and appropriateness of answers given by classmates to their questions. At the beginning of the next class, ask for a volunteer to read one of his or her questions to the class. Ask for volunteers to answer the question. The student who asked the question can then choose someone to answer it. That individual, in turn, must then pose one question. Continue until everyone in the class has asked and answered at least one question (as time permits). No one can answer a second question until everyone has answered at least one. Alternate the types of questions that are asked so that each of the four question types is given adequate coverage. Another variation of this questioning strategy is to have students predict what questions they believe will be asked on a unit test. Collect these questions and use them to generate a quiz or unit test.

Once you have whetted your students' appetites for generating well-conceived and thought-provoking questions in this activity, introduce them to other question typologies (e.g., recall, cause and effect, compare and contrast, and evaluation) with accompanying question stems or prompts. Posters 4.6 through 4.9 illustrate a variety of question prompts to scaffold students as they acquire the skill to generate their own questions. The posters can be used to generate either transparencies or student handouts. These prompts are especially effective for teaching difficult relationships like cause and effect and compare and contrast, skills usually covered on state assessments. Combine the prompts with various graphic organizers as shown in Posters 4.7 and 4.8 to help student access both the vocabulary and the images of these relationships.

THE PROSPECTOR: GRADES 4–8

Description

The Prospector is designed to introduce students to locating information on the Internet for the purpose of learning more about a specific topic under discussion or to write a report or research paper. It uses and facilitates students' acquisition of searching-selecting as well as the inferring, questioning, and summarizing strategies.

Recall Prompts

What happened first in the story?

Tell us about the sequence of events in the story.

What are some characteristics of _____?

How does the story end?

Retell the story for us.

What are the different kinds of _____ described in the article?

What are the important _____ of _____?

Cause and Effect Prompts

What caused _____ to happen?

What are the consequences of _____?

What is the effect of _____?

How does _____ affect _____?

What will be the result of _____?

What do you hypothesize will be the outcome of his actions?

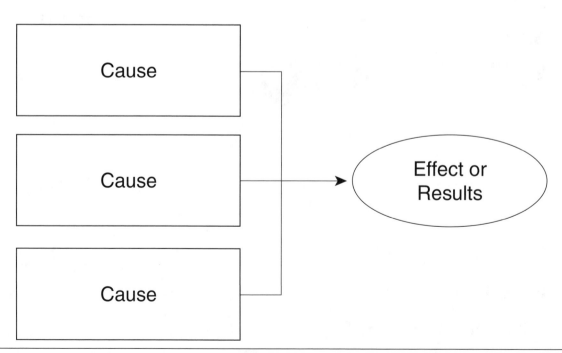

Compare and Contrast Prompts

How are _____
and _____ alike?

What are the
similarities between
_____ and _____?

Compare _____ and
_____with regard to
_____.

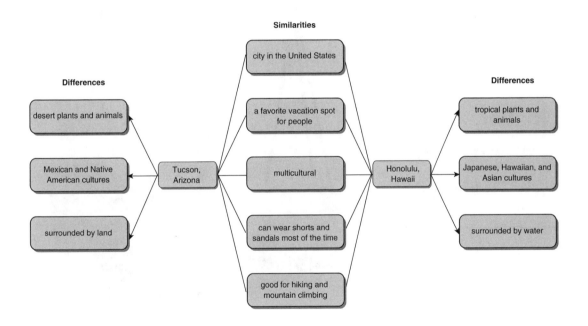

How would you
contrast _____
and _____?

How are _____and
_____different?

Evaluation Prompts

Which one is best:

_____ or _____? Why?

**What is your
opinion of
_____?**

**What are the
strengths and
weaknesses of
_____?**

**Do you agree or disagree with this
statement:_____?
Support your answer.**

Background Information

Most educators have the sense that engaging in research or searching on the Internet about subjects currently under study in the classroom is the ideal way to attract distractible but computer-savvy students to the exploration and understanding of new concepts. Educators often assume that students who spend hours surfing the Net must already know how to search, select, and detect. Consider the possibility, however, that the nonsequential and largely unedited nature of information on the Internet makes it far more challenging to understand than an edited textbook that is limited in scope and written specifically for a well-defined course or student reading level. The number of possible sites or documents that can be retrieved related to a single concept or topic while searching the Internet is overwhelming and may result in cognitive overload (Spires & Estes, 2002), an inappropriate focus on trivial or unrelated information (Birkets, 1995; Garner & Brown, 1992; Harp & Mayer, 1998), or inaccurate information. The editing process in textbook publishing houses screens out, for the most part, inaccurate, inflammatory, and highly biased text. Navigating the Web, however, requires a more cautious, if not suspicious, approach to retrieving information.

Anticipatory Set

Introduce this activity by reminding or telling students about the grizzly prospectors who roamed the Wild West searching for gold and other precious metals. They were savvy about where to look for these natural treasures and could readily recognize "fool's gold." Your students need to acquire the same kind of savvy that the prospectors demonstrated when they search the Internet for information. Poster 4.10 lists the steps to take when looking for information in all types of resources, but this activity focuses solely on using the Internet. There are few editorial safeguards on the Web, and anyone with a Web publishing program and a server is free to establish a Web site and disseminate information, whether reliable or not. So how can you tell if information on the Internet is reliable? You can trust WebQuest.

I Do It: Modeling and Explaining the Strategy (Activity) for Students

Although there is a searching-selecting teacher think-aloud in Chapter 3 based on an Internet search, the think-aloud you prepare for your students should relate to a specific topic featured in your content area. You will need Internet access projected through a laptop computer in order for your students to watch and listen as you frame your search goal, determine your search strategy, actually conduct a search, examine the top ten or twenty sites to select the ones that seem relevant to your search goal, and then determine whether the information you have found is credible.

How to Search and Select

 **Reflect** Determine what you are looking for and decide where to look.

 **Prospect** Go digging in library catalogs and on the Internet to identify prospective sources.

 **Detect** Review the books, Web sites, periodicals, and other resources you have found to determine which ones will give you what you need.

 **Select** Pick out what is most important in the sources you have found.

 **Connect** Put together what you have found to answer your questions.

We Do It: Further Explaining and Guided Practice

The We Do It portion of this activity features a WebQuest. A WebQuest is an inquiry-oriented activity in which some or all of the information that learners interact with comes from resources on the Internet that have been preselected by teachers or scholars, giving them a credibility that a list of sites retrieved by an average student would not have. The WebQuest model originated in the Department of Technology at San Diego State University, and their Web site offers a variety of problem-oriented Web-based activities developed by teachers from every grade level and content area around the country (Dodge, 2003). The advantage of using a predesigned WebQuest is that it provides a scaffolded experience for students by preselecting links as well as including hypertext levels of varying difficulty levels. Teachers are hard-pressed to provide this kind of experience for one student, much less four or five sections of thirty students each. The challenge is finding a WebQuest that meshes with your specific curricular objectives.

In a typical WebQuest, students work in cooperative teams for up to three days to solve their "problem" and complete their task. The team is given a scenario that places them in a particular time frame or role. If you are unfamiliar with WebQuests, here is just one example. It is an interdisciplinary unit suitable for middle school social students (Evans, 2003). The stage is set for students in the following description:

You are a team of newspaper reporters, living in the Civil War era. Battles are raging all around you: brother pitted against brother; father against son; neighbor against neighbor. Golden meadows and rolling hills you and your friends once played in are becoming soaked in crimson with the blood of a nation's most valued resource: its citizenry. What was once a courageous new union is now being torn apart before your own eyes.

Once students understand the setting, problem, and their role in it, they are assigned a task such as this one: *Your team is assigned the task of researching, writing, and editing a single edition of your newspaper that focuses on a specific battle during the Civil War. Include in this edition (1) a news article about the battle, (2) a human interest story, (3) an editorial, (4) and a letter to the editor from someone against the war (e.g., a soldier, a free black, a slave, a woman).*

Once they understand the problem and their assigned task, the team is free to click on and link to an eclectic collection of historical documents, primary sources, and current writings.

You Do It: Students Work in Small Groups or Individually

Whenever you and your students encounter an interesting question or problem in the course of reading and discussion, take that opportunity to model the search-select-detect activity, pointing out to students the importance of articulating their search question clearly, being able to scan large amounts of text to find key words or phrases that indicate the presence of desired information, and then knowing which information best answers the search question. If the WebQuest concept fires your imagination, head to a site called Filamentality (2003) where you can find out how to develop your own WebQuests with free available software and assistance.

THE SUMMARIZER'S FIVE C'S: GRADES 3–8

Description

The Summarizer's Five C's is designed to scaffold students' abilities to restate in their own words the meaning of something they have read. This instructional activity teaches summarizing with a five-step process articulated as one-word prompts. It also provides instruction and practice in monitoring-clarifying, inferring, and visualizing-organizing.

Background Information

There is no instructional activity that I use with teachers that is greeted with as much delight as this one. Summarizing is as difficult for teachers to teach as it is for their students to learn. I credit a slim volume with the unlikely title of *Textbooks and the Students Who Can't Read Them* (Ciborowski, 1992) for the idea of using a graphic organizer as an intermediary step on the way to writing a summary. The rules or steps for summary writing have been well researched (Anderson & Hidi, 1988/1989; Brown & Day, 1983; Hare & Borchardt, 1984; Rinehart et al., 1986). I have fine-tuned them and developed the prompts you will find in the instructional aids for this activity. Poster 4.11, How to Summarize Text, is suitable for putting on an easel, making a transparency, or using as student handouts.

Poster 4.12 introduces the Summarizer. He is *my* superhero and far more impressive, in my opinion, than either Superman or Spiderman. In fact, the Summarizer's cognitive powers can produce award-winning summaries in less time than it takes you and me to sharpen our pencils and get ready to read. Summarizing is a challenging cognitive task. It uses several cognitive strategies simultaneously, but in the beginning, you and your students should take them one at a time until both you *and* your students are feeling confident. If your students have difficulties with summarizing, they no doubt need to spend more time on monitoring-clarifying *and* inferring before they attempt to summarize text. A surefire way to be successful with summary writing, however, is to summarize easy text with which students are already familiar. Then they can concentrate on the nuances of summarizing because they already *comprehend*, the first "C" of Summarizing.

Anticipatory Set

The Summarizer is an engaging character. I created him to introduce this instructional activity to plant the idea in students' minds that they can become super summarizers if they will adopt the Summarizer's Five C's and practice

How to Summarize Text

Comprehend it. Read and understand it.

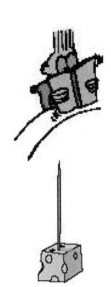

Chunk it. Divide it into parts.

Compact it. Make it even smaller by collapsing lists and deleting unimportant information.

Conceptualize it. Think of a key word that sums up each chunk.

Connect it. Combine the key words into a summary sentence.

The Summarizer's Five C's

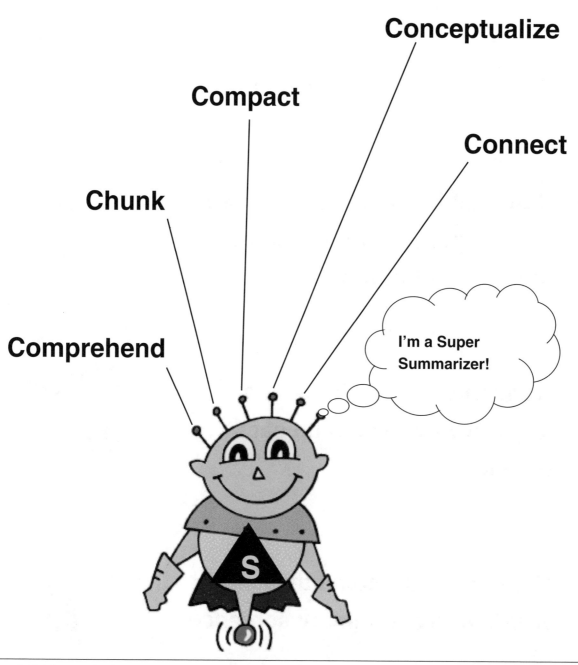

using them every day. In upper grades, the Summarizer may at first glance seem beneath your students, but let them know that when they can summarize like the Summarizer, they can make jokes about him. Review Roger Craig's introduction to summarizing in Chapter 2. Don't forget the additional instructional aids for summarizing that Roger used in his presentation (Figures 2.1–2.3).

I Do It: Modeling and Explaining the Strategy (Activity) for Students

The most effective way for you to learn how to summarize yourself is to carefully read and work through the summarizing think-aloud in Chapter 3. It leads you through each of the Summarizer's five steps and also explains the different ways to chunk text, information that is not found in this section. Practice writing summaries before you begin to teach summarizing to your students. Unless you exude confidence relative to writing summaries of what you read, your students may doubt the Summarizer's ability to get the job done. Your summaries don't have to be perfect. They will improve as you write more of them. Model summary writing numerous times before you move on to explaining the activity and then writing summaries together with your students.

We Do It: Further Explaining and Guided Practice

At this point, your students will have seen you model the writing of several different kinds of summaries. They will be eager to hear more about the Five C's as well as to try them out for themselves. But don't rush the process. You may need to spend several days on each of the Five C's before your students are ready to tackle summarizing a short story or expository article. Explain to them that this strategy will help them get better grades on classroom tests, score better on standardized tests, and help them do research and take notes when they are writing reports and papers.

If you do not feel completely confident about teaching the Five C's to your students, spend some more time studying the Teacher Think-Alouds and writing summaries of your own. Give your students copies of Poster 4.11 and look for opportunities to integrate mini-lessons that review the various steps of the activity. For example, as a recapping activity at the end of class, ask students to think of one word that describes the chapter that was covered. Or if you've just been to an assembly, ask them to think of three words that describe the performers or the performance. Remind students that what they are doing is the conceptualizing step of summarizing—reading a chapter, watching a movie, or attending a performance and then summing it up or boiling it down into a few key words.

You Do It: Students Work in Small Groups or Individually

After students have read and summarized text as homework, have them exchange summaries with classmates. After reading a classmate's summary, have each student answer the following questions: (1) If you hadn't read the text yourself, would you be able to understand what it was about from this summary? Why or why not? (2) Is there anything important that should be added to this summary? What is it? (3) Is there anything unimportant that should have been left out of the summary? What is it? After students have received feedback from peers, ask them to revise their summaries (Schoenbach et al., 1999, p. 89).

VISUALIZE A VIDEO: GRADES K–2

I strongly recommend introducing graphic organizers in kindergarten and adding one or two of the most useful organizers during each subsequent school year. Here's a good one for the kindergartners.

Description

Visualize a Video is designed to facilitate the development of the summarizing habit in pre- and emerging readers as they listen to stories or informational read-alouds. The summaries developed in this activity illustrate the grammar of a story in an organizer or illustrate the concepts of an informational book in a concept map. The activating and visualizing-organizing strategies are also stimulated and motivated through this activity.

Background Information

Summarizing is one of the most tested skills on performance assessments—usually at the third- or fourth-grade level. I meet many frantic teachers at these grade levels trying desperately to teach their students how to summarize in a year or two, often an impossible undertaking. The time to begin teaching students how to summarize is on the first day of kindergarten, and the best way to begin is by showing students how to "make mental movies," "visualize videos," or even "design DVDs." I developed this activity after some kindergarten teachers questioned a statement I made about teaching summarizing in kindergarten. The ability to make mental images is essential to extracting and constructing meaning from text, and students can be taught to increase their levels of visualization (Gambrell & Bales, 1986; Pressley, 1976).

Anticipatory Set

Explain to your students that when you read a story, you see (or even deliberately try to make) pictures in your mind. Sometimes your mental images (mental pictures, the pictures in your mind) are like photos taken with a camera, and sometimes they are actually moving pictures like a video, DVD, or TV show. Read a short descriptive excerpt and tell students what you see, hear, smell, and feel as you read it. Tell students that you are going to help them learn how to make a "mental movie" or "visualize a video," also. This activity is also suitable for use with informational picture books similar to the one used in the Teacher Think-Aloud for Visualizing in Chapter 3.

I Do It: Modeling and Explaining the Strategy (Activity) for Students

In the next chapter you will find a sample lesson plan in which a kindergarten teacher reads aloud *The Little Red Hen* (Galdone, 1973) to her students, and the students then develop a pictorial summary of the story in preparation for retelling it (see Figure 5.6). It is based on this instructional activity. Your think-aloud for this activity will draw on your artistic abilities to either create pictures on chart paper as you read or to select clip art or photos and develop some PowerPoint slides to illustrate the mental images evoked for you by the story. You may question the rationale for drawing or choosing additional pictures when the picture book you are reading is filled with professional artwork. However, the objective of this activity is to help your students realize the importance and acquire the habit of developing their own mental pictures through sharing the different ways in which we all picture what is happening in a story and then using those mental images to draw pictures or retell the story. Comparing their mental pictures to those of the illustrator is an excellent way to stimulate cognitive processing.

Tell students that you are going to think aloud for them about the visualizing processes going on in your brain as you read *The Little Red Hen* (or any story you select). As you read, describe what kind of pictures you see and then draw four pictures of the story (during or after your reading) that illustrate four components of the story: the main character, the setting, the problem, and the solution. Think-Aloud 4.6 shows one teacher's version.

We Do It: Further Explaining and Guided Practice

Explain to your students that as you read a story to them, you want them to make pictures in their minds, pictures about four very important things that they will hear about during the read-aloud: the main character of the story (who the most important person in the story is), the setting of the story (where the story takes place), the problem that the main character has, and how that problem gets solved (the solution).

Explain to your students some of the ways that you personally figure out who the main character of a story is (e.g., listening carefully to which person or animal is described in the most detail in the story, watching for which person or animal is pictured most often, or figuring out who has the most to say during the story). Also explain to students how you figure out the setting of the story (e.g., looking at the pictures and noticing what's in the background or seeing if there are buildings or objects that give clues). Explain that figuring out the problem and the solution takes more thinking (cognition, brain power) because you can't always point right to a picture and say, that's the problem or that's the solution, as you can with the main character or setting. Students will have to be detectives and look for clues regarding the story's problem and its solution. Maybe it will be something the main character is trying to do but can't because he or she keeps running into problems or can't seem to figure out how to do it. Ask your students to listen carefully to the story as you read it aloud, thinking about the mental pictures they can make to show the main character, the setting, the problem, and the solution.

Teacher Think-Aloud: Visualize a Video

Name   _Mrs. Smith_   Title   _The Little Red Hen_

	Main Character	Setting	Problem	Solution
W O R D S	The little red hen	A farm	None of the other farm animals would help the Little Red Hen take her wheat to the mill for grinding.	She decided to do it herself.
I M A G E S			Moo. I can't.	

Teacher Think-Aloud 4.6. Visualize a Video. *The Little Red Hen* (Galdone, 1973).

After you have read the story aloud and drawn some simple or very sketchy pictures in front of the class, ask them to suggest what kinds of pictures they would draw for showing the main character, setting, problem, and solution. Give a copy of Handout 4.5 to each student and instruct them to draw their own pictures in the appropriate spaces. Encourage students to draw pictures that are different from yours if they visualized something different. Once the pictures are completed, take time to debrief, talking about the variety of ways students have visualized a video for the story. Assure students that everyone makes different pictures in their minds because we all have had different experiences. The important thing is making the pictures whenever students hear or read a story.

You Do It: Students Work in Small Groups or Individually

Continue to use the same format several times a week. If individual students are having difficulty, pair them with students who have mental imagery to spare. Ask students who can readily visualize to work with classmates who are having problems. When students are comfortable with drawing their images, ask them to retell the stories you have read aloud using their Think-Aloud handout to prompt recall. Later, this activity can be adapted to the popular Somebody Wanted But So-Then prompt used to teach summarizing. Students who are ready to "write" a summary of the story can use their own picture prompts as well as the word prompts. A Teacher Think-Aloud (4.7) and Handout Form (4.6) are provided.

IT PAYS TO INCREASE YOUR WORD POWER: GRADES 2–8

Description

This activity uses graphic organizers to increase the vocabulary knowledge of students in Grades 2–8. Word Walls, dictionary definitions, and flash cards have their limitations in terms of making meaning last. This activity uses concept maps and semantic organizers that facilitate the learning of words in relationship to other words to develop concepts and build long-lasting and meaningful knowledge structures.

Background Information

Not long ago, a science teacher asked my opinion of giving weekly vocabulary assignments or tests. This kind of activity rarely produces meaningful and lasting learning because glossary definitions are often memorized by rote without first making connections. There are several more meaningful ways to acquire specialized vocabulary that are more effective (Novak, 1998; Novak & Gowin, 1984): (1) hearing words explained and used in conversation and context at least three to five times; (2) seeing words brought to life with pictures, models, and diagrams; and (3) constructing a graphic organizer that shows the relationship between words. This activity uses the third method.

Student Think-Aloud Form for Visualizing Story Grammar

Name _____

Title _____

Main Character	Setting	Problem	Solution

W
O
R
D
S

I
M
A
G
E
S

Teacher Think-Aloud: Somebody Wanted But So-Then

Name ___Mrs. Smith___   Title ___The Little Red Hen___

	Somebody	Wanted	But	So Then
W O R D S	The little red hen	Help from the other farm animals to take her wheat to the mill	None of the animals would help her	She decided to do it herself
I M A G E S				

Teacher Think-Aloud 4.7. Somebody Wanted But So-Then. *The Little Red Hen* (Galdone, 1973).

Student Think-Aloud Form for Visualizing Somebody Wanted But So-Then

Name _____   Title _____

Somebody	Wanted	But	So Then

W
O
R
D
S

I
M
A
G
E
S

Handout 4.6. Visualize a Video. Copyright © 2004 Corwin Press. All rights reserved. Reprinted from *Seven Strategies of Highly Effective Readers*, by E. K. McEwan. Thousand Oaks, CA: Corwin Press, www.corwinpress.com. Reproduction authorized only for the local school site that has purchased this book.

The activity gets its name from that well-known *Reader's Digest* feature, *It Pays to Increase Your Word Power.* I do not know the origin of this feature, but I assume the idea behind it is that people who know lots of words, especially "big" words, have the potential to be more effective communicators, be more successful in their work, and ultimately earn more money. We could definitely draw this conclusion if education equals word power, since the earning power of individuals with high school diplomas is usually greater than that for those individuals who do not have them. Increasing the word power of your students will certainly pay off for them in better comprehension if not more earning power.

Anticipatory Set

Introduce this activity by explaining where the name for the activity comes from. If you can dig up a *Reader's Digest*, make a transparency of the feature and show it to your students. Explain that to increase their word power in your classroom, they will be developing a variety of graphic organizers that portray the relationships between words. It's not enough to know just one definition of a word. Some words have a dozen or more definitions or synonyms (see *A Dozen Ways to Say Infer),* and the only way to learn these is not by memorizing them for the test on Monday and then forgetting them but through developing graphic organizers.

I Do It: Modeling and Explaining the Strategy (Activity) for Students

Model this activity by first completing a think-aloud similar to the Teacher Think-Aloud for Organizing in Chapter 3, a semantic word map of the brain. You can use a clear overhead transparency, a dry-erase board, chart paper on an easel, or Inspiration™ software to show your students how you think your way through its development. An example for primary students can be found in the Teacher Think-Aloud 3.8 in Chapter 3.

We Do It: Further Explaining and Guided Practice

Give students copies of Handout 4.7, a blank Semantic Word Map. Select a high-interest topic and complete the organizer with your students. Return to the I Do It phase of instruction and model the creation of a Semantic Features organizer. Teacher Think-Aloud 4.5 is an example for the topic of team sports. Then select (or let the students choose) a new and highly motivating category or concept (e.g., music genres, TV shows, or after-school snacks), develop a list of examples, and fill in Handout 4.8 together. Your students will no doubt be able to generate a list of descriptive features that would never have occurred to you.

You Do It: Students Work in Small Groups or Individually

Divide your class into teams to complete either a Semantic Features Organizer or a Semantic Word Map. Award a prize to the team that submits the most elaborate graphic organizer. Once they know how a semantic features

(text continues on page 128)

Teacher Think-Aloud: It Pays to Increase Your Word Power

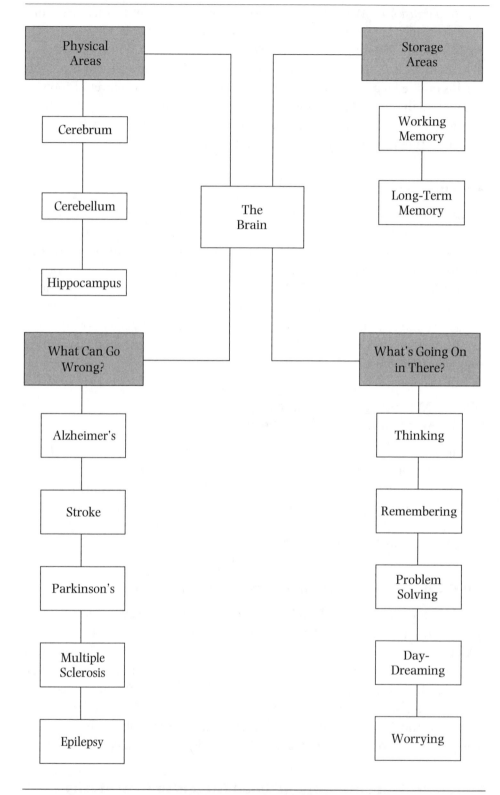

Semantic Word Map Organizer

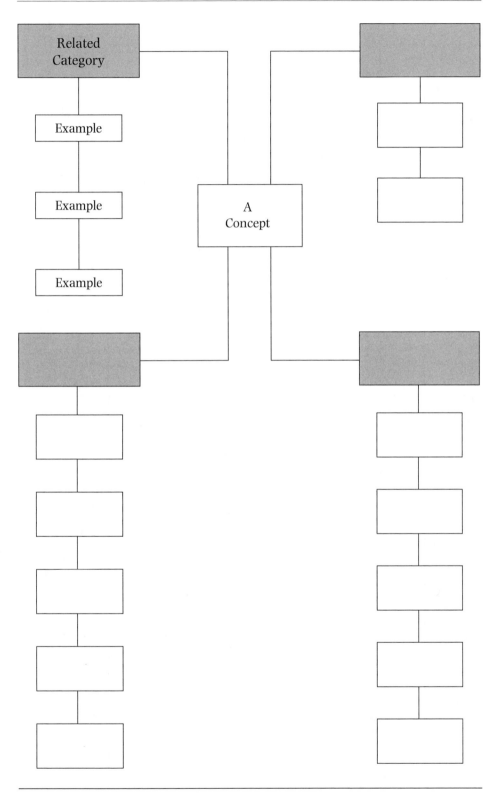

Teacher Think-Aloud: Semantic Features Organizer

	Played indoors	Referees	Umpires	Coaches	Managers	Fewer than ten players	More than ten players	Played with a net	Played with a glove	Played with a ball	Played with a puck	Lineup	Fouls	Penalties	Played on grass	Hat trick	Kicking	Hitting	Passing	Dribbling	Blocking	Spiking	Batting	Throwing	Played outdoors	Goals
Football																										
Baseball																										
Rugby																										
Volleyball																										
Soccer																										
Ice Hockey																										
Basketball																										

Semantic Features Organizer

organizer works with a high-interest topic, students can more readily develop organizers for your content area.

ORGANIZE IT: GRADES 3–8

Description

This instructional activity introduces organizing as a critical cognitive strategy and makes the case that getting organized is essential for learning and remembering. The activity also enhances the development of summarizing, inferring, and questioning.

Background Information

At its most expert level, organizing assumes the abilities to (1) read text, (2) determine which type of graphic organizer would be best suited for constructing a personal schema to better understand and remember large bodies of information, and (3) construct the organizer. A graphic organizer is a visual illustration of a verbal statement (Jones et al., 1988/1989, p. 20) and is useful for

- Organizing thoughts before writing
- Taking notes during lectures
- Taking notes during reading
- Organizing concepts or "big ideas" in preparation for a test
- Making sense of inconsiderate text

Anticipatory Set

Does someone in your life periodically threaten to get you organized, or are you the organizer in your family? No one, but especially teachers and students, can afford not to be organized. Graphic organizers are guaranteed, if used as directed by the teacher, to assist students in getting higher grades, more academic success, and a more enjoyable school career. There is no money-back guarantee, of course.

I Do It: Modeling and Explaining the Strategy (Activity) for Students

Depending on your grade level or the needs of your students, there are many ways to approach a think-aloud for organizing. Perhaps the textbook that you are expected to use is rather poorly written. In that case, model how you would graphically reorganize it for your students. Perhaps you have just finished a particularly challenging unit. Model for your students how you would develop a one-page organizer as a study guide (if you had to take your test). Many teachers hand out completed organizers to serve as study guides for their students and thus miss a golden opportunity to think aloud regarding its development. Your students will be spellbound to hear how you decided to organize the material and why you did it that way. In the course of your think-aloud, explain why you chose the type of organizer you did.

Explain that every graphic organizer has a frame: a set of questions or categories that are fundamental to understanding a given topic (Jones et al., 1988/1989, pp. 20–21).

Without their frames, graphic organizers are merely lines on a page. See Figure 4.6, Fishbone Organizers Without Frames. With the addition of frames to indicate which concepts go where, however, organizers come alive. See Figure 4.7, Fishbone Organizers With Frames. Meanwhile, begin to develop the organizer on chart paper displayed on an easel. Think aloud for your students as you move back and forth between the text and the organizer so that students can see how you are making decisions about where on the organizer to place information. Point out to students what you do when you discover "inconsiderate" text that is poorly organized or information that is irrelevant and does not "fit" into the organizer. Point out how the author could have benefited from using an organizer as he or she was writing. Point out the advantages of using organizers when writing a report.

One of the most useful tools for thinking aloud with graphic organizers is the Inspiration® software (2003). There is a version for primary students and another one appropriate for students in Grades 4 through adults. I used the software for the development of some of the organizers for this book, including the vocabulary organizer for *A Dozen Ways to Say "Infer"* and Teacher Think-Aloud 3.8.

We Do It: Further Explaining and Guided Practice

Tell students that you will be teaching them how to construct a graphic organizer to use during reading, research, or study. Tell them that you will be introducing the most important organizers of your discipline or grade level one at a time throughout the semester. Let the students know that constructing graphic organizers (either alone or in a cooperative group) will enable them to (1) organize large amounts of information into much smaller spaces making studying easier, (2) help them to understand and remember information more easily, (3) help them get better grades on classroom tests, and (4) assist them in organizing their thinking before writing reports and papers.

There are a multitude of graphic organizers. See Figure 4.8, Graphic Organizer Options. Choose four to five organizers that best fit your discipline or grade level, and consult one of the many fine books and articles that focus on using graphic organizers in the classroom (Alvermann, 1991; Alvermann & Boothby, 1986; Armbruster et al., 1991; Barton & Billmeyer, 1996; Eagan, 1999; Novak, 1998; Novak & Gowin, 1984; Ong, & Breneman, 2000). For example, after looking at Figure 4.8, English teachers might choose the story grammar to organize narrative text, the character map to study a character in-depth, a semantic word map for vocabulary study, and the Venn diagram to compare works of literature, characters, or genres. Math teachers might choose matrices, flow charts, diagrams, and pictures. Social studies and science teachers might choose time lines, continuums, cause-and-effect diagrams, webs, concept maps, why-because pursuit charts, and fishbone diagrams.

Fishbone Graphic Organizers Without Frames

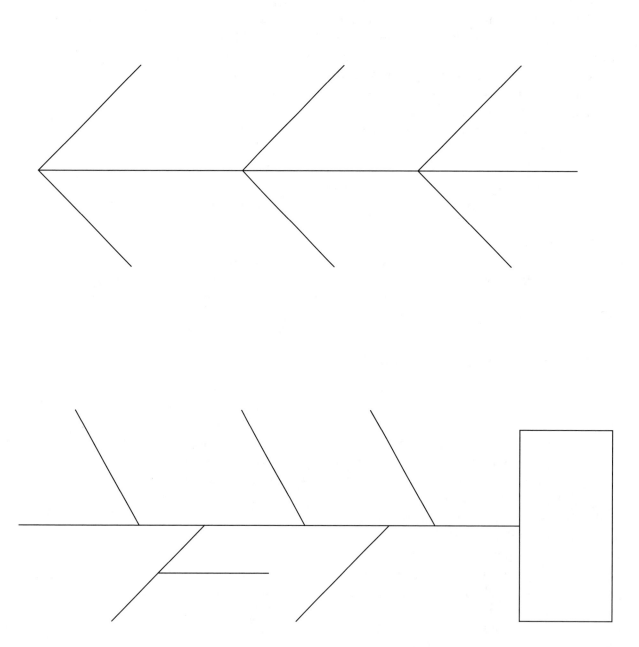

Fishbone Graphic Organizers With Frames

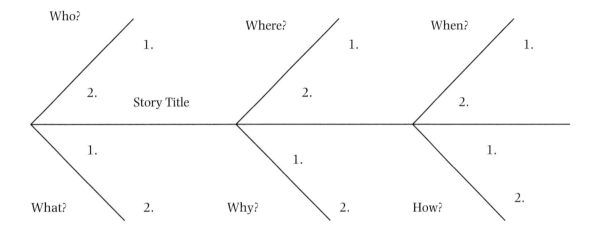

Use this fishbone to organize narrative text or a newspaper article.

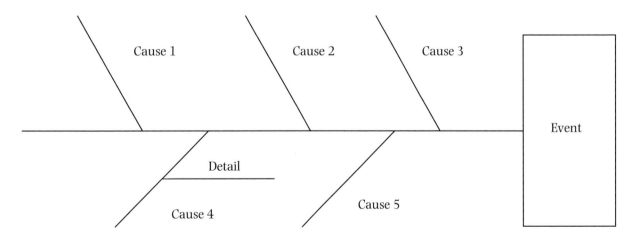

Use this fishbone to organize text that discusses causes leading up to a complex event (e.g., the Civil War). Put the event in the "head" of the fish and the multiple causes on the bones of the internal skeletal structure of the fish. Details related to each cause can be placed on horizontal lines leading from the bones.

Graphic Organizer Options

Nonfiction Organizers
Analogy organizer
Cause-effect
Chain of command
Chain of events
Chart
Compare-contrast matrix
Concept map
Concept wheel
Continuum
Crossword puzzle
Cycle
Diagram
Entailment meshes
Fishbone diagram
Flow chart
Frayer model
Grid
Hierarchy
Human interaction
List
Puzzle outline
Relay summary
Spider map

Fiction Organizers
Chain of events
Character map
Chart
Compare-contrast matrix
Matrix
Network tree
Picture
Problem-solution outline
Story frame
Story grammar
Story map
Talking drawings
Time line
Venn diagram
Web
Why-because pursuit chart

Mathematics Organizers
Chart
Diagram
Equation
Image
Matrix
Picture

Vocabulary Study Organizers
Concept map
Semantic word map
Semantic features analysis

Figure 4.6. Organize It. Copyright © 2004 Corwin Press. All rights reserved. Reprinted from *Seven Strategies of Highly Effective Readers*, by E. K. McEwan. Thousand Oaks, CA: Corwin Press, www.corwinpress.com. Reproduction authorized only for the local school site that has purchased this book.

First show the students blank organizers containing the frames (i.e., the set of questions that must be answered or the specific categories that must be filled in while reading the text). Then show the same organizer filled in with information from your textbook. Point out, for example, that a particular organizer summarizes an entire semester of learning or that another organizer summarizes a 250-page novel. Tell them that in the beginning, they will use the organizers and frames that you provide, but as the semester progresses, they will be free to suggest their own preferences for organizing texts to understand and remember them.

You Do It: Students Work in Small Groups or Individually

As your students acquire expertise in the use of a particular graphic organizer, assign a chapter, story, or article to organize. Once you have introduced and practiced a variety of organizers, students will be expected to choose the most appropriate one. However, the process is more important than the product in almost every case. One student might choose to organize a specific piece of text one way with one type of organizer while another student uses another organizer. When working with a new chapter in the text or a new piece of literature, ask students to preview the selection and suggest what organizer they believe might be most appropriate.

Remember to prompt, cue, remind, and encourage students to use organizers in their independent writing, research, and study. An organizer is only beneficial to the individual who actually processed the text and developed it.

WHAT'S AHEAD?

Thus far we have described and defined the seven strategies of highly effective readers, investigated the kinds of instructional methodologies that are most effective for teaching these strategies to students, and explored a variety of instructional activities to facilitate and motivate students' acquisition of the strategies. In Chapter 5, we will get even more specific as we look at how to organize your classroom for SRI.

NOTE

1. I recommend Easy-Stick Double Stick Adhesive (Removable Bond) for creating your own sticky pictures. Give each student two blocks of sticky pictures containing one of each kind, run a strip of the adhesive on the reverse side of the block, and ask students to cut them up into strips. The "sticky stuff" will last through two or three readings if the sticky pictures flags are handled carefully. Office supply stores carry the product. Call 1-800-321-0253 for further information.

Organizing for Strategic Reading Instruction in Your Classroom

Veteran educators are all too familiar with the following scenario: The principal (or a central office administrator) attends an inspiring workshop on Friday. He or she puts together a handout and cover memo over the weekend, and staff members get their marching orders on Monday: innovate. If you are one of those rare individuals who absorbs innovations like a sponge, you quickly shift gears and get going. The rest of us, however, need time to digest the prospect of change, ask the difficult questions, study the options, and think about the possibilities. This chapter is designed to help you do just that. It offers several frameworks and scripts for introducing students at various grade levels to SRI and provides answers to some of the most common questions teachers and administrators have regarding SRI implementation:

- When should strategy instruction begin?
- How should I introduce SRI to my students?
- Do I have to think aloud?
- Where will I find the time for SRI?
- How should SRI be paced and sequenced?
- What if an instructional activity doesn't work?
- How will I know if my students really are using the strategies?
- How can I keep track of everything?
- What does an SRI lesson plan look like?

Implementing SRI, as you have already begun to realize, entails far more than just developing a clever instructional activity or writing comprehensive lesson plans, although those two tasks are undeniably important. SRI demands a philosophical approach to instruction that may differ from the one you currently hold. Take a few moments to complete the SRI Teacher Behavior Inventory, Figure 5.1, to determine your personal readiness for implementing SRI. A score of 90% to 100% is Superior, 80% to 90% is Excellent, 70% to 80% is Good, 60% to 70% is Adequate. If you scored below 60%, your instructional philosophy and methodology may need some fine-tuning before you will feel comfortable implementing SRI.

You will find the biggest challenge of SRI to be maintaining a balance between the diverse and seemingly antithetical instructional components of SRI: direct explaining versus extracting and constructing meaning during the shared reading of authentic text with your students. Both are essential to achieve the ultimate goal of SRI: that students will become self-regulated readers who routinely employ cognitive strategies as needed to extract and construct meaning from text. Early researchers struggled with these same issues (Beck et al., 1997; Pearson, 1996), noting that some teachers objected to the use of rules and lists as being awkward and unrelated to natural reading. It is all too easy, having made the decision to implement SRI, to fall in love with the activities and forget about their raison d'être—constructing meaning and, ultimately, boosting student achievement.

Students do need to be taught the critical attributes of each of the cognitive strategies in a direct and explicit way, but *knowing* about or being able to *define* the strategies is nothing more than an interim instructional goal, similar to knowing which sounds correspond to the various letters of the alphabet. Just as the ability to decode without meaning is useless, knowledge about strategies is meaningless unless our students become independent strategic readers. Many educators who set out to implement SRI never get beyond learning *about* the strategies or implementing some disjointed activities. They miss out on the excitement of thinking aloud and the satisfaction of reading authentic text with students and joining them in extracting and constructing meaning. The essence of SRI occurs *during* reading (Trabasso & Magliano, 1996) as students and teachers process text together. That is not to say that the majority of students will not require ongoing coaching and skillful scaffolding to help them solidify and internalize cognitive strategies, but remember that *cognitive processing* during *real reading* is the essence of SRI.

WHEN SHOULD STRATEGY INSTRUCTION BEGIN?

There are two possible interpretations of this question. If the question pertains to when strategy instruction should begin in the K–12 sequence of instruction, the answer is *kindergarten*. If the question pertains to when you personally should begin SRI in your classroom or school, if you feel you are ready, the answer is ideally at the beginning of the school year. Let's examine the answers to these two questions in more depth.

Beginning in Kindergarten

The majority of five-year-olds are not ready to "read to learn" independently. Oh, there may be one or two students in the average kindergarten class who have miraculously made sense of the sound-spelling correspondences on their own, but most students are still learning how the sounds and letters relate to one another. On the other hand, all kindergarten students are quite capable of "listening to learn," particularly if the read-aloud experience is structured

SRI Teacher Behavior Inventory

1. Do I ask content-based questions that only focus on coming up with "right" answers (subtract 5 points for yes), or do I stress content-free questions that focus on strategy usage and problem solving that will lead to content acquisition in a more meaningful way (add 10 points for yes)?

2. Do I do all of the thinking, answering, and reading of text for my students (subtract 5 points for yes), or do I provide "wait" time for them to think, give cues and prompts as scaffolding to help them be successful on their own (add 10 points for yes)?

3. Do I keep a tight control over what is to be learned (subtract 5 points for yes), or do I encourage my students to gradually assume control of their own learning (add 10 points for yes)?

4. Do I emphasize getting things done and covering material (subtract 5 points for yes), or do I emphasize learning and understanding (add 10 points for yes)?

5. Do I decide ahead of time what will be difficult for students and avoid doing it or do it for them (subtract 5 points for yes), or do I ask them to tell me where they have had difficulties and provide scaffolding to ensure future success (add 10 points for yes)?

6. Do I focus on content recall (subtract 5 points for yes), or do I focus on understanding (add 10 points for yes)?

7. Do I keep students in the dark about my overall goals and plans for the school year or my learning outcomes for students (subtract 5 points for yes), or do I keep them fully informed about my goals and plans (add 10 points for yes)?

8. Do I avoid thinking aloud for my students and thus discourage them from thinking aloud (subtract 5 points for yes), or do I think aloud regularly and provide an affirming and supportive environment where students regularly share their thinking (add 10 points for yes)?

9. Do I deliberately choose easy material to make less work for everyone (subtract 5 points for yes), or do I present somewhat challenging material to continually keep up the academic press (add 10 points for yes)?

10. Do I use a "one size fits all" approach to reading assignments (subtract 5 points for yes), or do I show how different kinds of strategies can be used with different kinds of text (add 10 points for yes)?

Form 5.1. Adapted from Anderson and Roit (1993).

with that goal in mind. All students should ideally be introduced to SRI on the first day of kindergarten and experience some aspect of strategic reading or listening every day thereafter. Suggestions for introducing SRI in kindergarten are found later in this chapter.

Beginning at the Start of the School Year

Students often have the same reaction to changing direction in the middle of a semester that educators have when mandates come rolling out from the superintendent's or principal's office. Deshler and Schumaker (1993) point out that students in upper and middle grades who have become accustomed to one set of classroom norms may not take kindly nor be particularly supportive if the rules suddenly change. If you are a central office administrator or principal, a more humane and organizationally sound way to introduce SRI is to gradually begin with a book study, a task force, and some awareness activities, followed by opportunities for grade-level and content-area teams to try it out and become familiar with it. SRI as described in this book is not an "off-the-shelf," "paint-by-numbers" program. You cannot buy it and install it over a weekend. It is cognitively demanding for both teachers and students.

HOW SHOULD I INTRODUCE SRI TO MY STUDENTS?

The way in which you introduce SRI to your students will depend on the grade level you teach as well as your personal preferences and teaching style. This section describes several frameworks suitable for a range of grade levels. Nearly all of the frameworks are adaptable to other grade levels so be sure to read them all. There are two characteristics of the frameworks that are consistent regardless of grade level: the word *strategy* and the inclusion of explicit definitions and explanations of the strategies. In observations of experienced strategies teachers, researchers found the following:

> The term strategy was often included in the discussion as were the names of specific strategies. Teachers explicitly defined strategies in terms of their component processes. That is, students were presented an advanced vocabulary for talking about their new thinking. (Pressley, El-Dinary, Gaskins, et al., 1992, p. 528)

Introducing SRI in Preschool, Kindergarten, and Grade 1

As the parent of two children, two years apart in age, I spent some of the best years of my life investing in the cognitive development of my children through reading aloud and talking about books. Smolkin and Donovan (2000) call them "interactive read-alouds." I also spent some of the best years of my life as a library media specialist, conducting weekly read-alouds for preschool and primary students. Regrettably, I had two distinct read-aloud styles.

In my "mother" read-aloud mode, I frequently stopped along the way to help my children make sense of what we were reading by thinking aloud, anticipating their confusion because of an unfamiliar word or awkward sentence structure, adding information that was not in the text that I felt was needed for a more complete understanding, pulling ideas together and summarizing or recapping, articulating my own confusion or lack of knowledge about a word or concept that necessitated looking something up, and even commenting on the fact that what we were reading was poorly written or boring (if it seemed so to me). I was passionate about the power of reading aloud as a way to raise literacy levels— not only for my own children but for all children (McEwan, 1987, 2000). When I read aloud to students in the media center, however, I never interrupted the flow of a story to think aloud, question, or predict. I had been trained otherwise.

The daily interactions I had with my children were similar to those described by Cazden (1983) and later identified by Smolkin and Donovan (2000). Directly instructing and explaining, thinking aloud, and scaffolding pack a powerful cognitive punch when used to build comprehension skills and foster the acquisition of primary students' vocabulary and domain knowledge—especially when done in the context of reading aloud informational books.

Smolkin and Donovan's (2000) research showed that first-grade students were far more likely to engage in what they called "discourse moves" related to comprehension when they were listening to informational book read-alouds than when listening to storybooks. Although I never hesitated to interrupt my reading to talk about a book with my own children, during media center read-alouds, I felt compelled to read a book from start to finish before talking about it, and I focused almost exclusively on fiction during my weekly story hours.

If I had known then what I know now, I would have read far more informational books than picture books (at least four to one) and made the sessions as interactive as possible. During an interactive informational read-aloud, teachers model the seven strategies of highly effective readers and embed them in the context of real reading. Reading aloud a lot is *good.* Reading aloud interactively is *better.* And reading informational books aloud interactively is *best* (Duke, Bennett-Armistead, & Roberts, 2003).

If you are a teacher in the early grades, an administrator who supervises early childhood or primary education, or someone who trains early childhood educators, read Smolkin and Donovan's study (2000). This study plus what you have learned about SRI will give you the tools to begin planning a research-based program tomorrow.

Introducing SRI to Grades 1–3: Sally and Sam, the Strategic Readers

The first framework designed to introduce SRI to primary students features two strategic readers, Sally and Sam. Sally and Sam will help you explain to students how they use cognitive strategies whenever they read or listen to a read-aloud. The framework uses two posters to introduce these imaginary characters, Posters 5.1 and 5.2. The posters can be enlarged and displayed on an easel for use with a small group, photocopied so that students have their own copies to color, or reproduced on an overhead transparency or

PowerPoint slide for projection during your presentation. The following script offers suggestions for one possible way to explain SRI to primary students. If you find the script too difficult for first graders or too easy for third graders, adapt it, choose another framework, or best of all, design your own.

Class, when I am reading a book or listening to someone else read aloud to me, my brain is very busy processing [Introduce unfamiliar words to students before beginning the lesson.] *what I hear or read. The brain is the part of our body that thinks, learns, and remembers.* [You might wish to show a model of the brain from your science kit and point out its similarity in appearance to Sam's and Sally's brains as pictured on Posters 5.1 and 5.2.] *There are also other kinds of processing machines. If you have a food processor at home, you know what happens when your mother puts food into it and pushes the "on" button. It chops and stirs and smashes the food while mixing it all up.* [If your students are not likely to know what a food processor is, bring in a picture to explain, or delete this example.] *The processing that goes on in our brains isn't as noisy or messy as food processing, but there is definitely a lot of action in the brain when someone thinks about what they are reading or hearing. A* process *is something that our brains do to information so that we can understand and remember it.*

Another machine that does a lot of processing is my computer. It processes information just like our brains. My brain doesn't make noise like my computer does when I turn it on and it starts processing, but my brain is still processing—doing things with the ideas and facts and stories I read and see and hear. We call the processing that happens when we read strategic reading. *Notice the two posters I've put up on the bulletin board. Meet Sally and Sam, the Strategic Readers.* [See Posters 5.1 and 5.2.]

Now my brain and your brains are just like Sally's and Sam's brains, except the tops of our heads don't lift off so that we can look inside and see what's going on. But later this week [or next], *I'm going to think out loud for you while I read a story and you can hear about all of the things that are going on in my brain when I read. They are called* cognitive strategies. *I'm going to teach each of you how to become strategic readers and listeners this year.* [Pace this introduction to fit the needs of your students. You could stop here, and introduce the seven cognitive strategies in a subsequent lesson, or proceed.]

Boys and girls, remember that yesterday we talked about cognitive strategies— processes that go on in our brains to help us understand and remember what we read. I introduced you to my two friends, Sally and Sam. Today we're going to talk about the strategies that Sally and Sam use when they listen and think and read. Our brains do lots of things for us. They help us remember where we went on vacation. They help us remember what our favorite flavor of ice cream is. They even help us remember to take out the garbage and make our beds every morning. Doesn't your brain help you remember those things? And there are seven special things my brain does and your brain will also start doing once we begin learning and practicing. You can see the names of the seven cognitive strategies underneath the pictures of Sally and Sam. Follow along while I read the names of the strategies.

We're going to spend a lot of time this year learning how to use these strategies, and by the end of the year, you will be reading strategically every time you pick up a book or listen to a story. I'm going to tell you a little bit about each strategy.

Sally, the Strategic Reader

- **Activating**
- **Inferring**
- **Questioning**
- **Summarizing**

- **Monitoring-Clarifying**
- **Searching-Selecting**
- **Visualizing-Organizing**

Sam, the Strategic Reader

- **Activating**
- **Inferring**
- **Questioning**
- **Summarizing**

- **Monitoring-Clarifying**
- **Searching-Selecting**
- **Visualizing-Organizing**

The first cognitive strategy that Sam and Sally use is called Activating. [Point to the word on one of the posters and continue to point out each strategy on the posters as you introduce them to your students.] *When Sam's and Sally's brains are activating, it means that they are thinking of things they have learned about or read about some other time that connect to what they are hearing or reading. So, for example, if I read aloud a book to you about jellyfish, some of you might remember that you saw a jellyfish on the beach in Florida when you were on vacation. Some of you might remember seeing a jellyfish on a trip to an aquarium. Some of you haven't been on those trips but you saw a program on the Discovery Channel about jellyfish. Somebody else might have read a library book about jellyfish. When you are activating, you are connecting the things you already know to the new things you are reading or hearing about. Making connections like that helps you understand and remember what you read and hear.*

The second thing that Sally's and Sam's brains do is called inferring. *Inferring is one of the most magical things that our brains can do. For example, sometimes authors of books don't write down everything we need to know to understand a story. They leave things unsaid. So we have to infer. Inferring is figuring out what the author is trying to tell us by using clues—like a detective.*

The third strategy that Sally's and Sam's brains use has two parts. They are called monitoring *and* clarifying. *When Sally and Sam monitor and clarify, their brains are constantly figuring out if they really understand what they are hearing or reading, and if they don't, their brains help them fix up their mix-ups. For example, your dad's or mom's car has lots of monitors on it. There's a monitor (gauge) to tell if there's enough gas. There's a monitor (gauge) to tell if the car's temperature is too hot. There are also monitors in your brain that can tell if you are understanding or if you are confused. When Sally and Sam get confused, they know how to get help, and so will you when we finish learning about all of the cognitive strategies.*

The fourth strategy that Sam and Sally use is called questioning. *They ask lots of questions while they're reading or listening. They ask questions and then keep on reading to find answers. They ask their teachers questions. They ask their parents questions. They ask questions of their friends. Sometimes they even ask questions of the author of the book they are reading. Your parents have told me that all of you ask way too many questions at home, but here in this classroom, you can't ask too many of the right kind of questions. I'll show you how to do that very thing.*

[Depending on your students' attention spans, you may want to split the introduction into two sessions. If so, stop here and introduce the three remaining strategies later. Remember to review the first four strategies before introducing the remaining three.]

We have just three more cognitive strategies to talk about today, and then we'll see if you have any questions for Sam and Sally about their cognitive strategies. [If you're energetic, create puppets for Sam and Sally. They can do all of the talking and answering of questions while you sit on the sidelines and relax!] *Sam's and Sally's brains also use a strategy called* searching and selecting. *This strategy does two things: It helps them look for books that can answer questions and then helps them find the answers to their questions in the books. Some of you will be writing reports at the end of the year and will need to use the searching-selecting strategy. It's like the command on my computer that says FIND. When my brain is searching-selecting, it's scanning the page or the computer screen and looking for the answers or the information I want.*

The next strategy that Sally and Sam use is called summarizing. *I'm going to introduce you to a superhero called the Summarizer later on.* [Show students Poster 4.12 from Chapter 4, The Summarizer.] *The Summarizer taught Sally and Sam how to summarize, and he's going to teach you. Now after Sam and Sally have heard or read something, they can tell somebody all about it in their own words. It's one of the best things our brains can do.*

You've done a terrific job of paying attention, and we're on the last strategy— visualizing-organizing. *Sam likes the visualizing part of this strategy best because he can make really great pictures in his brain when he hears a story. He can imagine being in Africa on a safari, and he can see what all of the wild animals would look like and hear them, too. Sally likes the organizing part of the strategy best because she likes to make charts and webs and diagrams to help her remember what she has read.*

Let's review the seven strategies that strategic readers like Sally and Sam and you and I use. [Name the strategies once again, pointing to the words on the poster. Leave the posters showing Sally and Sam's cognitive strategies displayed in your classroom and look for opportunities during instruction to talk about one or more of the strategies. As you read aloud or read text, think aloud and refer to the strategies. Once you and your students feel comfortable with the vocabulary of the strategies, choose one of the instructional activities to teach a strategy in more depth.]

Introducing SRI to Grades 2–5: The Cognitive Tool Belt

A second possible framework for introducing SRI to students in Grades 2–5 uses the tool analogy introduced in Chapter 1. Poster 5.3 pictures a worker and some of his tools to illustrate the concept that cognitive strategies function like "mind tools" (Jonassen, 2000) or "tools of the mind." You might put your own creativity into this framework by bringing a tool belt and some well-used tools to your classroom.

Here's one way to introduce this concept to your students:

Class, when I read a book or listen to someone else read aloud to me, my brain must process what I hear or read, or I won't remember a thing. You may have heard the expression "in one ear and out the other," meaning you didn't hear a word somebody said because you weren't paying attention. That same thing can happen when you read. I call it "in one eye and out the other." When you're reading like that, you're not really reading, you're just staring at the page. The words are not being processed by your brain. No one can understand or remember if they read like that. To understand and remember, we have to use the tools in our minds—cognitive strategies to process what we read and hear.

Right now I'm going to explain what each of the cognitive strategies does in your brain. You know what a hammer does when a workman uses it. You know how to use a saw and a drill. You've seen tradespersons or your parents using these kinds of tools. Sometime later this week, you'll have a chance to see me use my cognitive tools. I'll do that by thinking aloud, telling you what's going on in my brain while I'm reading. It will be like a talking MRI or x-ray [explain this medical instrument if appropriate to your age level]. *We're going to spend a lot of time this year learning how to*

Cognitive Tools

Activating

Inferring

Monitoring-
Clarifying

Questioning

Searching-
Selecting

Summarizing

Visualizing-
Organizing

use these strategies, and by the end of the year, you will be using strategic reading every time you pick up a book or listen to a story.

The first cognitive strategy or mind tool that I personally use is called activating. [Point to the word on Poster 5.3 and continue to point out each subsequent cognitive strategy on the poster as you introduce them to students.] *When my brain is activating, it is thinking of things I have learned about or read about some other time that connect to what I am hearing or reading right now. So for example, if I'm reading a book about jellyfish, I might remember that I saw a jellyfish on the beach in Florida when I went there on vacation. Or I might remember seeing a jellyfish on a trip to an aquarium. If I haven't done either of those things, maybe I saw a program on the Discovery Channel about jellyfish or read another book about jellyfish. When I am activating, I am connecting the things I already know to the new things I am reading about in a book. Making connections like that helps me to understand and remember what I read and hear. Without making connections to prior knowledge that I activate, it's hard for me to remember new things.*

The second strategy or mind tool that I use is called inferring. *Inferring is one of the most magical things that my brain does. For example, sometimes authors of books don't tell me everything I need to know to understand a story so I have to infer. Inferring is figuring out what the author is trying to tell me by using clues—like a detective. Without my inferring tool, I would be confused a lot of the time.*

The third mind tool that I use a lot is a two-part tool. It is called monitoring and clarifying. *When I monitor and clarify, my brain is constantly figuring out if I really understand what I am hearing or reading, and if I'm confused, this tool helps me fix up my mix-ups. For example, your family car has lots of monitors or gauges on it. There's a monitor to tell if there's enough gas in the tank. There's a monitor to tell if the car's temperature is too high. There are monitors in my brain that can tell me if I understand or if I am confused. If I am, then I know it's time to use the clarifying part of the tool and fix up my mix-ups.*

The fourth mind tool or cognitive strategy I use is called questioning. *I ask lots of questions while I'm reading or listening. I ask questions and then keep on reading to find answers. When I was a student, I asked my teachers questions. I ask my friends questions about what I'm reading. Sometimes I'll even send an e-mail to an author and ask that person questions about their book. Your parents have told me that all of you ask way too many questions, but in this classroom, you can't ask too many of the right kind of questions. I'll show you how to do that very thing.*

Let's take a little stretching break and say the names of the mind tools (cognitive strategies) we've learned about so far. [Take a stretching break and say the names of the four strategies covered so far.] *We have just three more cognitive strategies to talk about. The next strategy I use all of the time is called* searching and selecting. *If I am searching and selecting, you would see me wandering around in the library, browsing through books and magazines, and looking up things on the Internet—looking for information I need to answer a question or help me prepare a lesson. This mind tool does two things: It helps me look for books that can answer questions and then helps me find the answers to my questions in the books. Searching and selecting is like using the FIND command on my computer. When my brain is searching-selecting, it's scanning the page or the computer screen and looking for the answers or the information I want.*

The next strategy or mind tool that I use is called summarizing. *After I read a book or a chapter in a book, I can write a one- or two-sentence version of what I read in my own words. It's one of the best things our brains can do, because if you can summarize, you can remember lots of information, but it won't take up so much room in your brain because you can summarize it.*

You've done a terrific job of paying attention, and we're on the last strategy— visualizing-organizing. *Some people like the visualizing part of this strategy the best because they can make really great pictures in their brains when they hear a story. A friend of mine can imagine being in Africa on a safari and what all of the wild animals would look like. I like the organizing part of the strategy the best because I find it very helpful to make charts and webs and diagrams to help me remember what I've read.*

The amazing thing about our brains is that they use all of these different tools to understand and remember. The more I practice using the strategies, the more I'm able to remember after I've read something.

Introducing SRI in Grades 4–8: Becoming a Smarter Person in Just Seven Steps

This framework presents SRI in the context of helping students become more effective learners and readers—in a word, smarter. Like Phyllis Hiemenez, the adult reader you met in Chapter 1, many students assume that reading comprehension is a function of intelligence. They presume that if they do not understand, the reason must be that they are not smart enough. While intelligence certainly impacts reading comprehension, the extent to which SRI can boost reading comprehension and student achievement, IQ notwithstanding, is well supported by research. I encounter many gifted students, who, if they had been taught the seven cognitive strategies of highly effective readers, would have been able to handle the rigors of their college honors courses with less stress and more success. Here's a sample introduction:

Our brains are pretty amazing. They can remember things, solve problems, forget upsetting experiences that we don't want to remember (e.g., when people get amnesia), and our brains are absolutely essential for doing something called strategic reading. *Some of you might think that teachers can just stare at a page of printed text and automatically remember it. You might also think that super-smart people just look at their textbooks and are ready for the test in a few minutes. No way! That is not true at all. Teachers, classmates, or your parents who seem super-smart just know about the seven strategies of highly effective readers, and they intentionally use them whenever they read.*

These strategies are processes that go on in the working memories of our brains and do things to the information that we read or hear to help us understand and remember it for longer than just a few seconds. I'm going to teach you those seven strategies during our first social studies (or science or math] unit, and I guarantee that if you listen carefully as I model the strategies for you so you can see how to use them, practice them with me in class, and use them in your own reading, you can become a smarter person by the end of the semester [year]. This is a better offer than the Bow-Flex or any of those deals they advertise on TV. Using the seven cognitive strategies has been shown by research to make a difference in grades in standardized test scores, and, who knows, they might even get you a scholarship to college if you work hard! Just stick with me, and with a little work, you can be a highly effective reader by the end of the year.

First, let me introduce you to the seven strategies, and then later I'll model each of the strategies to show you how they work in my brain. I won't have to do brain surgery for that. First, let's take a look at the strategies. I've handed out a sheet with the names of the strategies and some picture prompts to help you remember them. I am a very visual person, and I need mental images, organizers, and pictures to help me learn. [Give each student a copy of Handout 5.1, Seven Strategies of Highly Effective Readers.] *Research says that when you have both words and pictures, you learn much more effectively.* [Using the handout, explain each of the strategies, using examples from your particular grade level or discipline. Then choose some text that is related to your course content for thinking aloud. Model as many of the seven strategies as you can, during your think-aloud. Ask your students to check off the strategies they hear you model on the chart you handed out. Review the discussion on thinking aloud in Chapter 2, the Teacher Think-Alouds in Chapter 3, and a short discussion later on in this chapter relative to the critical importance of thinking aloud.]

Introducing SRI in Grades 5–8: Seven Reading Hats

One of my favorite thinking models comes from Edward DeBono's (1999) *Six Thinking Hats.* I have used this approach to help various kinds of teams appreciate the diversity and uniqueness of their thinking styles. To introduce this idea, I purchased six different hats in colors to correspond with the colors of the hats DeBono describes: a red beret, a white hard hat, a black cowboy hat—well, you get the picture. This same concept could be adapted to an attention-getting introduction, also called *Seven Reading Hats.* Your hats could come from your own private collection, be handmade to suit the seven strategies, or give you an excuse to go shopping. Just head to the hat store (I'm sure I saw one at the Mall of America in Minneapolis) and put the clerk to work looking for seven reading hats to wear when you introduce SRI to your students.

Here is a sample introduction for this age group:

Our brains are pretty amazing. They can remember things, solve problems, forget upsetting experiences that we don't want to remember (e.g., when people get amnesia), and our brains are absolutely essential for doing something called strategic reading. *Some of you might think that teachers can just stare at a page of printed text and automatically remember it. You might also think that super-smart people just look at their textbooks and are ready for the test in a few minutes. No way! That is not true at all. Teachers, classmates, or your parents who seem super-smart just know about the seven strategies of highly effective readers, and they intentionally use them whenever they read.*

These strategies are processes that go on in the working memories of our brains and do things to the information that we read or hear to help us understand and remember it for longer than just a few seconds. I'm going to teach you those seven strategies during our first social studies [or science or math] *unit, and I guarantee that if you listen carefully as I model the strategies for you so you can see how to use them, practice them with me in class, and use them in your own reading, you can*

The Seven Strataegies of Highly Effective Readers

Activating	Recalling what you already know and the experiences you have had so you can connect them to what you are reading in order to better understand and remember		How can I connect it?
Inferring	Bringing together what is spoken (written) in the text, what is unspoken (unwritten) in the text, and what is already known by the reader in the form of knowledge and experience in order to understand and remember the information and ideas in the text	What does it mean?	
Monitoring-Clarifying	Thinking about how and what you are reading both during and after the act of reading for purposes of determining if you are comprehending the text, combined with the ability to clarify and fix up any mix-ups if necessary		Is it clicking or clunking?
Questioning	Engaging in "conversations" with authors, peers, and teachers through self-questioning and question generation	Why did the author choose this setting for the story?	
Searching-Selecting	Searching a variety of sources to select appropriate information to answer questions, define words and terms, clarify misunderstandings, solve problems, or gather information		I need to know about the Civil War for a report.
Summarizing	Restating the meaning of text in your own words—different words from those used in the original text	What is the main idea of this book?	
Visualizing-Organizing	Constructing a mental image or graphic organizer for understanding and remembering the information and ideas found in text		What pictures do I see in my mind when I read?

become a smarter person by the end of the semester [year]. This is a better offer than the Bow-Flex or any of those deals they advertise on TV. Using the seven cognitive strategies has been shown by research to make a difference in getting better grades and standardized test scores, and, who knows, they might even get you a scholarship to college if you work hard! Just stick with me, and with a little work, you can be a highly effective reader by the end of the year. I want to have a little fun with the seven strategies, and I enjoy wearing funny hats. So I came up with the idea of having a different kind of hat to go with each of the seven strategies. If you want to bring some hats to wear on days that we're working on the strategies, I will personally suspend the "no hats in class" rule for those days. The only catch is that you have to make a connection between the hat you're wearing and one of the seven cognitive strategies. You don't have to bring or wear hats if you don't want to, but I definitely will be wearing each of the seven reading hats when I think aloud and model the cognitive strategies for you.

First let me introduce you to the seven strategies, and then later I'll model each of them (while wearing the corresponding hat) to show you how they work in my brain. First let's take a look at the strategy definitions. [Give each student a copy of Handout 5.1, Seven Strategies of Highly Effective Readers.] *Research says that when you have both words and pictures, you learn much more. I think a hat will serve the same purpose as a picture.*

[As you define and describe each cognitive strategy, wear its corresponding hat.] Here's a brief rationale for why I chose the hats I did:

• The Activating hat is a mortarboard worn by graduates who have studied long and hard to receive their diplomas. If anyone has background knowledge to activate, it is a high school or university graduate.

• The Inferring hat is a magician's top hat. I chose this metaphor for inferring because inferring meaning from an author's intent when it is not explicitly stated in the text is often as mysterious and magical as pulling a rabbit out of a top hat.

• The Monitoring-Clarifying hat is a chauffeur's cap. This strategy helps readers stay on the road to comprehension in much the same way that a chauffeur finds his or her way to unfamiliar locations. When the chauffeur is lost, he or she takes immediate action to get back on track, comparable to the clarifying part of this strategy.

• The Questioning hat is a police officer's cap, and I selected it because police officers are always asking questions: Can I see your driver's license? Where were you last Friday at 3:00 pm?

• The Searching-Selecting hat is an explorer's hat—the perfect choice for going on safari to find answers, solve problems, and gather information.

• The Summarizing hat is a fedora, traditionally worn by newspaper reporters. Students may have seen old movies in which a small cardboard pass with the word PRESS written on it gave reporters entrance into places where mere mortals were not allowed. No hat better exemplifies the summarizing strategy—boiling down a complicated story into a few paragraphs for the morning edition.

• The Visualizing-Organizing hat is a beret worn by an artist—someone who translates the real world into images on a canvas—images that represent the artist's interpretation.

DO I HAVE TO THINK ALOUD?

The most critical, albeit challenging, aspect of cognitive strategy instruction is *teacher modeling.* Thinking aloud is done so that students can observe *precisely* how skilled readers use a particular strategy as they read. It is the key to strategic teaching. The teacher serves as the "master reader (or thinker)" to their students, who are the cognitive apprentices. After you choose the text from which to model a specific strategy or group of strategies, rehearse the thinking-aloud process with a colleague or family member. Thinking aloud, as you will soon discover, is not a natural act. Our thoughts are ordinarily uncensored and unstructured while we are thinking. Teachers often feel awkward about making their thoughts available to students and frequently lapse into *explaining* what the text means or *lecturing* about how the strategy works rather than articulating their own thinking processes. Even though you will not be graded on your think-aloud, you will occasionally hear a small voice in your head telling you that your thinking is not "cognitive enough" or that your use of strategies is not clever enough. Ignore that voice and press on. Practice repeatedly until you can articulate your cognitive processes to students in a relaxed but detailed and specific way. Postpone actual strategy instruction until you are completely comfortable with this aspect of strategy instruction.

Reading text aloud for a primary-grade think-aloud is different from the usual read-aloud experience. You won't ask questions or point out interesting illustrations or specifically make connections for students. Your goal during the think-aloud is to give your students a peek into what is going on in *your* brain, (specifically your short- and long-term memory systems) that helps you extract and construct meaning from the text. Don't forget the goal of thinking aloud or slip into your teaching mode and start explaining, giving directions, or answering questions. Limit what you say to your thought processes while reading the text.

Choosing text from which to model your thinking aloud, as well as text for your students to read initially during guided practice after they have been introduced to an activity or strategy, is a matter of personal preference. If you choose text to model that is perceived as too easy by your students, they may dismiss your modeling efforts as playacting. If you choose text that is very difficult, students may become frustrated trying to understand what you are reading and fail to pay close attention to your thinking aloud. If you teach science, choose an article related to a unit you have just completed so you can connect it to prior knowledge. If you have read aloud several stories by Eric Carle or Leo Lionni, choose an informational book that adds new concepts to the ideas in the story to give you (and your students) the opportunity to make connections.

HOW SHOULD SRI BE PACED AND SEQUENCED?

The pacing and sequencing of SRI depends on the literacy and maturity levels of your students. There are four common problems that can derail SRI during your initial lessons: (1) failing to rehearse your thinking aloud, (2) overestimating the skill levels of your students and assuming they can do tasks on their own or understand concepts you are explaining when they can't, (3) planning too many steps for one lesson and thus overloading students' working memories, and (4) assuming students will understand your objectives and the reasons why you are using SRI without in-depth explaining.

Teaching cognitive strategies to students is far different from teaching a skill in which specific steps must be followed and one can teach these steps directly (e.g., a mathematical algorithm like addition or a decoding strategy). There are three phases to SRI, as you discovered in Chapter 4: (1) I Do It, in which the teacher models the strategy by thinking aloud for students; (2) We Do It, in which the class is divided into cooperative groups to practice using the strategy together with supportive instruction from the teacher or the whole class working together with the teacher in guided practice; and (3) You Do It, in which students are expected to use the strategy more independently, either in cooperative groups or individually, but still held up by the teacher's supportive scaffolding. Once your students have successfully completed these three phases in class, they are ready to apply the strategy in an independent homework assignment. The phases may well extend over several weeks (or even months) of instruction and will be filled with explanations, discussions, modeling, and practice, depending on the age and abilities of your students. Do not underestimate the amount of time you will need to spend on the "I Do It" and "We Do It" phases. Time invested in these two foundational phases will pay rich dividends for you and your students as you transition to You Do It and Apply It. Rushing the process will create confusion and frustration for both you and your students.

WHAT IF AN INSTRUCTIONAL ACTIVITY DOESN'T WORK?

If you develop what promises to be a lively instructional activity and find that it falls flat, consider the four instructional aspects of scaffolding described in Chapter 2 (people, text, tasks, and materials) and determine which one you need to adjust as you redesign your lesson. Perhaps your modeling wasn't specific and realistic enough. You didn't really *show* your students *how* to do it; you just *assumed* they could do it. It could be that the text you chose for students to read the first time you expected them to use the strategy in guided practice was too difficult, and their working memories were overloaded with new concepts leaving little cognitive power to learn a new strategy. Or perhaps in your eagerness to give your students "the whole enchilada," you fast-forwarded through some important prerequisite steps that needed to be mastered before moving on. Or maybe you pulled out the props and prompts too soon, and students were frightened to step out without a scaffold beneath them. Review the I Do It, We Do It, and You Do It instructional phases and be sure to include all of them.

HOW WILL I KNOW IF
MY STUDENTS ARE USING THE STRATEGIES?

You cannot determine if your students are using the seven strategies of highly effective readers by quizzing them on the definitions of the strategies or giving multiple-choice comprehension quizzes. The most definitive way to assess strategy usage is through student think-alouds (Afflerbach, 2002). You will know what kinds of text-processing activities are going on in students' working memories only if they can articulate them for you. The only way that your students will know how to model and think aloud regarding their own strategy usage is by hearing you think aloud and observing how you fix up your reading or thinking mix-ups, write summaries, search and select, and develop graphic organizers. You will notice a gradual improvement in comprehension, increased motivation, and a desire to talk about books and reading. If your students are using the seven strategies, their conversations and observations will become more metacognitive in nature. To assess cognitive strategy usage will require that you carefully listen and reflect on students' conversations about reading and meticulously note their behaviors and attitudes about reading.

WHERE WILL I FIND TIME FOR SRI?

If you feel that you don't have time for SRI, particularly if you are an upper-grade or middle school content teacher, take a moment to answer the following questions:

• Do all of your students "read to learn" using the seven strategies of highly effective readers, thus maximizing their learning and retention?

• Do your unit test grades, standardized test scores, and state assessments (in reading *and* your content area) reflect rising achievement that defies demographics?

If you are able to answer the foregoing questions in the affirmative, then keep on doing what you have been doing. However, if your students are not succeeding, change what you are doing. If your special education and remedial reading referrals are mounting, evaluate curriculum and instruction in the primary grades and begin SRI in preschool using interactive informational book read-alouds. If you are experiencing the dreaded fourth-grade drop-off in achievement (Hirsch, 2003), consider the implementation of SRI. If you have become a "talking textbook," explaining and translating your text for students, SRI is the answer.

HOW CAN I JUGGLE IT ALL?

As you initially plan for SRI, no matter what your grade level or content area, you may well find yourself on cognitive overload. Form 5.2 is a Lesson-Planning Matrix designed to scaffold your planning efforts. Take a moment to

Lesson-Planning Matrix

Title of Text _____   Date _____

Option	Before Reading	During Reading	After Reading
Cognitive strategy			
Instructional activity			
Teaching moves			
Student text reading			
Subject matter			
Text genre			
Student accountability-assessment			
Difficulty level of text			

preview it before we discuss each of the options listed. Your ultimate goal as you implement SRI is that your students will become independent, self-regulated readers, able to draw on a repertoire of cognitive strategies to the end of deep, meaningful, and lasting learning.

If you implement SRI schoolwide, strategy usage will soon become "institutionalized," and increasing numbers of students will arrive in your classroom each year with a foundation of cognitive strategy expertise. When that happy day arrives, your approach to strategy instruction can become less explicit and more facilitative. In the beginning, however, everyone is a novice—you and your students alike. Therefore, detailed planning is essential, and coordination with your colleagues (whether at the same grade, team, or content-area level) is a priority. We consider each of the aspects of the Lesson-Planning Matrix to prepare you for planning your first lesson.

Cognitive Strategies

One important decision to make when planning for SRI is which strategy or strategies to teach first. As you consider the role that each strategy plays in skilled reading, reflect on the developmental level of your students, the demands of your grade level or discipline, the assessment expectations that will confront your students in the near or not-too-distant future, and most immediately, which of the seven strategies is most essential or applicable to the next story, article, or book your students will be reading. All of these variables will determine how you choose the strategy or strategies to teach first. Undeniably, skilled readers employ at least five or six of the seven strategies almost all of the time they are reading a piece of challenging text. That will be your ultimate goal for students, but in the beginning, keep it simple.

You will discover as you become more aware of your own strategy usage that cognitive processing is more simultaneous than linear, adding to the challenge of SRI. You cannot teach students questioning without also touching on inferring, summarizing, activating, and monitoring. It is impossible to model summarizing without using questioning and inferring as well. SRI is not about starting at the beginning of the list and teaching one strategy a week. SRI is not about "coverage" or "completion." SRI is about modeling, explaining, coaching, and teaching all of the strategies, as needed, every day.

Instructional Activities

After you have chosen a cognitive strategy (or group of strategies) on which to focus a given sequence of instruction, the next decision is which activity to use. The best ones to use are of course those that get results. Figure 4.1, in Chapter 4, listed the instructional activity options available in this book, along with a matrix showing which cognitive strategies were used in each activity, but the suggestions found in *Seven Strategies of Highly Effective Readers* are not the only ones that can help you implement SRI. Every school needs a well-stocked professional library so that teachers can consult a variety of resources when they are developing the perfect lesson to teach summarizing in sixth-grade social studies or the most effective way to introduce questioning in second grade. The best lessons, however, are those developed by a grade-level team of teachers to meet a specific curricular goal.

As you evaluate the instructional activities in Chapter 4 as well as those of other authors and consultants, ask these questions: Did it work (get results)? Did my students become more confident readers? Were they able to think aloud about using a specific strategy as a result of the activity? Sometimes an excellent instructional activity can fail because we overestimate our students' background knowledge and experience. Begin simply. Go slowly. Build in success for yourself and your students from the outset. Form 5.3, Instructional Activity Planning Form, is useful for keeping track of the activities you develop on your own as well as those you adapt from other sources.

Instructional Groups

The next decision to make is how you will group students for the various instructional components of SRI. Figure 5.1 displays and defines a variety of grouping options. For example, if you have leveled reading groups, you may wish to model and explain strategy instruction in a whole-group setting while the teaching moves of scaffolding, coaching, facilitating, and constructing will go on in guided and leveled reading groups. Varying the makeup and size of your instructional groups during SRI will motivate students, make both individuals and small groups accountable for extracting and constructing meaning from text, and harness the research-confirmed power of cooperative learning (Johnson & Johnson, 1990).

Teaching Moves

The teaching moves that are essential for effective SRI implementation were described and defined in Chapter 2 (see Figure 2.4) along with a description of the *strategic teacher.* You may well already have assimilated all of these moves into your instructional repertoire. If not, your initial attempts at SRI will by necessity be more scripted and mechanical. Don't be impatient. The flow will eventually come as both you and your students discover the power of SRI.

Text Reading Options

It's time to put the worn-out round-robin reading approach out to pasture (Opitz & Rasinski, 1998). There are more motivating and productive ways for students to access text. Figure 5.2 lists a variety of ways for students to read text. At times, you will read a brief section of text aloud and then ask students to read it silently before you or your students think aloud about the strategies you have used. On other occasions, students will pair up and talk with each other. Or cooperative groups may use *Turn On Your CPU* (see Chapter 4) to read short sections of text and then talk with their team members about the connections they made with prior learning and experience or the parts of the text that confused and bewildered them.

Instructional Activity Planning Form
_____

Instructional activity: _____

Description: _____

_____

_____

Cognitive strategies: _____

Recommended usage: _____

Content area: _____

Props, prompts, and posters: _____

Text genre: _____

Anticipatory set: _____

_____

_____

_____

_____

Teacher think-aloud: _____

_____

Teacher input: _____

_____

Guided practice: _____

Student accountability-assessment: _____

_____

Follow-up activities: _____

_____

_____

Instructional Grouping Options

Option	Description
Cooperative group	Students working together in heterogeneous groups of 3–5 on a clearly defined task and including both group and individual accountability
Heterogeneous whole group	A self-contained classroom or ad hoc large group containing students of every ability level
Homogeneous whole group	A group of students at a similar skill level (e.g., flexible multigrade group, guided reading group, or ad hoc skill-level group)
Booster group	A small group of students constituted for the purpose of administering extra doses of instruction in a specific area of need
Enrichment group	A small group of students constituted for the purposes of enrichment or acceleration in a specific area of the curriculum
Student pairs	Pairs of students working together on a task (e.g., academic peers, buddies from another grade level, or an academically strong student peer-tutoring a student who needs help)
Individual student and tutor	Students working individually with a tutor or aide on a specific assignment (e.g., special education, ELL, Title I)
Jigsaw group	A group whose members are responsible for teaching one another different chunks of a topic or unit

Student Text Reading Options

Option	Description
Individual silent reading	One student reading text silently
Oral reading (choral or parts)	A group of students reading text aloud together or a group of students taking turns reading parts in a play or poem
Oral reading (pairs)	Back-and-forth oral reading between two students or choral reading of text in pairs
Listening to read-alouds	Listening to teacher, aide, peer, buddy, parent volunteer, or tutor reading text aloud
Silent read-pair-share	A pair of students reading the same portion of text silently and then thinking-aloud with each other
Read aloud with a tutor or volunteer	Student reading text aloud to someone else
Guided supportive reading	Students reading aloud or silently in a supportive, guided reading group taught by the teacher
Read aloud to a buddy	Student reading easy text aloud to a younger student
Repeated oral reading	Repeated oral reading of easy text for the purpose of building fluency and comprehension

Figure 5.2. Copyright © 2004 Corwin Press. All rights reserved. Reprinted from *Seven Strategies of Highly Effective Readers*, by E. K. McEwan. Thousand Oaks, CA: Corwin Press, www.corwinpress.com. Reproduction authorized only for the local school site that has purchased this book.

Text Genre and Difficulty Levels

Your choice of text genre may be dictated by the content you are expected to teach or the reading series you are mandated to use, but be sure to match the text genres you choose with the kind of text your students will encounter on their state and standardized assessments. If your students are linguistically needy or second language learners and need extra doses of vocabulary and knowledge instruction, spend more time reading expository text to supplement your science and social studies textbooks. Although most teachers have been led to believe that fiction is inherently more appealing to students of any age level, but particularly those in Grades K–2, Smolkin and Donovan (2000) found that children listening to information book read-alouds engaged in more "meaning-making" discourses with their teachers and each other than they did while listening to picture book read-alouds. Don't overlook the importance of introducing your students to a wide variety of text materials in addition to those that come with the territory. Figure 5.3 describes the possible options. Vary the difficulty level of the text you choose, as well. When introducing or using a strategy for the first time, choose text that is easier to read. Cognitive overload can occur when students are practicing the strategy while at the same time attempting to understand very challenging text. Figure 5.4 describes the difficulty level options.

Student Accountability and Assessment

Figure 5.5 displays a variety of ways to hold students accountable for their processing of text as well as to help you assess your students' progress in using the seven cognitive strategies. Accountability is essential to moving students to increasing levels of difficulty.

WHAT DOES A LESSON LOOK LIKE?

A Sample Kindergarten Lesson Plan

Figure 5.6 presents a sample lesson-planning matrix for a kindergarten lesson. The teacher plans to read aloud *The Little Red Hen* (Galdone, 1973) to the whole class. Before reading, she *explains* to students what she will be doing and why and then reminds them (activates prior knowledge) of the seven cognitive strategies they have been learning and using throughout the year so far. She points to the posters and pictures to prompt (refresh) their memories.

During her read-aloud, the teacher *models* how to summarize the story so that she (and her students) will be able to retell the story later in the lesson, in preparation for telling it once more during the day to someone they know (e.g., a reading buddy, parent, the afternoon aide, or the principal). The instructional activity is called *Visualize a Video* and uses the visualizing and summarizing strategies. After students have heard the story read aloud and the accompanying teacher think-aloud, they get into pairs and retell the story using the picture cues the teacher showed during her modeling (see Figure 4.8). The teacher keeps a lesson-planning matrix like the one shown in Figure 5.6 for each of her read-aloud strategy lessons so she can maintain a balance between informational and narrative texts as well as monitor the teaching moves she uses with her students.

Text Genre Options

Option	Description
Expository (nonfiction)	"Informational texts, including classroom textbooks that are used for teaching content areas such as social studies and science" (Beck et al., 1997, p. 8)
Narrative (fiction, literature)	"Fictional selections such as stories, novels, and fables, that typically involve characters attempting to resolve a conflict" (Beck et al., 1997, p. 8)
Periodical	Children's, young adult, and adult magazines issued periodically that cater to specialized tastes and interests
Newspaper	Daily or weekly news coverage in either print or online form
Hypertext	A collection of documents containing cross-references or 'links' which, with the aid of an interactive browser program, allow the reader to move easily from one document to another."
Practical text	Text that is typically found in real-life situations, such as recipes, manuals, directions, pamphlets, brochures, and advertising materials
Student-constructed text	Stories or books that have been edited and published by students for placement in the classroom or school library

Text Difficulty Level Options

Difficulty Level	Description
Independent	Text for which a student has the prerequisite word identification skills and appropriate background and vocabulary knowledge combined with cognitive strategy usage to read independently
Instructional	Text for which a student will need scaffolding to read: explanations of vocabulary and annotating (adding additional information) by the teacher
Frustration	Text that is too difficult for a student to read either independently or with scaffolding
Considerate	Text that is well organized and clearly written making it accessible to meaning making by students
Easy	Text for which students have prior knowledge and vocabulary as well as high-interest text that is motivating and engaging
Inconsiderate	Text that lacks clarity and coherence, tries to explain too many different concepts at one time, and lacks internal consistency

Figure 5.4. Copyright © 2004 Corwin Press. All rights reserved. Reprinted from *Seven Strategies of Highly Effective Readers*, by E. K. McEwan. Thousand Oaks, CA: Corwin Press, www.corwinpress.com. Reproduction authorized only for the local school site that has purchased this book.

Student Accountability-Asssessment Options

Option	Description
Graphic organizer	The generation of a visual illustration or representation of written text
Questions	Generating questions to ask the author, questions that the teacher might ask on a quiz, questions to ask classmates, or questions to ask oneself
Answers	Finding answers to questions asked by a textbook, teacher, or fellow student
Summary	Generating a one- or two-sentence thumbnail sketch of the text in one's own words
Oral retelling	Retelling a story, including the correct sequence of events along with the beginning, middle, end, and resolution of a problem
Interviewing	Generating questions about a topic to ask an expert
Reciprocal teaching	Taking a turn at being the leader or teacher of a group that is using strategic reading to extract and construct meaning
Brainstorming	Generating a list of possible ideas, questions, inferences, concepts, solutions, causes, effects, and so on
Thinking aloud	Describing one's thoughts during reading or solving problems encountered in the reading of text
Key words	Generating key words that summarize a character, conceptualize a chunk of text, or describe a theme or the main idea

Sample Lesson-Planning Matrix for Kindergarten

Title of Text: The Little Red Hen   Grade: Kindergarten   Date: January 27, 2004

Option	Before Reading	During Reading	After Reading
Cognitive strategy	Activating	Summarizing	Visualizing
Instructional activity			Visualize a Video
Grouping	Whole Group	Whole group	Pairs
Teacher input	Explaining	Modeling, giving directions	Facilitating, scaffolding
Student reading of text	Listening	Listening	
Subject		Language Arts	
Type of text		Narrative-Fairy Tale	
Student accountability-assessment			Student Think-Aloud Form, retelling
Difficulty level			

Figure 5.6. Copyright © 2004 Corwin Press. All rights reserved. Reprinted from *Seven Strategies of Highly Effective Readers*, by E. K. McEwan. Thousand Oaks, CA: Corwin Press, www.corwinpress.com. Reproduction authorized only for the local school site that has purchased this book.

A Sample Middle School Lesson Plan

Figure 5.7 is a sample lesson-planning matrix for a sixth-grade science lesson. The topic under study is endangered species. SRI was introduced at the beginning of the school year, and the teacher, Mr. Gray, has been modeling strategy usage regularly and integrating instructional activities into his content-area instruction. The instructional activity he has planned is the upper-grade version of the one selected by the kindergarten teacher, but it focuses on the organizing half of the strategy. Before the students receive their materials, Mr. Gray explains the activity and recaps what they have learned thus far about endangered species (and also what they have learned about summarizing and organizing). A variety of texts and difficulty levels are being used: an online article in the *New York Times* about adolescent condors raised in captivity and then released in the Grand Canyon National Park (Blakeslee, 2003), an article about the condor population in the Grand Canyon National Park (Grand Canyon Visitor's Guide, 2003), the applicable chapter in the science textbook, several informational books from the library about endangered species generally and condors specifically, and some full-color posters of condors at various stages of growth. Once the teacher has completed the initial explaining and recapping, the students assemble in their cooperative groups. They first divide the materials to be read among the group members, with each student taking responsibility for reading one article and using sticky arrows to note places in the text that need clarification or explanation by other group members (see Turn On Your CPU in Chapter 4). Group members who finish their articles first will also be responsible for searching-selecting passages in the available books (see The Prospector in Chapter 4) for use in constructing a group graphic organizer.

After reading, each team will use a classroom computer and Inspiration® Software to construct their organizer, summarizing the key ideas in the materials they have read. They have been introduced to the Inspiration templates previously and are free to choose the template that best fits the way their team has "pictured" and organized the materials they read (see Organize It in Chapter 4). They will have an additional class period to complete the organizer, and then a spokesperson for each group will present their organizer to the rest of the class.

Keeping track of the options chosen for a particular instructional activity or unit of study will ensure that all of the teacher input options are fully used and that as the year progresses, there is less explaining—more facilitating, less motivating-connecting—more coaching, and less recapping—more constructing. Keeping careful records of your SRI will also enable you to determine if you are giving the strategies "equal billing" or focusing on your favorites. It will also remind you of the various student accountability options available.

As a follow-up activity to this lesson, Mr. Gray asks students to prepare interview questions to ask an expert on condors (the author of one of the books they have read) who will "visit" the class via speakerphone during an upcoming class (see Do You Have Any Questions? in Chapter 4). At the end of the unit, each team will be responsible for generating three important questions that the members agree *should* be asked on the unit test. Mr. Gray will make the list of

Sample Lesson-Planning Matrix for Sixth Grade

Title of Text: Various   Grade: Sixth Grade   Date: March 15, 2004

Option	Before Reading	During Reading	After Reading
Cognitive strategy	Activating	Summarizing, searching-selecting	Organizing
Instructional activity		Turn On Your CPU	Organize It!
Grouping	Whole group	Jigsaw group	Cooperative teams
Teacher moves	Explaining, recapping	Facilitating, motivating-connecting	Assessing, coaching
Type of text reading		Oral-silent	
Subject		Science	
Text genre		Newspaper, periodicals, brochures, and textbooks	
Student accountability-assessment			Graphic organizer
Difficulty level of text		Instructional	

questions available to the students and give them an opportunity to ask the team that generated a particular question what its members believe is the most defensible and thoughtful answer. Then, he will choose several of the best questions and create his unit test.

The combination and permutations are endless, but you can readily see that with SRI, students will learn, understand, and remember. They will not only extract meaning from text but jointly construct it with their teachers and fellow students.

You now know a great deal of what you need to know to begin SRI implementation. It is time to put it into practice in your classroom. One of my stated goals in the Preface was to convince educators that strategy instruction done well is not more work but rather the most effective and important work a teacher can do. I trust I have made some progress toward that goal.

WHAT'S AHEAD?

Just ahead in Chapter 6 we'll examine how to implement schoolwide SRI, describe the six C's of school culture that are essential for successful implementation, and explain the important curricular components that support and enhance SRI.

Implementing Schoolwide Strategic Reading Instruction

As we enter the 21ˢᵗ century, many educators want to teach comprehension as the seamless, complex interaction of thoughts that good readers use. This instruction must be neither too prescriptive nor too free-flowing. When instruction is too teacher-dominated, students do not learn how to apply the skills without prompting. Alternatively, when instruction is too sparse or unmonitored, pupils do not develop tools to think strategically as they read.

Block, Schaller, Joy, and Gaine (2002, p. 43)

I sometimes fantasize about establishing a brand-new school, and I've already decided what to name it—the Strategic Reading Academy. SRI will be seamlessly woven into the fabric of every school day, and the mission statement will read as follows: *The Strategic Reading Academy is a learning community where every student learns to read, loves to read, and voraciously reads to learn in every content area.* To achieve this mission, the academy will give evidence of the following: (1) the six C's of school culture (commitment, cooperation, collaboration, conversation, communication, and coordination); (2) balanced instructional expertise that is characterized by the ability to meet all students' individual needs; and (3) curricular components that result in the acquisition of fluent word identification skills, deep vocabulary and domain knowledge, voracious reading habits characterized by sense making and accountability, and the acquisition and usage of the seven cognitive strategies of highly effective readers.

The three "big ideas" that characterize the as yet imaginary Strategic Reading Academy are the very qualities and practices that *you* will need to cultivate as you plan for SRI implementation in your classroom, school, or district.

SRI REQUIRES A PERVASIVE AND PERSUASIVE READING CULTURE

Before you make the decision to implement SRI, first evaluate your school's culture. Does it give evidence of the six C's of a pervasive and persuasive reading culture: (1) commitment, (2) cooperation, (3) collaboration, (4) conversation, (5) communication, and (6) coordination? In the absence of a culture that nurtures, supports, or even expects a pervasive and persuasive reading culture from administrators, staff, students, and parents, the implementation of schoolwide SRI as described in this chapter will be impossible.

Commitment

Effective cognitive strategy instruction will not flourish and mature in classrooms or schools without high levels of commitment—from administrators, teachers, students, and even parents. Recall a quotation in Chapter 1 regarding complex cognition in which Perkins (1992) advised that notching up cognitive expectations for students "introduces the discomforts of disorientation, as learners struggle to get their heads around difficult ideas" (p. 60). I submit that students are not the only ones who will be discomfited and disoriented. Teachers will struggle with cognitive dissonance and overload as well. They may feel that SRI is not in their job description or that it won't fit into already overloaded schedules.

Research has documented that teachers require at least three years to acquire cognitive strategy instruction expertise (Pressley, Schuder, SAIL Teachers, Bergman, & El-Dinary, 1992), typically moving through the following implementation phases: (1) a mechanical, rote approach to strategy instruction; (2) experimentation; and (3) internalization and personalization (Hall & Horde, 1987). Beginning SRI teachers need ongoing staff development, coaching, and instructional support if they are to achieve the final phase. If you are the kind of person who requires immediate personal gratification and instant success in your classroom, you will find SRI frustrating. You won't be satisfied with your own teaching (or administrative) performance immediately, and you won't get the results you want from students overnight, either. You will periodically feel as though you are failing. You will be tempted to give up and devote your energies to less demanding lessons where everyone is having more "fun." I know these statements to be true because I have experienced them personally while working with administrators, teachers, and students over the past four years. Remember, however, that you are investing for a long-term payoff. Commitment is the first and most important "C."

Cooperation and Collaboration

The second and third C's—cooperation and collaboration—are first cousins to each other. But for purposes of this discussion, I am making a distinction between them. Cooperation, in some contexts, is the opposite of *competition*. For a good share of my career in education, ability-based reading groups were the norm. These groups, cast in concrete in kindergarten, had little to do with skill- or strategy-based acceleration for students who needed a boost to catch up to their classmates. Neither did these ubiquitous groups provide enrichment and higher expectations for students who had already mastered the grade-level content. Usually reading groups as we knew them were a way to excuse low expectations, maintain the status quo, and keep the parents of gifted students happy. All concerned (even the students) knew that reading was *only* about the group: Students in the high reading groups somehow got high grades in reading no matter how they performed, while students in the low reading groups seemed to fail year after year, even if they improved.

Collaboration, the third "C," takes cooperation to the next level—a level in which teachers develop lessons and instructional activities jointly, plan together for the benefit of students regularly, and openly talk about teaching with a common language and shared excitement. Collaboration is the essence of a professional learning community (DuFour & Eaker, 1998), and it is essential to creating a persuasive and pervasive reading culture in which SRI can take root.

Conversation and Communication

Conversation, the fourth "C," is about talking with people—becoming acquainted, socializing, and sharing life stories. Communication, the fifth "C," on the other hand, means understanding, empathizing, and walking in another's boots, moccasins, or even Gucci loafers. Communication is about entrusting your ideas, hopes, and dreams to one another. Face-to-face conversation among stakeholders is important: Fun fairs, open houses, and potluck suppers to exchange ethnic specialties are the stuff that schools are made of. But there must also be the kind of communication in which all parties listen to what is being said and then endeavor to understand. In addition to daily conversations about teaching and learning among staff members, there must also be discussions about books and articles, deliberations about students and their needs, and encounters or even confrontations about what's working, what's not, and what to do about what's not working.

In SRI schools, students are also conversing. Rather than the typical Initiate-Response-Evaluate classroom dialogue routines so prevalent in many classrooms, students at an SRI school talk to each other and to their teachers about their reading and meaning making. They have opinions, ideas, goals, and desires and are not shy about sharing them with others. There are student literature circles, teacher lesson study groups, and parent book groups—all of them focused on maximizing the cognitive processing powers of all of the community's stakeholders.

Newsletters, bulletins, and memos constitute a very narrow definition of communication: Real communication occurs when all of the stakeholders in the school community are receptive to evaluative comments and input from other stakeholders and then agree to make changes in their behavior or attitudes based on the perceptions of others.

Coordination

The last "C" is coordination. The essence of coordination is *articulation.* Coordination means that teachers at the same grade level, on the same team, or in the same department are on the same page academically, instructionally, and behaviorally. They have an agreed-on set of expectations for students, which includes what they will learn, how they will be taught, and how they will treat their teachers and each other. Teachers have agreed on an articulated curriculum that spirals and builds each year, adding increasing amounts of vocabulary and domain knowledge.

All teachers feel strongly about the importance of students reading a lot, and no one teacher is permitted to lower those expectations or relax the standards for the sake of expediency. Teachers in an SRI school speak a common language as it relates to cognitive strategy instruction, and their instructional goals support and enhance the overall school mission. Administrators, staff, parents, and students believe in the necessity of working together. They do not point fingers of blame when failure looms but pull together to discover what else can be done to ensure success. No one individual is permitted to undermine the mission because of poor performance, and everyone is responsible for holding each other and all students accountable. Evaluation is not the sole prerogative of administrators. Teachers are willing to be courageous when it comes to confronting unacceptable behavior, whether from their colleagues, students, or their administrators. Administrators and teachers are willing to hold parents accountable for supporting their children in their intellectual endeavors, and parents are willing and able to hold their school accountable for their children's learning.

I have observed far too many schools in which well-intentioned attempts to bring about change, institute curricular innovations, establish whole-school reform, or raise achievement for low-performing students fail because of inattention to the cultural norms. If you want to nurture the seven cognitive strategies that boost student achievement, pay attention to the six C's of school culture.

SRI REQUIRES BALANCED INSTRUCTION

While many practitioners and scholars in the reading community continue to discuss and debate which methodologies constitute best practices in literacy instruction, hundreds of thousands of highly effective teachers continue to do what they have always done—balance their instruction in response to student needs, choosing from their extensive repertoires of effective and research-based models (McEwan, 2002c). Both the ability to modify teaching approaches on an as-needed basis and the willingness to do it are the hallmarks of highly effective teachers generally (Bryk & Thum, 1989; Edmonds, 1979; Good & Brophy, 1986; Rosenshine, 1979, 1997a). These qualities are also defining characteristics of highly effective *reading* teachers (Pressley et al., 1996; Pressley et al., 2001; Wharton-McDonald, Pressley, & Hampton, 1998).

Recall the major teaching moves of SRI that we discussed in Chapter 2 and further elaborated in Chapter 5. Placed on a continuum, these moves range from direct explaining to novices on the one hand to jointly constructing meaning with self-regulated experts (students) on the other. In addition to these contrasting but complementary instructional "book-ends," effective teachers skillfully use a wide range of other instructional moves to accomplish the goals of SRI.

SRI REQUIRES A RESEARCH-BASED CURRICULUM

In addition to a pervasive and persuasive reading culture that is characterized by the six C's *and* balanced instructional expertise that gets results, SRI also requires curricular components to ensure that all students acquire fluent word identification skills, a constantly increasing vocabulary, growing domain knowledge, and a voracious appetite for challenging text. The criteria for choosing such curricular components must be based on affirmative, research-based answers to the following questions: (1) Does it (the program, methodology, curriculum) work? (2) How does it work? (3) Will it work for me (in my classroom or school)? (4) Is it worthwhile (can I accomplish the same goals spending much less time and money)? (McEwan & McEwan, 2003, p. 4).[1]

Fluent Word Identification Skills

When I consult with middle and high school teachers and principals about raising achievement in their low-performing schools, one of the first pieces of advice I give (when asked) is to find the students who can't read and teach them to read (McEwan, 2001). While the benefits of SRI are most assuredly not limited to those students who already know how to read text fluently at their grade level or above, the *primary* purpose of cognitive strategy instruction is to help those students who are fluent readers but have somehow missed the point of reading: extracting and constructing meaning. Strengthening and enhancing the listening comprehension of emerging readers is a powerful way to increase vocabulary and knowledge, as well as build processing powers that will be sustained and enhanced in later grades. However, our goal as educators must be to teach all students to read independently (McEwan, 2002a; Pressley, 1998).

Vocabulary and Domain Knowledge

E. D. Hirsch, Jr. (1989), wrote in his preface to *A First Dictionary of Cultural Literacy,*

> Our schools' emphasis on skills rather than knowledge has . . . had the unintended effect of injuring disadvantaged students more than advantaged ones. Since more so-called skills are really based upon specific knowledge, those who have already received literate knowledge from their homes are better able to understand what teachers and textbooks are saying and are therefore better able to learn new things than are children from non-literate backgrounds. Consequently when schools emphasize skills over knowledge, they consistently widen the gap between the haves and have-nots instead of narrowing it. (p. xi)

More recently, Hirsch (2001, 2003) has spoken to the challenge that educators face in sustaining the early reading gains that disadvantaged students make as a result of intensive intervention and prevention programs. He suggested a way to narrow the widening achievement gap that exists between the richest (academically) and the poorest students: Teach knowledge. Pellegrino (2002) summarizes three key principles regarding the role of knowledge in science learning, and his principles apply to every discipline:

- Students come to the classroom with preconceptions about how the world works [both accurate and faulty], which include beliefs and prior knowledge acquired through various experiences;

- To develop competence in an area of inquiry, students must: (a) have a deep foundation of factual knowledge, (b) understand facts and ideas in the context of a conceptual framework, and (c) organize knowledge in ways that facilitate retrieval and application.

- A "metacognitive" approach to instruction can help students learn to take control of their own learning by defining learning goals and monitoring their progress in achieving them. (pp. 3–4)

Reading a Lot

Although most educators will agree that students should read more, there is really no agreed-on standard for exactly *how much* they should be reading—either at the elementary or secondary level. Many educators think in terms of words, pages, or books (Honig, 2001, p. 103), but Allington (2001) recommends, and I concur, that reading volume should be measured in *time*. To expect a beginning or slower reader to read the same number of pages or books as a more skilled reader can easily lead to frustration and discouragement for less voluminous readers. Since every student has the same amount of time available in the day, each one should be reading for the same amount of time. Actually, in order to catch up, struggling readers should be spending even more time reading than their peers who are reading fluently. Allington asserts that the volume of daily *in-school* reading that most elementary school children experience is far below an optimum level and suggests that students should be doing an absolutely mind-boggling ninety minutes of *actual* reading *in school* every day. Try that one on for size in your classroom, school, or district.

This ninety minutes would include any and all kinds of reading during the school day—content-area reading, reading done during reading instruction, silent reading, voluntary reading, assigned reading for which the student is held accountable, oral reading, repeated reading, guided reading, and buddy reading. Allington (2001) further recommends that teachers at each grade level jointly develop reading volume or time standards that are zealously adhered to by *every* staff member.

I would also recommend that *out-of-school* reading volume standards be established. We developed reading homework standards and expected every student to read for a certain period of time nightly (or weekly, depending on the grade level). This reading could include a read-aloud by an adult or older sibling to a student, listening to a commercially taped read-aloud, reading aloud by the student to an adult or sibling, repeated oral reading, or silent reading.

To summarize, the total amount of reading a lot that students do should ideally be composed of three kinds of reading: (1) guided and supervised reading during the school day (up to ninety minutes); (2) a staff agreed-on daily reading *homework* period in which students read anything they like but are held accountable for what they read in some minimal way (e.g., reading log, journal, or parent signature in homework book); and (3) *voluntary* (over and above what is required at school *or* for homework), *voracious* (enthusiastic and excited), and *voluminous* (lots and lots of books) *reading* outside of school that is facilitated and motivated by ongoing and meaningful incentives (Cameron & Pierce, 1994). Expecting students to do this much reading may sound unrealistic or even impossible, but you will never know if that is really so until you actually set forth the requirements and then expect your students and parents to "drop everything and read" *at home*!

Many teachers and administrators have succumbed to the seductive notion that all of their reading comprehension problems can be solved by adopting programs like *Accelerated Reader* (Renaissance Learning, 2002). While motivational reading programs like AR can, if used wisely and with full realization of their limitations, jump-start reading a lot in a school that doesn't read at all, they are no substitute for SRI by an expert teacher. The complex cognition that results from SRI is light-years beyond the kind of superficial reading that looks for easy answers to computerized recall questions.

IS YOUR SCHOOL OR DISTRICT READY FOR SRI?

You are ready to begin cognitive strategy instruction on a schoolwide or districtwide basis if

• All staff members (or the vast majority) agree that cognitive strategy instruction is essential for all students and have committed to instruction and training for themselves in advance of implementation.

• Staff members and administrators understand that the attainment of expertise in cognitive strategy instruction is a time-consuming process and will take at least two to three years of intense attention.

• The administration and staff realize that collaboration in the design of instruction is difficult and time-consuming and agree to intentionally collaborate, even when tempted to go it alone.

• All staff members understand that for cognitive strategy instruction to be meaningful, a common schoolwide vocabulary as well as a set of beliefs about reading instruction must be in place and that the achievement of this goal may be a difficult process.

• The administration is committed to providing time for grade-level or content-area teams to develop lessons, plan jointly, and observe in one another's classrooms.

• The administration is willing to provide instructional support either personally or in the form of a cognitive coach who will work at least three periods per day.

• Reading specialists are committed to cognitive strategy instruction as the means of improving reading achievement for at-risk and low-achieving students and will focus their efforts on providing in-class support, modeling, and feedback for teachers and students.

• A time line has been developed that provides materials, funding, and release time for a full three years.

• Staff members have been involved in a study discussion group using resource materials like this book to guide and stimulate discussion.

• Parental input has been solicited, and the new and more stringent expectations for students have been communicated to them.

• Students have been informed of the changes that will take place at the beginning of the next school year.

• Administration and staff recognize that strong instructional leadership for cognitive strategy instruction is derived from strong servant-leaders in both administrative and teacher-leader roles.

• Content-area teachers recognize that they alone are knowledgeable about the ways in which their disciplines are organized and presented in textbooks and are committed to developing the knowledge and skills they need to improve the comprehension of their students with regard to their discipline.

CONCLUSION

More than twenty years ago, Ron Edmonds (1981) made this compelling statement: "We can, whenever and wherever we choose, successfully teach all children whose schooling is of interest to us. We already know more than we need to do that. Whether or not we do it must finally depend on how we feel about the fact that we haven't so far" (p. 53). To paraphrase Edmond's statement, I believe, "We can, whenever and wherever we choose, successfully teach cognitive strategies to all children whose schooling is of interest to us. We already know more than we need to do that. The scientific research is clear and undeniable. Whether or not we do it must finally depend on how we feel about the fact that we haven't so far."

NOTE

1. Determining the answers to these questions prior to selecting a curriculum or program will enable you to meet the stringent requirements of the No Child Left Behind Act of 2002 (2002).

References

Adams, M. J. (1998). The three-cueing system. In F. Lehr & J. Osborn (Eds.), *Literacy for all issues in teaching and learning* (pp. 73–99). New York: Guilford.

Adler, M. (1940). *How to read a book.* New York: Simon & Schuster.

Afflerbach, P. (1990a). The influence of prior knowledge and text genre on readers' prediction strategies. *Reading Research Quarterly, 22,* 131–148.

Afflerbach, P. (1990b). The influence of prior knowledge on expert readers' main idea strategies. *Reading Research Quarterly, 25,* 31–46.

Afflerbach, P. (2002). Teaching reading self-assessment strategies. In C. C. Block & M. Pressley (Eds.). *Comprehension instruction: Research-based best practices* (pp. 96–111). New York: Guilford.

Afflerbach, P., & Johnston, P. H. (1984). Research methodology: On the use of verbal reports in reading research. *Journal of Reading Behavior, 16,* 307–322.

Afflerbach, P., & Walker, B. (1992). Main idea instruction: An analysis of three basal reader series. *Reading Research and Instruction, 32*(1), 11–28.

Alexander, P. A., & Murphy, P. K. (1998). The research base for APA's Learner Centered Psychological Principles. In N. M. Lambert & B. L. McCombs (Eds.), *How students learn: Reforming schools through learner-centered education* (pp. 25–60). Washington, DC: American Psychological Association.

Allington, R. L. (2001). *What really matters for struggling readers.* New York: Longman.

Alvermann, D. (1991). The discussion web: A graphic aid for learning across the curriculum. *The Reading Teacher, 45,* 92–99.

Alvermann, D. E., & Boothby, P. R. (1983). A preliminary investigation of the differences in children's retention of "inconsiderate" text. *Reading Psychology, 4*(3–4), 237–246.

Alvermann, D. E., & Boothby, P. R. (1986). Children's transfer of graphic organizer instruction. *Reading Psychology, 7*(2), 87–100.

Ambrose, S. (1994). *D-Day: June 6, 1944: The climactic battle of World War II.* New York: Simon & Schuster.

Andersen, H. C. (1875). The emperor's new clothes. In *Andersen's fairy tales: Short stories. The emperor's new clothes.* Retrieved July 18, 2003, from www.literaturepage.com.

Anderson, R. C., & Pearson, P. D. (1984). A schema-theoretic view of basic processes in reading. In P. D. Pearson (Ed.), *Handbook of reading research* (pp. 255–292). White Plains, NY: Longman.

Anderson, V., & Hidi, S. (1988/1989). Teaching students to summarize. *Educational Leadership, 46*(4), 26–28.

Anderson, V., & Roit, M. (1993). Planning and implementing collaborative strategy instruction with delayed readers in grades 6–10. *Elementary School Journal, 94*(2), 121–137.

Armbruster, B. B., Anderson, T. H., & Meyer, J. L. (1991). Improving content-area reading using instructional graphics. *Reading Research Quarterly, 26*(4), 393–416.

Armbruster, B. B., Anderson, T. H., & Ostertag, J. (1987). Does text structure/summarization instruction facilitate learning from expository text? *Reading Research Quarterly, 22,* 331–346.

Babbs, P. J. (1984). Monitoring cards help improve comprehension. *Reading Teacher, 18*(2), 200–204.

Baddeley, A. (1997). *Human memory: Theory and practice.* East Sussex, England: Psychology Press.

Baddeley, A., & Logie, R. H. (1999). Working memory: The multiple-component model. In A. Miyake & P. Shah (Eds.), *Models of working memory: Mechanisms of active maintenance and executive control* (pp. 2–61). Cambridge, UK: Cambridge University Press.

Bailey, C. S. (1949). *Old man rabbit's dinner party.* New York: Platt & Munk.

Baker, L. (2002). Metacognition in comprehension instruction. In C. C. Block & M. Pressley (Eds.), *Comprehension instruction: Research-based best practices* (pp. 77–95). New York: Guilford.

Baker, L., & Zimlin, L. (1989). Instructional effects on children's use of two levels of standards for evaluating their comprehension. *Journal of Educational Psychology, 81*(3), 340–346.

Barton, M. L., & Billmeyer, R. (1996). *Teaching reading in the content areas: If not me, then who?* Alexandria, VA: Association for Supervision and Curriculum Development.

Baumann, J. F. (1983). Children's ability to comprehend main ideas in content textbooks. *Reading World, 22*(4), 322–331.

Baumann, J. F. (1984). The effectiveness of a paradigm for teaching main idea comprehension. *Reading Research Quarterly, 20*(1), 93–115.

Baumann, J. F., Seifert-Kessell, N., & Jones, L. A. (1992). Effect of think-aloud instruction on elementary students' comprehension monitoring abilities. *Journal of Reading Behavior, 24*(2), 143–172.

Bean, T. W., & Steenwyk, F. L. (1984). The effect of three forms of summarization instruction on sixth graders' summary writing and comprehension. *Journal of Reading Behavior, 16*(4), 297–306.

Beatty, J. (2001). *The human brain: Essentials of behavioral neuroscience.* Thousand Oaks, CA: Sage.

Beck, I. L., McKeown, M. G., Hamilton, R. L., & Kucan, L. (1997). *Questioning the author: An approach for enhancing student engagement with text.* Newark, DE: International Reading Association.

Beck, I. L., Perfetti, C. A., & McKeown, M. G. (1982). Effects of long-term vocabulary instruction on lexical access and reading comprehension. *Journal of Educational Psychology, 74*, 506–521.

Bereiter, C., & Bird, M. (1985). Use of thinking aloud in identification and teaching of reading comprehension strategies. *Cognition and Instruction, 2*(2), 131–156.

Berkowitz, S. J. (1986). Effects of instruction in text organization on sixth-grade students' memory for expository reading. *Reading Research Quarterly, 21*(2), 151–168.

Birkets, S. (1995). *The Gutenberg elegies.* New York: Ballantine.

Blakeslee, S. (2003, June 3). Adolescent condors raised in captivity must be taught how adults behave. *New York Times.* Retrieved June 3, 2003, from www.nytimes.com/2003/06/03/science/03COND.html.

Block, C. C., Gambrell, L. L., & Pressley, M. (Eds.). (2002). *Improving comprehension instruction: Rethinking research, theory, and classroom practice.* San Francisco: Jossey-Bass.

Block, C. C., & Pressley, M. (Eds.). (2002). *Comprehension instruction: Research-based best practices.* New York: Guilford.

Block, C. C., Schaller, J. L., Joy, J. A., & Gaine, P. (2002). Process-based comprehension instruction. In C. C. Block & M. Pressley (Eds.), *Comprehension instruction: Research-based best practices* (pp. 42–61). New York: Guilford.

Bloom, B. S. (1980). The new direction in educational research: Alterable variables. *Phi Delta Kappan, 61*, 382–385.

Borduin, B. J., Borduin, C. M., & Manley, C. M. (1994). The use of imagery training to improve reading comprehension of second graders. *Journal of Genetic Psychology, 155*(1), 115–118.

Borokowski, J. G., & Muthukrishna, N. (1992). Moving metacognition into the classroom: "Working models" and effective strategy teaching. In M. Pressley, K. R. Harris, & J. T. Guthrie (Eds.), *Promoting academic competence and literacy in school* (pp. 477–501). San Diego: Academic Press.

Bransford, J. D. (1979). *Human cognition: Learning, understanding, and remembering.* Belmont, CA: Wadsworth.

Bransford, J. D. (1983). Schema activation—schema acquisition. In R. C. Anderson, J. Osborn, & R. C. Tierney (Eds.), *Learning to read in American schools* (pp. 258–272). Hillsdale, NJ: Lawrence Erlbaum.

Bransford, J. D., Brown, A. L., & Cocking, R. R. (Eds.). (2000). *How people learn: Brain, mind, experience, and school.* Washington, DC: National Academy Press.

Brown, A. L., & Campione, J. C. (1994). Guided discovery in a community of learners. In K. McGilly (Ed.), *Classroom lessons: Integrating cognitive theory and classroom practice* (pp. 229–270). Cambridge: MIT Press.

Brown, A. L., & Campione, J. C. (1996). Psychological theory and the design of innovative learning environments: On procedures, principals, and systems. In L. Schauble & R. Glaser (Eds.) *Innovations in learning: New environments for education* (pp. 289–325). Mahwah, NJ: Erlbaum.

Brown, A. L., & Day, J. D. (1983). Macrorules for summarizing texts: The development of expertise. *Journal of Verbal Learning and Verbal Behavior, 22,* 1–14.

Brown, A. L., Day, J. D., & Jones, E. S. (1983). The development of plans for summarizing texts. *Child Development, 54(4),* 968–979.

Brown, R., Pressley, M., Van Meter, P., & Schuder, T. (1996). A quasi-experimental validation of transactional strategies instruction with low-achieving second-grade readers. *Journal of Educational Psychology, 88(1),* 18–37.

Brown, A. L., Smiley, S. S., Day, J. D., Townsend, M. A. R., & Lawton, S. D. (1977). Intrusion of a thematic idea in children's comprehension and retention of stories. *Child Development, 48,* 1454–1466.

Bryk, A. S., & Thum, Y. M. (1989). The effects of high school organization on dropping out: An exploratory investigation. *American Educational Research Journal, 26,* 353–383.

Cain, K., & Oakhill, J. (1998). Comprehension skill and inference-making ability: Issues and causality. In C. Hulme & R. M. Joshi (Eds.), *Reading and spelling: Development and disorders* (pp. 329–342). London: Erlbaum.

California Department of Education. (2001). Grade Four English-Language Arts content standards. Retrieved April 12, 2003, from http://www.cde.ca.gov/standards/reading/grade4.html.

Cameron, J., & Pierce, W. E. (1994). Reinforcement, reward, and intrinsic motivation: A meta-analysis. *Review of Educational Research, 64,* 363–423.

Carr, E. M., & Ogle, D. M. (1987). K-W-L Plus: A strategy for comprehension and summarization. *Journal of Reading, 30,* 626–631.

Cazden, C. (1983). Adult assistance to language development: Scaffolds, models, and direct instruction. In R. P. Parker & F. A. David (Eds.), *Developing literacy: Young children's use of language* (pp. 3–18). Newark, DE: International Reading Association.

Cecil, N. L. (1995). *The art of inquiry: Questioning strategies for K–6 classrooms.* Winnipeg, Manitoba: Peguis.

Ciborowski, J. (1992). *Textbooks and the students who can't read them.* Cambridge, MA: Brookline.

Collins, C. (1991). Reading instruction that increases thinking abilities. *Journal of Reading, 34,* 510–516.

Collins, A., Brown, J. S., & Holum, A. (1991, Winter). Cognitive apprenticeship: Making thinking visible. *American Educator,* 6–11, 38–41.

Collins, A., Brown, J. S., & Newman, S. E. (1990). Cognitive apprenticeship: Teaching the crafts of reading, writing, and mathematics. In L. Resnick (Ed.), *Knowing, learning, and instruction: Essays in honor of Robert Glaser* (pp. 453–494). Hillsdale, NJ: Erlbaum.

Collins, W., Dritsas, L., Frey, P., Howard, A. C., McClain, K., Molina, D., Moore-Harris, B., Ott, J. M., Pelfrey, R., Price, J., Smith, B., & Wilson, P. S. (2002). *Glencoe mathematics: Applications and connection, Course 2.* New York: Glencoe McGraw-Hill.

Cross, D. R., & Paris, S. G. (1988). Developmental and instructional analyses of children's metacognition and reading comprehension. *Journal of Educational Psychology, 80*(2), 131–142.

Cunningham, J. W., & More, D. W. (1986). *The confused world of the main idea.* In J. F. Baumann, *Teaching main idea and comprehension* (Ed). (pp. 1-17). Newark, DE: International Reading Association.

Davey, B. (1983). Think aloud—Modeling the cognitive processes of reading comprehension. *Journal of Reading, 27*(1), 44–47.

Davey, B., & McBride, S. (1986). Effects of question-generation on reading comprehension. *Journal of Educational Psychology, 78,* 256–262.

DeBono, E. (1999). *Six thinking hats.* Boston: Little, Brown.

Deshler, D. D., & Schumaker, J. B. (1993). Strategy mastery by at-risk students: Not a simple matter. *The Elementary School Journal, 94*(2), 153–167.

Dewitz, P., Carr, E. M., & Pathberg, J. P. (1986). Effects of inference training on comprehension and comprehension monitoring. *Reading Research Quarterly, 22,* 109–119.

Dickinson, D. K., & Smith, M. W. (1994). Long-term effects of preschool teachers' book reading on low-income children's vocabulary and story comprehension. *Reading Research Quarterly, 29,* 104–122.

Dickson, S. V., Collins, V. L., Simmons, D. C., & Kameenui, E. J. (1998). Metacognitive strategies: Instructional and curricular basics and implications. In D. C. Simmons & E. J. Kameenui (Eds.), *What reading research tells us about children with diverse learning needs* (pp. 361–380). Hillsdale, NJ: Erlbaum.

Dillon, J. T. (1988). *Questioning and teaching: A manual of practice.* New York: Teachers College Press.

Dodge, B. (2003). Some thoughts about WebQuests. San Diego, CA: San Diego State University. Retrieved June 9, 2003, http://edweb.sdsu.edu/courses/edtec596/about_webquests.html.

Dole, J. (2000). Explicit and implicit instruction in comprehension. In B. M. Taylor, M. F. Graves, & P. van den Broek (Eds.), *Reading for meaning: Fostering comprehension in the middle grades* (pp. 52–69). New York: Teachers College Press.

Dole, J. A., Valencia, S. W., Greer, E. A., & Wardrop, J. L. (1991). Effects of two types of prereading instruction on the comprehension of narrative and expository text. *Reading Research Quarterly, 26*(2), 142–159.

Dreher, M. J. (1993). Reading to locate information: Societal and educational perspectives. *Contemporary Educational Psychology, 18,* 129–138.

Dreher, M. J. (2002). Children searching and using information text: A critical part of comprehension. In C. C. Block & M. Pressley (Eds.), *Comprehension instruction: Research-based best practices* (pp. 289–317). New York: Guilford.

Dreher, M. J., & Guthrie, J. T. (1990). Cognitive processes in textbook search tasks. *Reading Research Quarterly, 25*(4), 323–339.

Duffy, G. G. (1993). Rethinking strategy instruction: Four teachers' development and their low achievers' understandings. *Elementary School Journal, 93*(3), 231–247.

Duffy, G. G. (2002). The case for direct explanation of strategies. In C. C. Block & M. Pressley (Eds.), *Comprehension instruction: Research-based best practices* (pp. 28–41). New York: Guilford.

Duffy, G. G., & Roehler, L. R. (1989). The tension between information-giving and mediation: Perspectives on instructional explanation and teacher change. In J. Brophy (Ed.), *Advances in research on teaching* (Vol.1, pp. 1–33), New York: JAI.

Duffy, G. G., Roehler, L. R., Sivan, E., Rackliffe, G., Book, C., Meloth, M., Vavurs, L., Wesselman, R., Putnam, J., & Bassiri, D. (1987). The effects of explaining the reasoning associated with using reading strategies. *Reading Research Quarterly, 22*(3), 347–368.

DuFour, R., & Eaker, R. (1998). *Professional learning communities at work: Best practices for enhancing student achievement.* Bloomington, IN: National Educational Service.

Duke, N. K., Bennett-Armistead, V. S., & Roberts, E. M. (2003). Filling the great void: Why we should bring nonfiction into the early-grade classroom. *American Educator.* Retrieved April 7, 2003, from www.aft.org/american_educator/spring2003/void.html.

Duncker, K. A. (1926). A qualitative experimental and theoretical study of productive thinking (solving of comprehensible problems). *Pedagogical Seminary, 33,* 642–708.

Duncker, K. A. (1945). On problem solving. *Psychological Monographs, 58,* 1–113 (Whole No. 270).

Eagan, M. (1999). Reflections on effective use of graphic organizers. *Journal of Adolescent and Adult Literacy, 42*(8), 641–645.

Edmonds, R. (1979). Effective schools for the urban poor. *Educational Leadership, 37*(1), 15–24.

Edmonds, R. (1981). Making public schools effective. *Social Policy, 12,* 53–60.

Elliott-Faust, D. J., & Pressley, M. (1986). Self-controlled training of comparison strategies to increase children's comprehension monitoring. *Journal of Educational Psychology, 78,* 27–32.

Engle, R. W., Cantor, J., & Carullo, J. J. (1992). Individual differences in working memory and comprehension: A test of four hypotheses. *Journal of Experimental Psychology: Learning, Memory, and Cognition, 18*(3), 972–992.

Engle, R. W., Kane, M. J., & Tuholski, S. W. (1999). Individual differences in working memory capacity and what they tell us about controlled attention, general fluid intelligence, and functions of the prefrontal cortex. In A. Miyake & P. Shah (Eds.), *Models of working memory: Mechanisms of active maintenance and executive control* (pp. 102–134). Cambridge, UK: Cambridge University Press.

Engle, R. W., Tuholski, S. W., Laughlin, J. E., & Conway, R. A. (1999). Working memory, short-term memory, and general fluid intelligence: A latent-variable approach. *Journal of Experimental Psychology: General, 128*(3), 309–311.

Evans, J. (2003). *Civil War gazette.* San Bernadino, CA: Instructional Technology Development Consortium. Retrieved June 9, 2003, from www.itdc.sbcss.k12.ca.us/curriculum/civilwar.html.

Fielding, L. G., & Pearson, P. D. (1994). Reading comprehension: What works. *Educational Leadership, 51*(5). Retrieved April 12, 2003, from www.ascd.org/readingroom/edlead/9402/fielding.html.

Filamentality. (2003). Retrieved June 9, 2003, from www.filamentality.com.

The Free Online Dictionary of Computing. (February 9, 2002). Retrieved February 7, 2004 from www.dict.die.net.

Galdone, P. (1973). *The little red hen.* New York: Seabury.

Gambrell, L. B., & Bales, R. J. (1986). Mental imagery and the comprehension-monitoring performance of fourth- and fifth-grade poor readers. *Reading Research Quarterly, 21,* 454–464.

Garner, R., & Brown, R. (1992). Seductive details and learning from text. In A. K. Remington, S. Holt, & A. Krapp (Eds.), *The role of interest in learning and development* (pp. 239–254). Hillsdale, NJ: Erlbaum.

Gaskins, I. W., & Elliot, T. T. (1991). *Implementing cognitive strategy instruction across the school: The Benchmark manual for teachers.* Cambridge, MA: Brookline.

Gaskins, I. W., Laird, S. R., O'Hara, C., Scott, T., & Cress, C. A. (2002). Helping struggling readers make sense of reading. In C. C. Collins, L. B. Gambrell, & M. Pressley (Eds.), Improving comprehension instruction: Rethinking research, theory, and classroom practice (pp. 370-383).

Gilbar, S. (Ed.). (1990). *The Reader's quotation book: A literary companion.* Wainscott, NY: Pushcart.

Goldstein, R. (2002, October 14). Stephen Ambrose dies at 66. *The New York Times.* Retrieved April 3, 2003, from www.nytimes.com.

Good, T. L., & Brophy, J. E. (1986). School effects. In M. C. Wittrock (Ed.), *Handbook of research on teaching* (3rd ed., pp. 570–602). New York: Macmillan.

Goodwin, D. K. (1987). *The Fitzgeralds and the Kennedys: An American saga.* New York: Simon & Schuster.

Grand Canyon National Park. (2003, Spring). Spring in condor country. *Visitor's Guide,* p. 7. Grand Canyon, AZ: Author.

Guthrie, J. T., & Kirsch, I. S. (1987). Distinctions between reading comprehension and locating information in text. *Journal of Educational Psychology, 79*(3), 220–227.

Guthrie, J. T., & Mosenthal, P. (1987). Literacy as multi-dimensional: Locating information and reading comprehension. *Educational Psychologist, 22,* 279–297.

Guthrie, J. T., Van Meter, P., Hancock, G. R., Alao, S., Anderson, E., & McCann, A. (1998). Does concept oriented reading instruction increase strategy use and conceptual learning from text? *Journal of Educational Psychology, 90*(2), 261–278.

Hall, G. E., & Horde, S. M. (1987). *Change in schools: Facilitating the process.* Albany: State University of New York Press.

Hansen, J. (1981). The effects of inference training and practice on young children's reading comprehension. *Reading Research Quarterly, 16,* 391–417.

Hansen, J., & Pearson, P. D. (1983). An instructional study: Improving the inferential comprehension of good and poor fourth grade readers. *Journal of Educational Psychology, 75*(6), 821–829.

Hare, V., & Borchardt, K. M. (1984). Direct instruction of summarization skills. *Reading Research Quarterly, 21,* 62–78.

Harp, S. F., & Mayer, R. E. (1998). How seductive details do their damage: A theory of cognitive interest in science learning. *Journal of Educational Psychology, 90*(3), 414–434.

Harvey, S., & Goudvis, A. (2000). *Strategies that work: Teaching comprehension to enhance understanding.* York, ME: Stenhouse.

Herber, H. L., & Herber, J. N. (1993). *Teaching in content areas with reading, writing, and reasoning.* Boston: Allyn & Bacon.

Hirsch, E. D., Jr. (Ed.). (1989). *A first dictionary of cultural literacy.* Boston: Houghton Mifflin.

Hirsch, E. D., Jr. (2001). Make better use of the literacy time block. *American Educator, 25*(2), 4, 6–7.

Hirsch, E. D., Jr. (2003). Reading comprehension requires knowledge—of words and the world. *American Education, 27*(2), 11–29, 44–45.

Hoffman, J. V., McCarthey, S. J., Abbott, J., Christian, C., Corman, L., Curry, C., Dressman, M., Elliott, B., Matherne, D., & Stahle, D. (1994). So what's new in the new basals? A focus on first grade. *Journal of Reading Behavior, 26,* 47–73.

Honig, B. (2001). *Teaching our children to read: The role of skills in a comprehensive reading program.* Thousand Oaks, CA: Corwin.

Hornblow, L., & Hornblow, A. (1970). *Reptiles do the strangest things.* New York: Random House.

Ihnot, C. (2001). *Read naturally.* Retrieved September 2001, from www.read-naturally.com.

Inspiration Software. (2003). Inspiration [Computer software]. Portland, OR: Author.

James, W. (1890). *The principles of psychology.* New York: Holt.

Jefferson T. (1803). Transcript of Letter: Thomas Jefferson to Meriwether Lewis. Retrieved September 2003 from www.loc.gov/exhibits/Jefferson/168.html.

Johnson, D. D., & Johnson, B. V. H. (1986). Highlighting vocabulary in inferential comprehension instruction. *Journal of Reading, 28*(5), 444–447.

Johnson, D. W., & Johnson, R. T. (1990). Cooperative learning and achievement. In S. Sharan (Ed.), *Cooperative learning: Theory and research* (pp. 23–37). New York: Praeger.

Jonassen, D. H. (2000). *Computers in the classroom: Mindtools for critical thinking.* Englewood Cliffs, NJ: Prentice Hall.

Jones, B. F., Pierce, J., & Hunter, B. (1988/1989). Teaching students to construct graphic representations. *Educational Leadership, 46*(4), 20–25.

Just, M. A., & Carpenter, P. A. (1987). *The psychology of language and reading comprehension.* Newton, MA: Allyn & Bacon.

Kamberelis, G. (1998). Relations between children's literacy diets and genre development: You write what you read. *Literacy Teaching and Learning, 3,* 7–53.

King, A. (1989). Effects of self-questioning training on college students' comprehension of lectures. *Contemporary Educational Psychology, 14,* 366–381.

King, A. (1990). Improving lecture comprehension: Effects of a metacognitive strategy. *Applied Educational Psychology, 29,* 331–346.

King, A. (1992). Comparison of self-questioning, summarizing, and note taking–review as strategies for learning from lectures. *American Educational Research Journal, 29,* 303–325.

King, J. R., Biggs, S., & Lipsky, S. (1984). Students' self-questioning and summarizing as reading study strategies. *Journal of Reading Behavior, 16*(3), 205–218.

Kirkpatrick, D. D. (2002, April 9). Pulitzer Prizes and plagiarism. *The New York Times,* p. A22.

Klingner, J. K., Vaughn, S., & Schumm, J. S. (1998). Collaborative strategic reading during social studies in heterogeneous fourth grade classrooms. *Elementary School Journal, 99*(1), 3–22.

Kobasigawa, A. (1983). Children's retrieval skills for school learning. *Alberta Journal of Educational Research, 29,* 259–271.

Kuhlthau, C. C. (1988). Development of a model of the library search process: Cognitive and affective aspects. *Reference Quarterly, 28,* 232–242.

LaBerge, D., & Samuels, S. J. (1974). Toward a theory of automatic information processing in reading. *Academic Press, 6,* 293–323.

Lysynchuk, L. M., Pressley, M., & Vye, N. J. (1990). Reciprocal instruction improves standardized reading comprehension performance in poor grade-school comprehenders. *Elementary School Journal, 90*(5), 469–484.

Manzo, A. V., Manzo, U. C., & Estes, T. H. (2001). *Content area literacy: Interactive teaching for active learning.* New York: John Wiley.

Markman, E. M. (1977). Realizing that you don't understand: A preliminary investigation. *Child Development, 46,* 986–992.

Marks, M., Pressley, M., Coley, J. D., Craig, S., Gardner, R., DePinto, T., & Rose, W. (1993). Three teachers' adaptations of reciprocal teaching in comparison to traditional reciprocal teaching. *The Elementary School Journal, 94*(2), 267–283.

Marzano, R. J., Pickering, D. J., & Pollock, J. E. (2001). *Classroom instruction that works: Research-based strategies for increasing student achievement.* Alexandria, VA: Association for Supervision and Curriculum Development.

Mason, J., Roehler, L. R., & Duffy, G. G. (1984). A practitioner's model of comprehension instruction. In G. G. Duffy, L. R. Roehler, & J. Mason (Eds.), *Comprehension instruction: Perspectives and suggestions* (pp. 299–314). New York: Longman.

McEwan, E. K. (1987). *How to raise a reader.* Elgin, IL: David C. Cook.

McEwan, E. K. (1998). *The principal's guide to raising reading achievement.* Thousand Oaks, CA: Corwin.

McEwan, E. K. (2000). *How to raise a reader* (2nd ed.). Grand Rapids, MI: Baker Book House.

McEwan, E. K. (2001). *Raising reading achievement in middle and high schools: Five simple-to-follow strategies for principals.* Thousand Oaks, CA: Corwin.

McEwan, E. K. (2002a, July 10). Cognitive strategies lead to better comprehension. *The Northwest Explorer,* pp. 27, 29.

McEwan, E. K. (2002b). *Teach them all to read: Catching the kids who fall through the cracks.* Thousand Oaks, CA: Corwin.

McEwan, E. K. (2002c). *The ten traits of highly effective teachers.* Thousand Oaks, CA: Corwin.

McEwan, E. K. & McEwan, P. J. (2003). *Making sense of research: What's good, what's not, and how to tell the difference.* Thousand Oaks, CA: Corwin.

McGuinness, C., & McGuinness, G. (1998). *Reading reflex.* New York: Simon & Schuster.

McKeown, M. G., Beck, I. L., Omanson, R. D., & Perfetti, C. A. (1983). The effects of long-term vocabulary instruction on reading comprehension: A replication. *Journal of Reading Behavior, 15,* 3–18.

McKeown, M. G., Beck, I. L., Omanson, R. D., & Pople, M. T. (1985). Some effects of the nature and frequency of vocabulary instruction on the knowledge and use of words. *Reading Research Quarterly, 20,* 522–535.

Mehan, H. (1979). *Learning lessons: Social organization in the classroom.* Cambridge, MA: Harvard University Press.

Mercer, C. D., & Campbell, K. U. (2001). *Great leaps.* Gainesville, FL: Diarmuid. Retrieved September 15, 2001, from www.greatleaps.com/default.asp.

Mikulecky, L. (1982). Job literacy: The relationship between school preparation and workplace actuality. *Reading Research Quarterly, 17*(3), 400–419.

Miller, G. E. (1985). The effects of general and specific self-instruction training on children's comprehension monitoring performances during reading. *Reading Research Quarterly, 20*(5), 616–628.

Miller, G. E. (1987). The influence of self-instruction on the comprehension monitoring performance of average and above-average readers. *Journal of Reading Behavior, 19*(3), 303–317.

Miyake, A., & Shah, P. (1999). Toward unified theories of working memory: Emerging general consensus, unresolved theoretical issues, and future research directions. In A. Miyake & P. Shah (Eds.), *Models of working memory: Mechanisms of active maintenance and executive control* (pp. 442–481). Cambridge, UK: Cambridge University Press.

Moats, L. C. (1999, June). *Teaching reading is rocket science: What expert teachers of reading should know and be able to do.* Washington, DC: American Federation of Teachers. Retrieved August 15, 2001, from www.aft.org/edissues/rocketscience.htm.

Morrow, L. M., Tracey, D. H., Wood, D. G., & Pressley, M. (1999). Characteristics of exemplary first-grade literacy instruction. *Reading Teacher, 52,* 462–476.

National Reading Panel. (2000). *Report of the National Reading Panel: Teaching children to read: An evidence-based assessment of the scientific research literature on reading and its implications for reading instruction.* Reports of the Subgroups. Rockville, MD: National Institute of Child Health and Human Development.

Neuman, S. B. (1988). Enhancing children's comprehension through previewing. *National Reading Conference Yearbook, 37,* 219–224.

New Jersey Department of Education. (2002). New Jersey core curriculum content standards for language arts literacy. Retrieved April 12, 2003, from www.state.nj.us/njded/cccs/02/s3_lal.htm.

New York Times Notable Books 2002. (2003). Review of *Blessings.* Retrieved April 4, 2003, from www.nytimes.com/2002/12/08/books/review/2002/notablefiction.html?ex=1049605200&en=5d24c1bb36c3da09&ei=5070.

No Child Left Behind Act. (2002, January 8). Public Law 107–110 115 STAT.1425 H. R. 1. Retrieved May 28, 2002, from www.ed.gov.legislation/ESEA02/.

Nolte, R. Y., & Singer, H. (1985). Active comprehension: Teaching a process of reading comprehension and its effects on reading achievement. *The Reading Teacher, 39,* 24–31.

Novak, J. D. (1998). *Learning, creating, and using knowledge: Concept maps as facilitative tools in schools and corporations.* Mahwah, NJ: Lawrence Erlbaum.

Novak, J. D., & Gowin, D. B. (1984). *Learning how to learn.* Cambridge, UK: Cambridge University Press.

Oakhill, J., Cain, K., & Yuill, N. (1998). Individual differences in children's comprehension skill: Toward an integrated model. In C. Hulme & R. M. Joshi (Eds.), *Reading and spelling: Development and disorders* (pp. 343–367). London: Erlbaum.

Ogle, D. (1986). K-W-L: A teaching model that develops active reading of expository text. *The Reading Teacher, 26,* 564–570.

Ong, F., & Breneman, B. (2000). *Strategic teaching and learning: Standards based instruction to promote content literacy in grades four through twelve.* Sacramento, CA: California Department of Education.

Olson, L., & Viadero, D. (2002, January 30). Law mandates scientific base for research. *Education Week, 21*(20), 14–15.

Opitz, M. F., & Rasinski, T. V. (1998). *Good-bye round robin: 25 effective oral reading strategies.* Portsmouth, NH: Heinemann.

Palincsar, A., & Brown, A. L. (1984). Reciprocal teaching of comprehension fostering and monitoring activities. *Cognition and Instruction, 1*(2), 117–175.

Palmatier, R. A. (1973). A notetaking system for learning. *Journal of Reading, 17,* 36–39.

Paris, S. G., Cross, D. R., & Lipson, M. Y. (1984). Informed strategies for learning: A program to improve children's reading awareness and comprehension. *Journal of Educational Psychology, 76*(6), 1239–1252.

Paris, S. G., Saarnio, D. A., & Cross, D. R. (1986). A metacognitive curriculum to promote children's reading and learning. *Australian Journal of Psychology, 38*(2), 107–123.

Pearson, P. D. (1996). Reclaiming the center. In M. F. Graves, P. van den Broek, & B. Taylor (Eds.), *The first R: Every child's right to read* (pp. 259–274). New York: Teachers College Press, and Newark, DE: International Reading Association.

Pearson, P. D., & Fielding, L. (1991). Comprehension instruction. In R. Barr, M. L. Kamil, P. Mosenthal, & P. D. Pearson (Eds.), *Handbook of reading research* (Vol. 2, pp. 815–860). New York: Longman.

Pearson, P. D., & Gallagher, M. C. (1983). The instruction of reading comprehension. *Contemporary Educational Psychology, 8,* 317–344.

Pearson, P. D., & Johnson, D. D. (1978). *Teaching reading comprehension.* New York: Holt, Rinehart & Winston.

Pearson, P. D., Roehler, L. R., Dole, J. A., & Duffy, G. G. (1992). Developing expertise in reading comprehension. In J. Samuels & A. Farstup (Eds.), *What research has to say about reading instruction* (pp. 145–199). Newark, DE: International Reading Association.

Pellegrino, J. (2002, February). *Understanding how students learn and inferring what they know: Implications for the design of curriculum instruction, and assessment.* A paper presented at the Annual NSF K–12 Math, Science Curriculum and Implementation Projects Conference, Herndon, VA.

Perfetti, C. (1985). *Reading ability.* London: Oxford University Press.

Perkins, D. N. (1992). *Smart schools: Better thinking and learning for every child.* New York: Free Press.

Pressley, M. (1976). Mental imagery helps eight-year-olds remember what they read. *Journal of Educational Psychology. 68*(3), 355–259.

Pressley, M. (1998). *The case for balanced reading instruction.* New York: Guilford.

Pressley, M. (2000). Comprehension instruction in elementary school: A quarter-century of research progress. In B. M. Taylor, M. F. Graves, & P. van den Broek (Eds.), *Reading for meaning: Fostering comprehension in the middle grades* (pp. 32–51). New York: Teachers College Press.

Pressley, M., & Afflerbach, P. (1995). *Verbal protocols of reading: The nature of constructively responsive reading.* Hillsdale, NJ: Erlbaum.

Pressley, M., El-Dinary, P. B., & Brown, R. (1992). Skilled and not-so-skilled reading: Good information processing and not-so-good information processing. In M. Pressley, K. R. Harris, & J. T. Guthrie (Eds.), *Promoting academic competence and literacy in school* (pp. 91–127). San Diego, CA: Academic Press.

Pressley, M., El-Dinary, P. B., Gaskins, I., Schuder, T., Bergman, J. L., Almasi, J., & Brown, R. (1992). Beyond direct explanation: Transactional instruction of reading comprehension strategies. *Elementary School Journal, 92,* 513–556.

Pressley, M., El-Dinary, P. B., Marks, M. B., & Stein, S. (1992). Good strategy instruction is motivating and interesting. In K. A. Renninger, S. Hidi, & A. Krapp (Eds.), *Role of interest in learning and development* (pp. 333–358). Hillsdale, NJ: Erlbaum.

Pressley, M., Goodchild, F., Fleet, J., Azjchowski, R., & Evans, E. D. (1989). The challenges of classroom strategy instruction. *Elementary School Journal, 89*(3), 301–342.

Pressley, M., Johnson, C. J., Symons, S., McGoldrick, J. A., & Kurita, J. A. (1989). Strategies that improve children's memory and comprehension of text. *Elementary School Journal, 90*(1), 3–22.

Pressley, M., Rankin, J., & Yokoi, L. (1996). A survey of instructional practices of primary teachers nominated as effective in promoting literacy. *Elementary School Journal, 96*, 363–384.

Pressley, M., Schuder, T., Teachers in the SAIL Program, Bergman, J., & El-Dinary, P. B. (1992). A researcher-educator collaborative interview study of transactional comprehension strategies instruction. *Journal of Educational Psychology, 84*, 231–243.

Pressley, M., Wharton-McDonald, R., Mistretta-Hampton, J., & Echevarria, M. (1998). The nature of literacy instruction in ten 4/5 classrooms in upstate New York. *Scientific Studies of Reading, 2*, 159–194.

Pressley, M., Wharton-McDonald, R., Allington, R., Block, C. C., Morrow, L., Tracey, D., Baker, K., Brooks, G., Cornin, J., Nelson, E., & Woo, D. (2001). A study of effective first-grade literacy instruction. *Scientific Studies of Reading 5*(1), 35–58.

Pressley, M., Woloshyn, V., Burkell, J., Cariglia-Bull, T., Lysynchuk, L., McGoldrick, J. A. K. Schneider, B., Snyder, B. L., & Symons, S. (1995). *Cognitive strategy instruction that really improves children's academic performance.* Cambridge, MA: Brookline.

RAND Reading Study Group. Catherine Snow, Chair. (2002). *Reading for understanding: Toward an R & D program in reading comprehension.* Santa Monica, CA: RAND Corporation.

Raphael, T. (1982, November). Question-answering strategies for children. *The Reading Teacher,* 186–190.

Raphael, T. (1984). Teaching learners about sources of information for answering questions. *Journal of Reading, 27*(4), 303–311.

Raphael, T. E., & Gavelek, J. R. (1984). Question-related activities and their relationship to reading comprehension: Some instructional implications. In G. G. Duffy, L. R. Roehler, & J. Mason (Eds.), *Comprehension instruction: Perspectives and suggestions* (pp. 234–250). New York: Longman.

Raphael, T., & Pearson, P. D. (1985). Increasing students' awareness of sources of information for answering questions. *American Educational Research Journal, 22*, 217–236.

Raphael, T. E., & Wonnacott, C. A. (1985). Heightening fourth-grade students' sensitivity to sources of information for answering comprehension questions. *Reading Research Quarterly, 25*, 285–296.

Renaissance Learning. (2002). *Research summary.* Wisconsin Rapids, WI: Author.

Reutzel, D. R., & Hollingsworth, P. M. (1988). Highlighting key vocabulary: A generative-reciprocal procedure for teaching selected inference types. *Reading Research Quarterly, 23*(3), 358–378.

Rinehart, S. D., Stahl, S. A., & Erickson, L. G. (1986). Some effects of summarizing on reading and studying. *Reading Research Quarterly, 21*(4), 422–436.

Robbins, C., & Ehri, L. C. (1994). Reading storybooks to kindergartners helps them learn new vocabulary words. *Journal of Educational Psychology, 86*, 54–64.

Roberts, T. A. (1988) Development of pre-instruction versus previous experience: Effects on factual and inferential comprehension. *Reading Psychology, 9*(2), 141–157.

Roehler, L. R., & Duffy, G. G. (1984). Direct explanation of comprehension processes. In G. G. Duffy, L. R. Roehler, & J. Mason (Eds.), *Comprehension instruction: Perspectives and suggestions* (pp. 265–280). New York: Longman.

Rosenshine, B. (1979). Content, time, and direct instruction. In P. L. Peterson & H. J. Walberg (Eds.), *Research on teaching: Concepts, findings, and implications* (pp. 28–56). New York: Longman.

Rosenshine, B. (1997a). Advances in research on instruction. In J. W. Lloyd, E. J. Kameenui, & D. Chard (Eds.), *Issues in educating students with disabilities* (pp. 197–221). Mahwah, NJ: Lawrence Erlbaum.

Rosenshine, B. (1997b, March 24–28). The case for explicit, teacher-led, cognitive strategy instruction. Paper presented at the annual meeting of the American Educational Research Association, Chicago, IL.

Rosenshine, B., & Meister, C. (1984). Reciprocal teaching: A review of nineteen experimental studies. *Review of Educational Research, 64*(4), 479–530.

Rosenshine, B., Meister, C., & Chapman, S. (1996). Teaching students to generate questions: A review of the intervention studies. *Review of Educational Research, 66*(2), 181–221.

Schank, R. (1999). *Dynamic memory revisited.* Cambridge, UK: Cambridge University Press.

Schmitt, M. C. (1988). The effects of an elaborated directed reading activity on the metacomprehension skills of third graders. *National Reading Conference Yearbook, 37,* 107–123.

Schoenbach, R., Greenleaf, C., Cziko, C., & Hurwitz, L. (1999). *Reading for understanding: A guide to improving reading in middle and high school classrooms.* San Francisco: Jossey-Bass.

Schunk, D. H., & Rice, J. M. (1985). Verbalization of comprehension strategies: Effects on children's achievement outcomes. *Human Learning: Journal of Practical Research and Applications, 4*(1), 1–10.

Secretary's Commission on Achieving Necessary Skills. (1992). *What work requires of schools: A SCANS report for America 2000.* Washington, DC: U.S. Department of Labor.

Shriberg, L. K., Levin, J. R., McCormick, C. B., & Pressley, M. (1982). Learning about "famous" people via the keyword method. *Journal of Educational Psychology, 74,* 238–247.

Simpson, M. L. (1986). PORPE: A writing strategy for studying and learning in the content areas. *Journal of Reading, 29,* 407–414.

Sinatra, G. M., Stahl-Gemake, J., & Berg, D. N. (1984). Improving reading comprehension of disabled readers through semantic mapping. *Reading Teacher, 38*(1), 22–29.

Singer, H., & Dolan, D. (1982). Active comprehension: Problem-solving schema with question generation of complex short stories. *Reading Research Quarterly, 17,* 166–186.

Smolkin, L. B., & Donovan, C. A. (2000). The contexts of comprehension: Information book read alouds and comprehension acquisition. Ann Arbor: University of Michigan School of Education, Center for the Improvement of Early Reading Achievement.

Spires, H. A., & Estes, T. H. (2002). Reading in web-based learning environments. In C. C. Block & M. Pressley (Eds.), *Comprehension instruction: Research-based best practices* (pp. 115–125). New York: Guilford.

Squire, L. R., & Kandel, E. R. (1999). *Memory: From mind to molecules.* New York: Scientific American Library.

Stanovich, K. E. (1993). Does reading make you smarter? Literacy and the development of verbal intelligence. In H. Reese (Ed.), *Advances in child development and behavior* (pp. 134–180). San Diego, CA: Academic Press.

Stanovich, K. E., & Cunningham, A. E. (1993). Where does knowledge come from? Specific associations between print exposure and information acquisition. *Journal of Educational Psychology, 85,* 211–229.

Symons, S., MacLatchy-Gaudet, H., Stone, T. D., & Reynolds, P. L. (2001). Strategy instruction for elementary students searching information text. *Scientific Studies of Reading, 5,* 1–33.

Taylor, B. M. (1986). Teaching middle-grade students to read for main ideas. In J. A. Niles & R. V. Lalik (Eds.), *Solving problems in literacy: Learners, teachers, and researchers* (pp. 99–108). Rochester, NY: National Reading Conference.

Taylor, B. M., Graves, M., & van den Broek, P. (Eds.). (2000). *Reading for meaning: Fostering comprehension in the middle grades.* New York: Teachers College Press.

Taylor, B. M., Pearson, P. D., Clark, K. F., & Walpole, S. (1999). Effective schools/ accomplished teachers. *Reading Teacher, 53*(2), 156–159.

Taylor, B. M., Pearson, P. D., Clark, K., & Walpole, S. (2000). Effective schools and accomplished teachers: Lessons about primary-grade reading instruction in low-income schools. *Elementary School Journal, 101,* 121–165.

Texas Education Agency. (2002). PowerPoint™ Presentation. Retrieved March, 2003, from www.tea.state.tx.us/curriculum/sstaks.ppt.

Tharp, R. G. (1982). The effective instruction of comprehension: Results and description of the Kamehameha Early Education Program. *Reading Research Quarterly, 17*(4), 503–527.

Thorndike, E. (1917). Reading as reasoning: A study of mistakes in paragraph reading. *Journal of Educational Psychology, 8,* 323–332.

Tovani, C., & Keene, E. O. (2000). *I read it but I don't get it: Comprehension strategies for adolescent readers.* Portland, ME: Stenhouse Publishers.

Towse, J. N., & Houston-Price, C. M. T. (1999). Reflections on the concept of the central executive. In J. Andrade (Ed.), *Working memory in perspective* (pp. 240–260). New York: Taylor & Francis.

Trabasso, T., & Bouchard, E. (2000). *Text comprehension instruction. Report of the National Reading Panel, Report of the Subgroups* (Chap. 4, Pt. 2, pp. 39–69). NICHD Clearinghouse.

Trabasso, T., & Bouchard, E. (2002). Teaching readers how to comprehend text strategically. In C. C. Block & M. Pressley (Eds.), *Comprehension instruction: Research-based best practices* (pp. 176–200). New York: Guilford.

Trabasso, T., & Magliano, J. P. (1996). How do children understand what they read and what can we do to help them? In M. F. Graves, P. van den Broek, & B. M. Taylor (Eds.), *The first R: Every child's right to read* (pp. 160–188). New York: Teachers College Press, and Newark, DE: International Reading Association.

Twain, M. (1876). *The adventures of Tom Sawyer.* Leipzig: Bernhard Tauchnitz.

Twenty-First Independent Parachute Company. (2003). Retrieved August 15, 2003, from www.extraplan.demon.co.uk/batt_ind_coy.htm.

University of Washington Psychology Writing Center. (2003). *Plagiarism and student writing.* Retrieved April 13, 2003, from http://depts.washington.edu/psywc/handouts. shtml.

USA Today. (2003, April 8). Summary of Duke-Kansas Basketball Game. Author, p. 7C.

van den Broek, P. (1994). Comprehension and memory of narrative texts: Inference and coherence. In M. A. Gernsbacher (Ed.), *Handbook of psycholinguistics* (pp. 539–588). San Diego, CA: Academic Press.

van den Broek, P., Young, M., Tzeng, Y., & Linderholm, T. (1999). The landscape model of reading: Inferences and the online construction of a memory representation. In H. van Oostendorp & S. R. Goldman, *The construction of mental representations during reading* (pp. 71–98). Mahwah, NJ: Lawrence Erlbaum.

Van Someren, M. W., Barnard, Y. F., & Sandberg, J. (1994). *The think-aloud method: A practical guide to modeling cognitive processes.* San Diego, CA: Academic Press.

Venezky, R. L. (2000). The origins of the present-day chasm between adult literacy needs and school literacy instruction. *Scientific Studies of Reading, 4,* 19–39.

Vygotsky, L. S. (1979). *Mind in society: The development of higher psychological processes.* Cambridge, MA: Harvard University Press.

Wade, S. E. (1990). Using think-alouds to assess comprehension. *The Reading Teacher, 43*(3), 442–451.

Weaver, C. (1994). *Reading process and practice: From socio-linguistics to whole language* (2nd ed.). Portsmouth, NH: Heinemann.

Weinstein, C. E., & Hume, L. M. (1998). *Study strategies for lifelong learning.* Washington, DC: American Psychological Association.

Weinstein, C. E., & Mayer, R. E. (1986). The teaching of learning strategies. In M. C. Wittrock (Ed.), *Handbook of research on teaching* (pp. 315–327). New York: Macmillan.

Wharton-McDonald, R., Pressley, M., & Hampton, J. M. (1998). Literacy instruction in nine first-grade classrooms: Teacher characteristics and student achievement. *The Elementary School Journal, 99*(2), 101–128.

Wharton-McDonald, R., Pressley, M., Rankin, J., Mistretta, J., Yokoi, L., & Ettenberger, S. (1997). Effective primary grades literacy instruction: Balanced literacy instruction. *Reading Teachers, 50,* 518–521.

Williams, J. P. (2002). Using the theme scheme to improve story comprehension. In C. C. Block & M. Pressley (Eds.), *Comprehension instruction: Research-based best practices* (pp. 126–139). New York: Guilford.

Wisconsin Department of Public Instruction. (2003). Wisconsin model academic standards. Fourth grade. Retrieved April 14, 2003, from www.dpi.state.wi.us/standards/elaa4.html.

Wolf, M., & Bowers, P. G. (1999). The double-deficit hypothesis for developmental dyslexias. *Journal of Educational Psychology, 91,* 415–438.

Wolf, M., & Bowers, P. G. (2000). Naming-speed processes and developmental reading disabilities: An introduction to the special issue on the double-deficit hypothesis. *Journal of Learning Disabilities, 33*(4), 322–324.

Wong, R. Y. L., Wong, W., Perry, N., & Sawatsky, D. (1986). The efficacy of a self-questioning summarization strategy for use by underachievers and learning disabled adolescents. *Learning Disability Focus, 2,* 20–35.

Wood, E. G., Winne, P., & Pressley, M. (1988, April). *Elaborative interrogation, imagery, and provided precise elaborations as facilitators of children's learning of arbitrary prose.* Paper presented at the American Educational Research Association, New Orleans.

Wood, E., Woloshyn, V. E., & Willoughby, T. (Eds.). (1995). *Cognitive strategy instruction for middle and high schools.* Cambridge, MA: Brookline.

Wooden, J., & Jamison, S. (1997). *Wooden: A lifetime of observations and reflections on and off the court.* Chicago: Contemporary Books.

Yoshida, M. (1999). *Lesson study: An ethnographic investigation of school-based teacher development in Japan.* Doctoral dissertation, University of Chicago.

Index

**CORWIN
PRESS**

The Corwin Press logo—a raven striding across an open book—represents the union of courage and learning. Corwin Press is committed to improving education for all learners by publishing books and other professional development resources for those serving the field of K–12 education. By providing practical, hands-on materials, Corwin Press continues to carry out the promise of its motto: **"Helping Educators Do Their Work Better."**